D0001408

Visual C++ 6
Core Language

Little Black Book

Bill McCarty

CORIOLIS

Publisher
Keith Weiskamp

Acquisitions Editor
Stephanie Wall

Marketing Specialist
Diane Enger

Project Editor
Jeff Kellum

Technical Reviewer
Andrew Indovina

Production Coordinator
Meg E. Turecek

Layout Design
April Nielsen

Cover Design
Jody Winkler

Visual C++ 6 Core Language Little Black Book

Limits Of Liability And Disclaimer Of Warranty

The author and publisher of this book have used their best efforts in preparing the book and the programs contained in it. These efforts include the development, research, and testing of the theories and programs to determine their effectiveness. The author and publisher make no warranty of any kind, expressed or implied, with regard to these programs or the documentation contained in this book.

The author and publisher shall not be liable in the event of incidental or consequential damages in connection with, or arising out of, the furnishing, performance, or use of the programs, associated instructions, and/or claims of productivity gains.

Trademarks

Trademarked names appear throughout this book. Rather than list the names and entities that own the trademarks or insert a trademark symbol with each mention of the trademarked name, the publisher states that it is using the names for editorial purposes only and to the benefit of the trademark owner, with no intention of infringing upon that trademark.

The Coriolis Group, LLC
14455 N. Hayden Road, Suite 220
Scottsdale, Arizona 85260

602/483-0192
FAX 602/483-0193
http://www.coriolis.com

Library of Congress Cataloging-in-Publication Data
McCarty, Bill, 1953-
    Visual C++ 6 core language little black book / by Bill McCarty
        p.   cm.
    Includes index.
    ISBN 1-57610-389-7
    1. C++ (Computer program language).   2. Microsoft Visual C++.   I. Title.
QA76.73.C153M3286   1999
005.13'3–dc21   99-17357
                                                            CIP

Printed in the United States of America
10 9 8 7 6 5 4 3 2 1

Dear Reader:

Coriolis Technology Press was founded to create a very elite group of books: the ones you keep closest to your machine. Sure, everyone would like to have the Library of Congress at arm's reach, but in the real world, you have to choose the books you rely on every day *very* carefully.

To win a place for our books on that coveted shelf beside your PC, we guarantee several important qualities in every book we publish. These qualities are:

- *Technical accuracy*—It's no good if it doesn't work. Every Coriolis Technology Press book is reviewed by technical experts in the topic field, and is sent through several editing and proofreading passes in order to create the piece of work you now hold in your hands.

- *Innovative editorial design*—We've put years of research and refinement into the ways we present information in our books. Our books' editorial approach is uniquely designed to reflect the way people learn new technologies and search for solutions to technology problems.

- *Practical focus*—We put only pertinent information into our books and avoid any fluff. Every fact included between these two covers must serve the mission of the book as a whole.

- *Accessibility*—The information in a book is worthless unless you can find it quickly when you need it. We put a lot of effort into our indexes, and heavily cross-reference our chapters, to make it easy for you to move right to the information you need.

Here at The Coriolis Group we have been publishing and packaging books, technical journals, and training materials since 1989. We're programmers and authors ourselves, and we take an ongoing active role in defining what we publish and how we publish it. We have put a lot of thought into our books; please write to us at **ctp@coriolis.com** and let us know what you think. We hope that you're happy with the book in your hands, and that in the future, when you reach for software development and networking information, you'll turn to one of our books first.

Keith Weiskamp
President and Publisher

Jeff Duntemann
VP and Editorial Director

My long-suffering family continues to bear with my authoring habits beyond any reasonable expectation. My wife (Jennifer), son (Patrick), and daughter (Sara) are in that very significant sense co-authors of this book, for without their patience it would not have come to be. Thanks for all the blessings we enjoy as a family to Jesus Christ, fully man and fully God, who graciously did for us what we could not do for ourselves, living a perfect life and dying in our place, in order that we might have perfect fellowship with the Father, who accepts us as His own, despite our many serious and manifest faults.

—Bill McCarty

About The Author

Bill McCarty is an Associate Professor of Management Information Systems and former Associate Professor of Computer Science at Azusa Pacific University in Azusa, California. Bill has written numerous books on a plethora of topics, including two other books for Coriolis: *Visual Developer SQL Database Programming With Java,* and *Visual C++ 6 Programming Blue Book* (with Stephen D. Gilbert). Bill has programmed professionally since the mid-1970s, when mainframe computers had 32KB of memory and programs, like their programmers, were made of sterner stuff. Bill, his wife Jennifer, son Patrick, and daughter Sara, live in La Mirada, California.

Acknowledgments

Former Yankee teammates of baseball great Yogi Berra swear that one night, baseball's greatest catcher was horrified to see a baby falling from the roof of a nearby apartment. Berra's well-honed baseball skills enabled him to instantly calculate the toddler's trajectory. Dashing to the proper spot, he saved the child by making the most miraculous catch of his career. But, alas, force of habit proved too much for the would-be hero: He immediately straightened up and threw the baby to second base.

Though the team assembled to bring this book safely home had all of Berra's skill, its members (thankfully) had better control of their reflexes. They managed to point out or fix error after error, but never once did they throw the baby to second base. My thanks to Stephanie Wall, Acquisitions Editor; Jeff Kellum, Project Editor; Andrew Indovina, Technical Reviewer; and Meg E. Turecek, Production Coordinator. My thanks also to those who worked in the dugout, without whose help the stars wouldn't have been on the field: Joanne Slike, Copy Editor; and Bob LaRoche, Proofreader.

—Bill McCarty

Table Of Contents

Part II   The C++ Libraries

Part III   The Visual C++ IDE

Chapter 15
Projects 313

Chapter 16
Working With ClassView 331

Introduction

I wrote this book because I grew tired of reaching for language and library references and shuttling CD-ROMs back and forth from case to drive as I programmed using Visual C++ 6. Perhaps a few savants manage to learn everything about C++, its libraries, and the Visual C++ development environment. But surely only a handful manage to retain that information at their fingertips, poised for instant recall. The rest of us spend a goodly portion of our programming time looking up information that we can't recall. This book is intended to save us time and effort, by combining in one relatively small book information about the C++ language, the C/C++ libraries, and the Visual C++ environment and tools.

Who This Book Is For

If you're an intermediate or advanced programmer, I'm confident you'll find this book useful. However, this is not a book for beginners. I wrote as clearly as I know how and a team of editors called into question every ambiguous or incomplete construction that got past me. But, the original meaning of the word *manual* was a book that fit in one's hand, and I wanted this book to be a manual in exactly that sense of the word. Others have written multivolume works that address a mere fraction of the material presented in this book. Using such books is inconvenient at best. However, making this book a manual required me to leave out examples and long-winded explanations that are sometimes essential to beginners unfamiliar with the territory. The chief value of this book is in helping you recall what you once knew and helping you apply your already considerable knowledge to some less familiar areas of the C++ language, its libraries, and the Visual C++ environment.

The Structure Of This Book

Part I of the book summarizes the syntax and semantics of the C++ language. Railroad diagrams, long a staple in the Pascal community, are used to simply and clearly present the syntax of C++. Use Part I, for example, to refresh or clarify your understanding of C++ exception handling.

Part II of the book summarizes the principal C/C++ libraries, compactly describing each constant, type, and routine they define. Use Part II, for example, to refresh your recollection of the function and parameters of a string-handling library routine or to discover which routine performs a needed function.

Part III of the book summarizes the Visual C++ 6 development environment, describing its tools and the techniques required to use them. Use Part III, for example, to learn how to create an image resource or change its properties.

How To Use This Book

This book is designed for use as a reference book; I don't anticipate that you'll read it from beginning to end. Instead, you'll open it when you need help with a specific problem. To help you find relevant information as quickly as possible, each chapter of this book contains the following elements:

- A "jump table," which is a list of the most important Immediate Solutions presented in the chapter. You can use the jump table as a mini table of contents for the chapter, jumping directly to the page that addresses your need.

- An In Brief section, which presents an overview of the chapter contents. You can read this section to quickly refresh your memory of the chapter contents and to learn general information that applies to a variety of problems and situations.

- An Immediate Solutions section, which provides "quick fixes" to specific needs or problems. In some chapters, an Immediate Solution takes the form of a step-by-step procedure that you can use to accomplish a specific task. In other chapters, an Immediate Solution describes the function, operation, and parameters of a specific C++ library routine.

- Cross-reference tables, which help you quickly locate related information contained elsewhere in the book.

Conventions

This book uses *italic font* to highlight the definitions of important terms and to indicate placeholders, such as macro and function arguments. Brief code phrases that appear within text are shown using a **bold font**. Code examples are shown using a monospaced font:

```
// This is a line of code.
```

Throughout this book, you'll find tips, notes, and warnings:

- Tips provide information intended to help you work with Visual C++ more efficiently and effectively.

- Notes provide additional details that may prove useful in special or infrequent circumstances.

- Warnings point out risks and obstacles so that you can avoid problems.

Feedback

I hope that you find this book useful and that it helps you work more efficiently. Your comments and suggestions for corrections, improvements, and additions are most welcome; please send them to me via email, at **ctp@coriolis.com**. Please include the title of this book in your message.

Part I

The C++ Language

Language Elements

In Brief

Writing Programs And Declarations

A Visual C++ program consists of one or more source files that are linked. Each file contains a series of declarations, each of which can do the following:

- Introduce an identifier
- Specify the storage class, type, or linkage of a function or object
- Declare a new type or specify a synonym for an existing type
- Specify the initial value of an object
- Name a constant
- Define a class
- Define a function

You use identifiers to refer to:

- Objects
- Variables
- Classes, structures, or unions
- Enumerated types
- Members of a class, structure, or union
- Functions or member functions
- **typedef** statements
- Labels
- Macros or macro parameters

Some identifiers cannot be used by programmers because they have a preassigned meaning. Such operators are called *keywords*.

In addition to identifiers, a C++ program includes punctuators, operators, and literals. Punctuators guide the compiler in interpreting a program. Operators specify operations performed on one or more operands. Each operator has an associated precedence and associativity, which determine how the operator evaluates its operands. Literals specify constant values.

A program may also contain comments, which are ignored by the compiler. A program generally defines a function named **main( )**, which is the starting point of the program. A **return** statement or a call to the **exit( )** function typically terminates the program.

Immediate Solutions

Forming Identifiers

Visual C++ uses identifiers to refer to constructs such as classes, class members, enumerations, functions, **typedef** statements, and preprocessor macros. The first character of an identifier must be an alphabetic character, which may be uppercase or lowercase, or an underscore. Each subsequent character must be an alphabetic character, a digit, or an underscore. Identifiers are case-sensitive. For example, the identifier **Dog** is distinct from **dog**.

Identifiers have no maximum length, but Visual C++ considers only the first 247 characters of an identifier to be significant. Visual C++ defines a number of keywords that may not be used as identifiers. These are shown in Table 1.1. Visual C++ also defines for its own use many identifiers that begin with an underscore. To avoid conflicts with these internal identifiers, you should not normally define identifiers that begin with an underscore.

Table 1.1   The Visual C++ keywords.

__asm	__based	__cdecl	__declspec
__except	__fastcall	__finally	__inline
__int16	__int32	__int64	__int8
__leave	__multiple_inheritance	__single_inheritance	__stdcall
__try	__uuidof	__virtual_inheritance	allocate
asm	auto	bad_cast	bad_typeid
bool	break	case	catch
char	class	const	const_cast
continue	default	delete	dllexport
dllimport	do	double	dynamic_cast
else	enum	except	explicit
extern	false	finally	float
for	friend	goto	if
inline	int	long	mutable
naked	namespace	new	nothrow

(continued)

Table 1.1   The Visual C++ keywords (continued).

operator	private	property	protected
public	register	reinterpret_cast	return
selectany	short	signed	sizeof
static	static_cast	struct	switch
template	this	thread	throw
true	try	type_info	typedef
typeid	typename	union	unsigned
using	uuid	virtual	void
volatile	while		

Writing Comments

Visual C++ programs may include comments, which are treated by the compiler as white space. You can write either of two kinds of comment:

- The C-style or multiline comment consists of slash, asterisk characters (/*), followed by any sequence of characters (including new-line characters), followed by */. C-style comments cannot be nested; the first occurrence of */ ends the comment.

- The C++-style or single-line comment consists of double slash characters (//) followed by any sequence of characters. A new-line character not immediately preceded by a backslash character (\) terminates the comment.

Writing Declarations And Definitions

Declarations tell the compiler that a specified name or program element exists. Definitions tell the compiler what the name describes. If a declaration does one of the following, it is a mere declaration; otherwise, it is a definition:

- Declares a class name (for example, **class TheClass;**)

- Declares a function without specifying the function body

- Declares a static data member

- Contains the **extern** specifier, but no initializer or function body

- Is a **typedef** statement

A program element can be declared multiple times; however, each such declaration must be identical. For example, a variable cannot be declared as both an **int** and a **float**.

Introducing A Class Or Function Name

Suppose you have two classes, call them **A** and **B**, that reference each other. Suppose you define the class **A** first. The definition of class **A** must reference class **B**, but when the compiler processes the definition, it won't yet know that **B** is a class. Therefore, the compilation will fail.

To remedy this situation, you must tell the Visual C++ compiler that **B** refers to a class. You do so by placing this line of code before the definition of class **A**:

```
class B;
```

This line of code introduces the name **B** and tells the compiler that **B** refers to a class.

You use this same technique to tell the compiler about functions that you prefer to define after they're used, or in another source file. For example, suppose your program includes a function named **area** that takes two **float** arguments representing the width and length of a rectangle and returns the area of the rectangle as a **float** value. To introduce the name **area** to the compiler you write:

```
float area(float width, float length);
```

After introducing the name **area**, you may write functions that invoke the **area** function. The compiler knows the types of the arguments of the **area** function and its return type, so the compiler generates the appropriate code.

Defining Program Elements

It's generally more convenient and therefore more common to define program elements than to merely declare them. When you define a program element, you can specify its type, storage class, access, linkage, and other attributes.

Choosing Data Types

Visual C++ provides a variety of fundamental (built-in) data types, as shown in Table 1.2. Integral types represent whole numbers, whereas floating-point types represent values with fractional parts. The table gives the precision of each type as implemented by the Visual C++ compiler. The C++ standard does not fix the precision of the fundamental types, which may differ from one C++ implementation to another.

In choosing a data type, you should select a type that's large enough to accommodate every anticipated value of your variable. However, you should not select a type that's unnecessarily large, because that wastes storage.

In addition to its fundamental data types, C++ lets you work with derived types and class types. Derived types include pointers, references, arrays, and functions. Whenever you define a C++ class, structure, or union, you introduce a new class type that you may subsequently use to define objects.

Defining Variables

To define a variable, you merely specify its name and type. For example:

```
int x;          // an int variable named x
char c;         // a char variable named c
float radius;   // a float variable named radius
```

In addition, you can specify such characteristics as storage class, access, and linkage.

Specifying Storage Class

Visual C++ provides four storage classes:

- Automatic
- Static
- Register
- External

Objects with automatic storage are visible only within the block of code within which they're declared. Visual C++ allocates storage for such objects when the program enters the containing block and frees storage when the program exits the containing block. If the program defines multiple instances of the containing block, each such instance will have distinct instances of its automatic objects. Visual C++

Table 1.2   The Visual C++ data types.

Type	Characteristics
void	The **void** type describes an empty set of values. You cannot specify a variable of type **void**. The main use of the **void** type is to declare functions that return no value or that return a value of arbitrary type.
char	The **char** type is a 1-byte signed integral type that represents the values of the ASCII character set. Its values range from –128 to 127.
signed char	The **signed char** type is a 1-byte signed integral type that represents the values of the ASCII character set. Its values range from –128 to 127. Although both the **signed char** and **char** types are 1-byte signed values, the types are distinct.
unsigned char	The **unsigned char** type is a 1-byte unsigned integral type that represents the values of the ASCII character set. Its values range from 0 to 255.
short	The **short**, **short int**, **signed short**, or **signed short int** type is a 2-byte signed integral type. Its values range from –32768 to 32767.
unsigned short	The **unsigned short** or **unsigned short int** type is a 2-byte unsigned integral type. Its values range from 0 to 65535.
int	The **int** or **signed int** type is a 4-byte signed integral type. Its values range from –2147483648 to 2147483647.
unsigned int	The **unsigned int** type is a 4-byte unsigned integral type. Its values range from 0 to 4294967295.
__intn	The **__intn** type is an integral type having the number of bits specified by n, which may be 8, 16, 32, or 64.
long	The **long**, **long int**, **signed long**, or **signed long int** type is a 4-byte signed integral type. Its values range from –2147483648 to 2147483647.
unsigned long	The **unsigned long** or **unsigned long int** type is a 4-byte unsigned integral type. Its values range from 0 to 4294967295.
float	The **float** type is a 4-byte floating point type that provides approximately six decimal digits of precision. The minimum positive value is 1.175494351e–38F and the maximum positive value is 3.402823466e+38F.
double	The **double** type is an 8-byte floating point type that provides approximately 15 decimal digits of precision. The minimum positive value is 2.2250738585072014e–308 and the maximum positive value is 1.7976931348623158e+308.
long double	The **long double** type is an 8-byte floating point type that provides approximately 15 decimal digits of precision. The minimum positive value is 2.2250738585072014e–308 and the maximum positive value is 1.7976931348623158e+308. Although **double** and **long double** have the same size and precision, they are distinct types.

1. Language Elements

assigns automatic storage by default to objects specified within blocks. To explicitly specify that an object has automatic storage, you include the keyword **auto** in the object's definition:

```
auto int x;  // an int variable with automatic storage
```

Objects with static storage are initialized when the program is loaded or when the containing block is entered, and they retain their values throughout execution of the program. Visual C++ assigns static storage by default to objects specified outside all blocks. To explicitly specify that an object has static storage, you include the keyword **static** in the object's definition:

```
static int y;  // an int variable with static storage
```

An object with static storage has the same value in all instances of its containing block, even if the block is entered recursively.

Like objects with automatic storage, objects with register storage exist only during the execution of the containing block. Only function arguments and local variables may be assigned the register class. Some compilers attempt to assign variables with register storage to hardware registers; the Visual C++ compiler does not do so. To specify that an object has register storage, you include the keyword **register** in the object's definition:

```
register int n;  // an int variable with register storage
```

You declare an object with external storage when the object is defined in a source file other than the one that references the object (or when the object is defined in an enclosing scope). To specify external storage, you use the keyword **extern**. For example, the following statement refers to an **int** variable defined in another source file:

```
extern int NotHere;  // an int variable with external storage
```

The linker—not the compiler—resolves references to objects with external storage.

Specifying Access

You specify the allowable access to an object by using the keywords **public**, **protected**, and **private**. (See the section "Defining A Class, Structure, Or Union" later in this chapter.)

Specifying Linkage

Objects and functions have either internal linkage, external linkage, or no linkage. Objects and functions with internal linkage are unique to a source file and can be referenced only within that source file. All references to an object or function with external linkage refer to the same object throughout the program, even if the references are within distinct source files. Objects with no linkage are unique to the containing block and may not be referenced outside it.

The rules governing the specification of linkage are somewhat complicated. If an object or function is first declared outside all blocks, it has either internal or external linkage. Its linkage is internal if the declaration includes the keyword **static**; otherwise, its linkage is external. An object or function declared within a block has either external linkage or no linkage. Its linkage is external if the declaration includes the keyword **extern**; otherwise, it has no linkage. Table 1.3 summarizes these rules.

Using Other Qualifiers

Visual C++ provides two additional qualifiers that you can include in a declaration: **volatile** and **const**. The keyword **volatile** specifies that the value of an object may be changed by something outside the control of the program, such as a concurrently executing thread. The keyword **const** specifies that the value of an object should not be modified; the Visual C++ compiler will flag as an error any operation that attempts to modify the value of a **const** object. Because the value of a **const** object cannot be modified, the declaration generally specifies an initial value for the object. Here are examples showing how these qualifiers may be used:

```
volatile int status;              // an int that may be
                                  // modified asynchronously
const    int triangle_sides = 3;  // an unmodifiable int
```

Table 1.3   Linkage rules.

Type	How Declared	Where Referenced
External	Outside all blocks, without **static**	Throughout program
	Inside a block, with **extern**	
Internal	Outside all blocks, with **static**	Within containing source file
None	Inside a block, without **extern**	Within containing block

Defining Arrays

Visual C++ lets you define arrays, which contain multiple elements of a specified type. For example, to define an array of 100 **ints** you can write:

```
int scores[100];  // an array of 100 ints
```

The type of the elements of an array need not be a fundamental type: You can create arrays of elements of a nonfundamental type. For example, suppose your program defines a class named **CheckerPiece**. You can define an array of 100 **CheckerPiece**s by writing:

```
CheckerPiece thePiece[100];  // an array of 100 CheckerPieces
```

Visual C++ does not provide multidimensional arrays; however, you can simulate a multidimensional array by defining an array whose elements are arrays (an "array of arrays"). For example, here's an array that represents the squares of a checkerboard:

```
int occupied[8] [8]; //  an array of arrays
```

C++ does not provide a fundamental type that represents strings of text characters; in C++, you use an array of **char**s to represent text.

Defining Pointers And References

Visual C++ lets you define objects called *pointers*, which hold the memory address of an object or function. To define a pointer to an object of a given type, write a definition for an object of the given type, and then precede the name of the object with an asterisk (*). For example, to define a pointer to an **int**, you can write:

```
int *x;  // a pointer to an int
```

You can also define a pointer to a class member of a given type. For example, suppose the **CheckerPiece** class contains an **int** member named **location** that holds an identifier for the checkerboard square that the piece occupies. You can define a pointer to the **location** member by writing:

```
CheckerPiece::*location p;  // p points to a location member
```

To access the object to which a pointer refers, you use a dereference operator, as described in Chapter 2.

Visual C++ also lets you define *references*. Like pointers, references hold the memory address of an object or function. However, unlike pointers, references need not be dereferenced: Each use of a reference is translated by the compiler to access the object or function to which the reference points. You define a reference much like you define a pointer, only you use an ampersand (**&**) rather than an asterisk. For example, to define a reference to an **int** you write:

```
int &x;  // a reference to an int
```

Using the keyword **const**, you can define a reference that lets you access an object but prohibits you from modifying the object. For example, the following definition creates a **const** reference to an **int**:

```
const int &x;
```

You may find it useful to declare the arguments of a function as **const** references, which causes the arguments to be efficiently passed by reference but prevents the function from modifying the arguments' values:

```
float computeSquare(const float &x)
{
   return x * x;
}
```

Using Initializers And Initializer Lists

A declaration may specify the initial value of an object; for a **const** object, a declaration must specify the initial value of the object, because the value of the object cannot be modified. C++ provides two constructs for initializing objects: one that assigns an initial value to an object and one that invokes an object's constructor (see Chapter 4). The latter can be used only where such a constructor exists; it cannot be used, for example, to initialize the value of a variable having a fundamental type, such as an **int**.

To assign an initial value to an object, follow the definition of the object with an assignment operator (**=**) and an expression that computes the desired initial value. For example, to initialize an **int** variable to the value 100, you write:

```
int x = 100;  // an int initialized to 100
```

For more information on forming expressions, see Chapter 2.

To initialize an object by invoking an appropriate constructor, follow the definition with a function-type invocation of the constructor. For example, suppose that your program includes a constructor that initializes a **CheckerPiece** given its color and square. You could initialize a **CheckerPiece** as follows:

```
CheckerPiece thePiece(red, 15); // initialize a red
                                // CheckerPiece on square 15
```

You can initialize an array by specifying a list of values for its elements. For example, to initialize a five-element array in which each cell contains the square of its index, you can write:

```
int squares[] = { 0, 1, 4, 9, 16 };
```

When you initialize an array in this fashion, you may—but don't need to—specify the number of elements in the array. The compiler can determine the proper number of elements by examining the list of initial values. If you specify a number of elements larger than the number of values in the initialization list, the remaining elements of the array are initialized to zero. If you specify a number of elements smaller than the number of values in the initialization list, the compiler will flag the initialization as an error.

You can initialize an array of arrays by using nested lists of initial values. For example, suppose you need an array of arrays that simulates a two-dimensional array in which the elements contain sequential values. You can write a definition like the following:

```
int sequence[3][2] = { {1, 2}, {3, 4}, {5, 6} };
```

This definition specifies an array that resembles a multidimensional array of three rows of two columns each.

You can initialize arrays of type **char** either of two ways. For example, you can initialize an array to contain the name of the company that implemented Visual C++ by writing either

```
char ms1[] = { 'M', 'i', 'c', 'r', 'o', 's', 'o', 'f', 't' };
```

or:

```
char ms2[] = "Microsoft";
```

The second form is generally more readable and convenient. By convention, a string of text contains as its final character the character whose ASCII value is 0 (the null character). The first form of initialization does not include this delimiting character in the array, but the second form does. To use the first form but include the delimiting character, you can write:

```
char ms1[] = { 'M', 'i', 'c', 'r', 'o', 's', 'o', 'f',
               't', 0 };
```

For more information on writing initial values, see the section "Specifying Literal Values" later in this chapter.

Defining Enumerations

An enumeration is a user-defined integral type that takes as its values the members of a set of integer constants. Here's an example definition of a simple enumeration:

```
enum Side { TOP, BOTTOM, LEFT, RIGHT };
```

The example assigns arbitrary values to the enumerators **TOP**, **BOTTOM**, **LEFT**, and **RIGHT**. You can assign explicit values by including a constant initialization expression, for example:

```
enum Side { TOP=1, BOTTOM=2, LEFT=3, RIGHT=4 };
```

Once you've defined an enumeration, you can create variables that have its type in the usual way. For example:

```
Side theSide = 3;   // refers to the LEFT side
```

Using **typedef** statements

The C++ **typedef** statement lets you introduce a synonym for a type. For example, the following statement introduces **BIG** as a synonym for **long**:

```
typedef long BIG;
```

The **typedef** statement can help you simplify a series of definitions by letting you write the complicated part only once. For example, suppose you want to define a series of two-dimensional **int** arrays that represent checkerboard positions. You can do so as follows:

```
typedef int[8, 8] checkerboard;
checkerboard current_move;
checkerboard previous_move;
checkerboard next_move;
```

Specifying Literal Values

A literal value is one that stands literally for itself. Unlike a variable, you can determine the value of a literal by merely reading it. Visual C++ lets you specify literals of four types:

- Integer
- Floating point
- Character
- String

Forming Integer Literals

To specify a decimal integer value, write a series of digits that begins with a digit other than zero. Follow the literal with **u** or **U** to specify an unsigned value; follow the literal with **l** or **L** to specify a long value. For example, the following definitions include valid literals:

```
unsigned int i = 123U;
long j = 123L;
```

In specifying a **long** literal, it's better to use **L** than l, because the latter closely resembles the digit 1.

You can also use an octal or hexadecimal value to specify a literal. To specify an octal value, begin the literal with the digit zero and follow the initial digit with a series of octal digits (0-7). To specify a hexadecimal value, begin the literal with **0x** or **0X** and follow the initial digit with a series of hexadecimal digits (0-f or 0-F). For example, the following definitions include value octal or hexadecimal literals:

```
unsigned int i = 0173U;   // decimal value 123
long j = 0X7bL;           // decimal value 123
```

Forming Floating-Point Literals

To specify a floating-point literal, you can write the value using a decimal point. For example, 123.0 is a value floating-point literal. You can also specify a floating-point literal using exponential notation. To do so, write a fractional constant, followed by **e** or **E**, followed by an optionally signed exponent that specifies the power of 10 by which the fractional constant is multiplied to arrive at the value of the literal. For example, the literals 1.23E2, 1.23e2, and 1.23E+2 all have the value 123. By default, a floating-point literal has type **double**. You can follow a floating point literal with **f** or **F** to indicate that the type of the literal is **float**, or with **l** or **L** to indicate that the type of the literal is **long double**.

Forming Character Literals

Visual C++ supports three types of character literals:

- Normal

- Multicharacter

- Wide-character

Normal character literals have type **char** and may include only a single character. Multicharacter values have type **int**. Wide-character values have a special type, **wchar_t**, defined by a **typedef**. Microsoft recommends that you use wide-character literals rather than multicharacter literals to ensure program portability. To write a normal character or multicharacter literal, enclose the characters within single quotes. To write a wide-character literal, write an **L**, followed by a series of characters enclosed between single quotes. Here are some example definitions that include character literals:

```
char c1 = 'a';      // a normal character literal
int  c2 = 'ab';     // a multicharacter literal
wchar_t c3 = L'ab'; // a wide-character constant
```

Forming String Literals

A string literal may contain an arbitrary number of characters. The last character of a string literal is always the null character (ASCII value 0). To write a string literal, enclose a series of characters between double quotes. For example, the string literal "Hi" consists of three characters: an "H", an "i", and a null.

Using Escape Sequences

Visual C++ provides a set of escape sequences that let you conveniently specify values of nonprinting and special characters within character and string literals. Table 1.4 describes the available escape sequences. As an example, the following defines a string terminated by a carriage return and line feed:

```
char message[] = "Hi Mom!\r\n";
```

Escape sequences are especially useful for embedding a single quote within a character literal ('\'') or a double quote within a character string ("\"**This is a quote.**\"").

Table 1.4   Escape sequences.

Sequence	ASCII Value	Definition
\0	0	Null character
\a	7	Alarm
\b	8	Backspace
\t	9	Horizontal tab
\n	10	New-line (linefeed)
\v	11	Vertical tab
\f	12	Form feed
\r	13	Carriage return
\"	34	Double quote
\'	39	Single quote
\?	63	Question mark
****	92	Backslash
\ooo	Varies	The number given by the octal digits *ooo*
\xhhh	Varies	The number given by the hexadecimal digits *hhh*

Defining A Class, Structure, Or Union

Visual C++ lets you define three class types:

- Classes
- Structures
- Unions

Classes and structures are quite similar; the most significant difference is that the members of a class have private access by default, whereas the members of a structure have public access by default. Unions let you specify multiple members, but at runtime, a union contains only one of its defined members. The members of a union have public access by default. For more information on classes, structures, and unions, see Chapter 4.

Briefly, to define a C++ class, structure, or union, begin with the appropriate keyword: **class** for a class, **struct** for a structure, or **union** for a union. Follow the keyword with the name of the class, structure, or union.

You can follow the name of the class with information that specifies the base class from which the class derives. See Chapter 4 for details.

The definition of a class includes a list of optional class member definitions, enclosed within a pair of curly braces ({}). The members may be data members or function members. The definition of a member may be preceded by an access specifier: **public**, **protected**, or **private**. Here's an example definition of a class that includes only data members:

```
class TheClass {
public:
    int x;
    int y;
private:
    int size;
};
```

Defining A Function

You can define a function outside all blocks, or within a class or structure, in which case the function is called a *member function*. Briefly, a function definition consists of:

- An optional storage class (**auto**, **register**, **static**, or **extern**)
- A type, which may be fundamental or nonfundamental
- The function name
- An argument list, enclosed between parentheses
- A function body, which consists of a compound statement (see Chapter 3)

The definitions of special functions, such as constructors, may contain additional information. Here's an example definition of a simple function:

```
float square(float x)
{
    return x * x;
}
```

Conversions, Expressions, And Operators

In Brief

Writing Expressions

Visual C++ lets you combine literals and variables (referred to as *operands*) with operators to form expressions. You can also form expressions by combining other expressions.

You use an expression to compute a value from the values of the literals, variables, and expressions (called *terms*) that compose it. The terms may be of the same type or different types. When all the terms of an expression have the same type, the value computed by the expression also has this type. (Expressions built using the conditional operator pose an exception: A conditional expression returns 1 or 0—representing true and false, respectively—regardless of the types of the expression's terms).

Conversions

When the terms of an expression have different types, Visual C++ applies a series of conversion rules that determine the type of the expression result. These rules change the type of a term within the expression; however, they do not change the value or type of the operands of the expression.

Here's a simple example:

```
int x = 1;
float y = x;
```

This segment of code assigns the value of **x** (an **int**) to **y** (a **float**). Because the bit representations of **int**s and **float**s are quite different, Visual C++ does not merely store the bits of **x** in **y**'s storage location. Instead, Visual C++:

- Determines the value represented by the bits of **x**
- Forms a **float** value with an integer part having the same value as **x** and a fractional part having the value zero
- Stores the **float** value in **y**'s storage location

Notice that Visual C++ does not disturb the stored value of **x**.

Evaluating Expressions

Just as Visual C++ has rules that determine the type of an expression result, it also has rules that determine the value of the result. For example, consider this simple example:

```
int x = 1 + 2 * 3;
```

If you recall the rules of algebra, you expect Visual C++ to calculate the value of the expression as though it were written like this:

```
int x = 1 + (2 * 3);
```

The rules of algebra specify that the multiplication operation is performed before the addition operation. Because the rules of algebra are so widely known, Visual C++ uses them to determine how to calculate expressions. However, Visual C++ provides many more operators than algebra. Therefore, Visual C++'s rules for evaluating expressions are more numerous than those of algebra.

Of course, Visual C++ understands parentheses, and so you can use them just as you do in ordinary algebra. For example, suppose you wanted the expression given earlier to perform the addition first. You can simply rewrite the expression like this:

```
int x = (1 + 2) * 3;
```

In this chapter, you'll learn how Visual C++'s conversion and evaluation rules work. Understanding the conversion and evaluation rules will help you write expressions accurately and concisely.

Immediate Solutions

Promotion

Visual C++ lets you use a **signed** or **unsigned char**, **signed** or **unsigned short**, enumeration, object of enumeration type, or bit-field wherever an **int** is allowed. Visual C++ automatically *promotes* the type of such an operand to **int**. If a **signed int** can't accommodate all the possible values of the type of its operand, the value is converted to an **unsigned int**. If the value of the operand is large and negative, this conversion may change the sign of the value.

Other Integer Conversions

Integer conversions can also involve converting unsigned values to signed values. When the value of an unsigned operand can be represented using a signed type, its value is unchanged. Otherwise, the value is implementation-dependent. In such cases, Visual C++ converts the value of the operand to a signed representation that has the same bit pattern as that of the operand.

For example, consider the following code fragment:

```
unsigned int u = 2147483649;
signed   int n = u;
```

This code assigns the value –2147483647 to **n**, because this value has the same 32-bit representation as that of 2147483649.

Floating Conversions

Because the **double** type uses more bits to represent value than does the **float** type, the set of possible **float** values is a subset of the set of possible **double** values. As a result, conversion of a **float** to a **double** does not change the value.

However, converting a **double** to a **float** may result in a change of value. This can occur if the **double** value is too large or too small to be represented as a **float**. In this case, the result is undefined. Even if the **double** value is within the range of valid **float** values, a change of value will occur if the **double** value does not correspond to a valid **float** value. In such a case, Visual C++ assigns the closest (next smaller or next larger) **float** value.

Mixed-Integer Floating-Point Conversions

When Visual C++ converts a floating value to an integral type, it discards the fractional part of the floating value without performing any rounding. For example, the floating value 1.9999999 becomes the integer value 1.

Many programmers erroneously believe that conversion of an integer value to a floating-point type never results in a change of value. When Visual C++ converts a large integer value to a floating type, the value may change. For example, consider the following code fragment:

```
int n = 2147483647;
float f = n;
```

The **float** type provides only about six decimal digits of precision. The result of this conversion is 2.14748e+009; several digits of the original value cannot be represented within the available precision of a **float** value.

Arithmetic Conversions

Visual C++ defines a series of rules called "the usual arithmetic conversions." It applies these rules whenever it computes an expression, examining the operands of each arithmetic operator:

- If either operand is of type **long double**, the other is converted to **long double**.
- Otherwise, if either operand is of type **double**, the other is converted to type **double**.
- Otherwise, if either operand is of type **float**, the other is converted to type **float**.

2. Conversions, Expressions, And Operators

- Otherwise, the operands must both be of integral type. Visual C++ promotes the operands as follows:

  - If either operand is of type **unsigned long**, the other is converted to type **unsigned long**.

  - Otherwise, if either operand is of type **long** and the other is of type **unsigned int**, both operands are converted to type **unsigned int** (or **unsigned long**, if either value is too large to be represented as an **unsigned int**).

  - Otherwise, if either operand is of type **long**, the other operand is converted to type **long**.

  - Otherwise, if either operand is of type **unsigned int**, the other operand is converted to type **unsigned int**.

  - Otherwise, both operands are converted to type **int**.

Pointer And Reference Conversions

Whenever Visual C++ initializes, assigns, or compares pointers to objects or functions, it may perform the following conversions:

- When Visual C++ attempts to convert the value of an expression to a pointer, it checks the type and value of the expression. If it finds that the expression is a constant expression that has the value zero, it converts the expression to a special pointer value commonly called the *null pointer*. Visual C++ ensures that the null pointer does not point to any object.

- Visual C++ may convert a pointer to any object type (other than a **const** or **volatile** type) to a **void***.

- Visual C++ may convert a pointer to a function to a **void***, provided that a **void*** has sufficient bits to hold the resulting value.

- Visual C++ may convert a pointer to a class to a pointer to any base (parent) class of that class if two conditions apply:

  - The conversion must be unambiguous. This condition restricts some classes that inherit more than once from participating in the conversion.

  - The public members of the base class must be accessible.

    The result of the conversion is a pointer to the base class subobject of the object pointed to. If the original pointer is null, the resulting pointer is null.

- Visual C++ may convert an expression that refers to an array to a pointer of the same type as the array. The resulting pointer refers to the initial element of the array.

- Visual C++ may convert an expression that refers to a function to a pointer that refers to the function. However, Visual C++ will not perform such a conversion when the original expression is used as an operand of the address-of operator **&** or the function call operator ().

Visual C++ converts a reference to a class to a reference to a base (parent) class of that class if the conversion can be performed unambiguously. The result of the conversion is a reference to the base class subobject of the object referenced. As in the case of a pointer to a class, the condition that the conversion be unambiguous restricts some classes that inherit more than once from participating in the conversion.

Whenever Visual C++ initializes, assigns, or compares pointers to members, it may perform the following conversions:

- Visual C++ may convert a constant expression that has the value zero to the null pointer.

- Visual C++ may convert a pointer to a member of a class to a pointer to a member of a derived (child) class if two conditions apply:

  - The conversion from the derived class to the base class pointer is accessible.

  - The conversion is unambiguous. As before, this precludes some multiply derived classes from participating in such conversions.

Notice that a pointer to a member is not the same as a pointer to an object or a function. The conversion rules that apply to pointers to objects or functions do not generally apply to pointers to members.

Type Casts

Visual C++ performs some conversions automatically. However, by specifying a type cast, you can explicitly instruct Visual C++ to perform a desired conversion. Visual C++ lets you specify a type cast either of two ways:

- Using functional notation
- Using cast notation

To write a type cast using functional notation, you write the name of the desired type, followed by the target expression, which you enclose within parentheses. For example, the following code fragment casts the type of **n** to **short**:

```
int    n = 100;
short s = short (n);
```

To write a type cast using cast notation, you enclose the name of the desired type within parentheses, followed by the target expression. For example, the following code fragment casts the type of **n** to **short**:

```
int    n = 100;
short s = (short) n;
```

Visual C++ permits only type casts that satisfy the following rules:

- A type can be automatically converted to another type can be cast to that type.

- A pointer can be cast to any integral type large enough to hold it.

- An integral value can be cast to a pointer.

- A pointer to one object type can be cast to a pointer to another object type. However, the resulting pointer is not generally guaranteed to be valid. A pointer to a derived class can be safely cast to a pointer of a base (parent) class. But, in the general case, addressing exceptions may occur if the resulting pointer refers to an object that is not suitably aligned in storage.

- An object can be cast to a reference type if a pointer to that object can be cast to a pointer of the same type. For example, you can cast an object to reference type **X&** if you can cast a pointer to that object to type **X***.

- A pointer to a function can be cast to a pointer to an object type, provided that the object pointer type has sufficient bits to hold the result.

- A pointer to an object type can be cast to a pointer to a function, provided that the function pointer type has sufficient bits to hold the result.

- A pointer to a function of one type can be cast to a pointer to a function of a different type.

- An object or value can be cast to a class object only if the class provides an appropriate constructor or conversion operator.

- A pointer to a member can be cast to a different pointer-to-member type, provided that both types are pointers to members of the same class or pointers to member functions of a class and one of its (unambiguously) derived classes.

- A pointer to a **const** object can be cast to a pointer to a non-**const** type. Similarly, an object of **const** type or a reference to such an object can be cast to a reference of a non-**const** type. However, attempting to modify that object via the resulting pointer or reference may cause an addressing exception, because that operation is implementation-dependent.

- A pointer to a **volatile** object can be cast to a pointer to a non-**volatile** type. Similarly, an object of **volatile** type or a reference to such an object can be cast to a reference of a non-**volatile** type.

Primary Expressions

You use expressions to compute values by combining *primary expressions*, which include literals, variables, and other expressions. Visual C++ lets you use any of the following as a primary expression:

- A literal.

- The keyword **this**, which represents the current object for which the nonstatic member function was invoked.

- The scope resolution operator followed by an identifier. The identifier refers to a type, object, function, or enumerator of file scope. This device lets you refer to such a program object even if its identifier has been hidden.

- The scope resolution operator followed by an operator function name. An operator function name consists of the keyword **operator**, followed by an operator other than the member operator (.), the pointer-to-member operator (.*), the scope resolution operator, or the conditional operator (?:). This device lets you refer to an operator function of file scope, even if its identifier has been hidden. Here's an example of a reference to an operator function at file scope:

```
::operator =
```

- The scope resolution operator followed by a qualified name, which consists of a qualified class name, followed by the scope resolution operator, followed by a name. A qualified class name is a class name, or a qualified class name followed by the scope resolution operator and a name. This recursive definition lets you daisy-chain a series of class names to form a primary expression such as **::a::b::c::d**. Such an expression refers to a class **a** at file scope, which contains a class **b**, which contains a class **c**, which defines the identifier **d**.

- An expression enclosed within parentheses.

- A name, which can be an identifier, a conversion function name, the name of a destructor, a qualified name, or an operator function name. An operator function name consists of the keyword **operator** followed by the name of a class or type.

Operators

Table 2.1 summarizes the operators provided by Visual C++ and groups them into 17 categories, ordered by precedence. Operators within a category have the same precedence. The scope operator has a higher precedence than any of the postfix operators, which have a higher precedence than the unary operators, and so on.

Recall that the precedence of an operator determines the order in which an expression is evaluated (except where parentheses explicitly specify the order of evaluation). Within an expression, the operator with highest precedence is evaluated first.

When an expression includes operators of equal precedence, Visual C++ applies rules of associativity. Most Visual C++ operators are left-to-right associative. For example, the addition operator is left-to-right associative, and so the following two expressions have the same order of evaluation:

```
a + b + c    // expression #1
(a + b) + c  // expression #2
```

The Visual C++ operators that are right-to-left associative are:

- The type cast operator
- The conditional operator
- The assignment operators

Table 2.1   Visual C++ operators by category.

Category	Operator	Operator Name
Scope	::	Scope resolution
Postfix	.	Member
	->	Member pointer
	[ ]	Index
	( )	Function call
	++	Increment
	- -	Decrement
Unary	++	Increment
	- -	Decrement
	!	Not
	~	Complement
	sizeof	Size of
	+	Unary plus
	-	Unary minus
	*	Pointer dereference
	&	Address of
	(type)	Type cast
	new	New operator
	delete	Delete operator
Membership	->*	Pointer-to-member
	.*	Pointer-to-member
Multiplicative	*	Multiplication
	/	Division
	%	Modulus (remainder)
Additive	+	Addition
	-	Subtraction
Shift	<<	Left-shift
	>>	Right-shift
Relational	<	Less than
	<=	Less than or equal to
	>	Greater than
	>=	Greater than or equal to
Equality	==	Equality
	!=	Inequality
Bitwise AND	&	Bitwise AND
Bitwise XOR	^	Bitwise exclusive OR (XOR)
Bitwise OR	I	Bitwise inclusive OR
Logical AND	&&	Logical AND

2. Conversions, Expressions, And Operators

(continued)

Table 2.1   Visual C++ operators by category (continued).

Category	Operator	Operator Name
Logical OR	||	Logical OR
Conditional	?:	Conditional
Assignment	=	Assignment
	*=	Multiplication assignment
	/=	Division assignment
	%=	Modulus assignment
	+=	Addition assignment
	-=	Subtraction assignment
	&=	Bitwise AND assignment
	^=	Bitwise XOR assignment
	|=	Bitwise OR assignment
	<<=	Left-shift assignment
	>>=	Right-shift assignment
Comma	,	Comma

For example, the following two expressions involving the assignment operator have the same order of evaluation:

```
a = b = c    // expression #1
a = (b = c)  // expression #2
```

The unusual associativity of the assignment operators lets you conveniently initialize a series of variables by writing a statement expression such as:

```
a = b = c = 1;
```

This *expression statement* (as an expression followed by a semicolon is called) first assigns the value 1 to the variable **c**. The evaluation of the subexpression **c = 1** produces the result 1, which is then assigned to the variable **b**. The evaluation of the subexpression **b = c = 1** therefore produces the result 1, which is assigned to the variable **a**. The evaluation of the subexpression **a = b = c = 1** produces the result 1; but this is the final subexpression. Therefore, Visual C++ does nothing with this final result, transferring control to the next sequential statement.

Postfix Operators

Visual C++ has six postfix operators:

- The member operator (**.**)
- The member pointer operator (**->**)

- The index (subscript) operator ([])
- The function call operator (())
- The increment operator (++)
- The decrement operator (--)

You can use the member operator to refer to the value of a member of a class object (a class, structure, or union). For example, suppose that **X** is a class object that defines the member **m**. Then, the expression **X.m** refers to the member **m** of the class object.

You can use the member pointer operator to dereference a pointer to a class object. For example, suppose that **p** points to an instance of **X**, which is a class that defines the member **m**. Then, the expression **p->m** points to the member **m** of the instance **X**.

You can use the index operator to refer to an element of an array. For example, suppose that **A** is an array. Then, the expression **A[0]** refers to the first element of the array **A**. The subscript operator can also be used with a pointer. The effect is to increment the value of the pointer by the specified amount and dereference the result. For example, suppose that **p** is a pointer. Then, the expression **p[1]** is equivalent to ***(p + 1)**.

A *function call* is an expression that evaluates to a function (for example, a function name or a dereferenced pointer to a function), followed by parentheses containing a comma-separated list of actual arguments to the function. If the function has no arguments, the list can be omitted, but the parentheses are always present.

The increment operator increases the value of its argument by 1; the related decrement operator decreases the value of its operand by 1. Notice in Table 2.1 that increment and decrement operators appear in two categories: postfix and unary. Either operator is considered postfix when it follows its operator, or unary when it precedes its operands. For example, the expression **n++** includes a postfix increment operator, and the expression **++n** includes a unary increment operator.

When used as a postfix operator, the increment operator and decrement operator return the value of their operand (that is, the value of the operand before the operator is applied). When used as a postfix operator, the increment operator and decrement operator return the value of their operand after the operator is applied. For example, consider the following code fragment:

```
int m1 = 1;
int n1 = m1++;
int n2 = 1;
int m2 = ++n2;
```

The fragment assigns the value 1 to **n1** and the value 2 to **m2**.

Unary Operators

Unary operators take only a single operand. In addition to the unary increment and decrement operators, Visual C++ provides 10 additional unary operators:

- *The NOT operator (!)*—This operator returns 1 (a true value) if its argument is false (zero) and returns zero (false) otherwise. The type of the operand must be arithmetic or pointer.

- *The complement operator (~)*—This operator returns the 1's complement of its operand, which must have integral type.

- *The unary plus operator (+)*—This operator returns the value of its operand, which must have arithmetic or pointer type.

- *The unary minus operator (-)*—This operator returns the negation of its operand, which must have arithmetic type.

- *The **sizeof** operator*—This operator returns the size, in bytes, of its operand.

- *The pointer dereference operator (*)*—This operator returns the object to which its operand—which must have pointer type—points.

- *The address-of operator (&)*—This operator returns a pointer to its operand.

- *The type cast operator ((**type**))*—This operator explicitly converts the type of the value of its operand.

- *The **new** operator*—This operator allocates a new instance of the specified object type.

- *The **delete** operator*—This operator deallocates the specified object previously created by the **new** operator.

Membership Operators

Visual C++ provides two membership operators—.* and ->*—each referred to as the pointer-to-member operator. Each operator returns the value of the member (specified by the right operand, which must be a pointer to a member) of an object (specified by the left operator). The left operand of the **.*** operator refers to a class, whereas the left operand of the **->*** operator refers to a pointer to a class. For example, suppose that **X** is a class object and **m** is a pointer to a member of **Y**, which is an unambiguous and accessible base class of class **X**. Then, the expression **X.*m** refers to a pointer to the **m** member of **X**. Suppose that **p** has the type pointer to class **X**. Then, the expression **p->*m** refers to a pointer to a member of **Y**.

Multiplicative Operators

Visual C++ provides three multiplicative operators:

- The multiplication operator (*****)
- The division operator (**/**)
- The modulus (remainder) operator (**%**)

These operators perform their usual algebraic operations. The modulus operator computes the modulus or remainder. For example, the expression **10%3** has the value 1, the remainder of the integer division of 10 by 3.

Additive Operators

Visual C++ provides two additive operators:

- The addition operator (**+**)
- The subtraction operator (**-**)

Like the multiplicative operators, the additive operators perform their usual algebraic operations.

Shift Operators

Visual C++ provides two shift operators:

- *The left-shift operator (**<<**)*—This operator shifts the bit representation of the value of its left operand a specified number of positions to the left. For example, the expression **2<<1** has the value 4, the result of shifting the value 2 one bit position to the left.

- *The right-shift operator (**>>**)*—This operator shifts the bit representation of the value of its left operand a specified number of positions to the right. For example, the expression **4>>1** has the value 2, the result of shifting the value 4 one bit position to the right.

Relational Operators

Visual C++ provides four relational operators:

- The less than operator (<)
- The less than or equal to operator (<=)
- The greater than operator (>)
- The greater than or equal to operator (>=)

These operators perform their usual algebraic operations.

Equality Operators

Visual C++ provides two equality operators:

- The equality operator (==)
- The inequality operator (!=)

These operators perform their usual algebraic operations. The equality operator returns 1 (a true value) if its operands have the same value and returns zero (false value) otherwise. The inequality operator returns 1 if its operands have different values and returns zero otherwise.

Bitwise Operators

Visual C++ provides three bitwise operators:

- *The bitwise AND operator (&)*—This operator combines the bits of its left and right operands by using the AND operation. A bit of the result will be a 1 bit if the corresponding bit is 1 in each operand.

- *The bitwise exclusive OR operator (^)*—This operator combines the bits of its left and right operands by using the exclusive OR operation. A bit of the result will be a 1 bit if the corresponding bit is 1 in exactly one of the operands.

- *The bitwise inclusive OR operator (l)*—This operator combines the bits of its left and right operands by using the OR operation. A bit of the result will be a 1 bit if the corresponding bit of either operand is 1.

Logical Operators

Visual C++ provides two logical operators:

- *The logical AND operator (&&)*—This operator combines the values of its left and right operands by using the logical AND operation. The result will be 1 if both operands have true (non-zero) values; otherwise, the result will be 0.

- *The logical OR operator (||)*—This operator combines the values of its left and right operands by using the logical OR operation. The result will be 1 if either operand has a true (non-zero) value; otherwise, the result will be 0.

The Conditional Operator

The conditional operator is a ternary operator, taking three operands. Two tokens, a question mark, and a colon are used to represent the conditional operator. For example, the expression **(a == 1) ? b : c** is a conditional expression that tests the value of the subexpression **a == 1**, which is interpreted as a logical (true-false) expression. If the subexpression evaluates true, the conditional expression returns the value **b**; otherwise, it returns the value **c**.

Assignment Operators

Visual C++ provides 11 assignment operators:

- The (simple) assignment operator (=)
- The multiplication assignment operator (*=)
- The division assignment operator (/=)
- The modulus assignment operator (%=)
- The addition assignment operator (+=)
- The subtraction assignment operator (-=)
- The bitwise AND assignment operator (&=)
- The bitwise exclusive OR assignment operator (^=)
- The bitwise inclusive OR assignment operator (!=)
- The left-shift assignment operator (<<=)
- The right-shift assignment operator (>>=)

The simple assignment operator (=) assigns the value of its right argument to its left argument. Each remaining assignment operator is equivalent to an expression involving the simple assignment operator and another operator. Suppose that an assignment expression has the form **x *op*= y**, where ***op*=** is an assignment operator other than simple assignment. Such an assignment expression is equivalent to the expression **x = x *op* y**. For example, consider the assignment expression given in the following code fragment:

```
int m = 1;
int n = 0;
n += m;  // equivalent to n = n + m;
```

The assignment stores the value 1 in **n**.

The Comma Operator

You can use the comma operator to join two expressions. Visual C++ will evaluate the left expression and then evaluate the right expression. The value returned by the comma operator is the value of the right expression. For example, the expression **n = ((a = 1), (b = 2))** assigns 1 to **a**, assigns 2 to **b**, and returns the value 2. The comma operator is not often used except as a way of performing multiple operations within the expressions of a loop statement (see Chapter 3). Although the arguments of a function are separated by commas, such commas are not instances of the comma operator.

Statements, Functions, And Scope

In Brief

Defining Statements

Statements declare program objects, perform computations, and control the flow of program execution. Figure 3.1 summarizes the types of statements that Visual C++ provides.

The Visual C++ *declaration statement* lets you declare or define one or more program objects. It consists simply of a declaration. Because every declaration ends with a semicolon, every declaration statement also ends with a semicolon. An important type of declaration statement defines a function. Declaration statements and function definitions are described in more detail in the Immediate Solutions section of this chapter. The point at which a program object is defined determines the *scope*, or visibility, of the program object. The topic of scope is presented in more detail in Immediate Solutions as well.

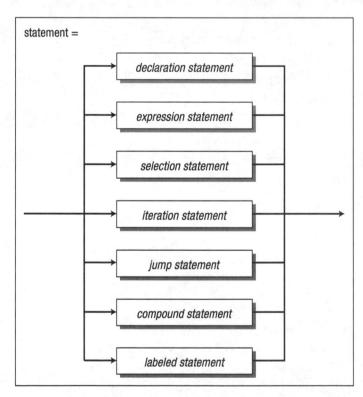

Figure 3.1   Statement syntax.

Figure 3.2 shows the syntax of the declaration statement by using a so-called *railroad track* diagram. A railroad track diagram uses three elements: rounded rectangles, ordinary rectangles, and tracks. The rounded rectangles denote C++ *terminal symbols*: reserved words, punctuators, operators, and other C++ tokens that appear in programs exactly as shown in the diagram. The ordinary rectangles denote C++ *non-terminal symbols*: higher-level syntactic elements composed of non-terminal and terminal symbols. The arrows and tracks show one or more paths through the diagram, which may include forks and loops. Because the C++ declaration statement is so simple, its railroad track diagram requires only a single non-terminal symbol and a single track.

The Visual C++ *expression statement* evaluates an expression. Such expressions often contain an assignment operator that stores the value of the expression in a program variable. An expression statement can contain no operators or operands; such an expression statement is called a *null statement*. The null statement does nothing; it's merely a placeholder that you can use anywhere a statement is allowed. Figure 3.3 shows the syntax of the expression statement, which consists of an optional expression followed by a semicolon.

Visual C++ generally executes statements sequentially, but selection, iteration, and jump statements let you alter your program's flow of execution. *Selection statements* (the **if** and **switch**) let you skip execution of a statement based on the value of a test expression. *Iteration statements* (the **while**, **do**, and **for**) let you execute a statement

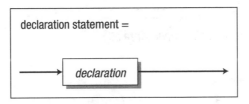

Figure 3.2   Declaration statement syntax.

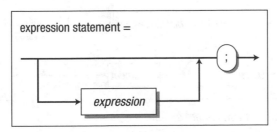

Figure 3.3   Expression statement syntax.

3. Statements, Functions, And Scope

repeatedly, based on the value of a test expression. *Jump statements* (the **break**, **continue**, **return**, and **goto**) let you transfer program control to a nonsequential statement. Selection, iteration, and jump statements are described in detail in the Immediate Solutions section of this chapter.

You can combine a series of statements into a single *compound statement* (also called a *block*) by enclosing the series within curly braces. Figure 3.4 shows the syntax of the Visual C++ compound statement. Notice that you can define an empty compound statement, which is a compound statement that includes no subordinate statements within its braces. Such a compound statement appears as a mere pair of curly braces ({}).

Visual C++ lets you label a statement so that a **goto** statement can transfer control to it. The **switch** statement lets you label statements and conditionally execute them based on the value of a test expression. Figure 3.5 shows the syntax of the labeled statement.

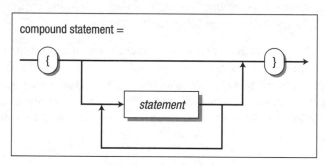

Figure 3.4   Compound statement syntax.

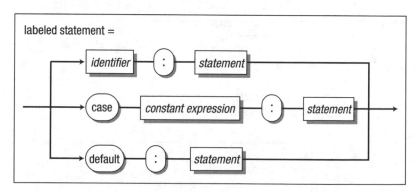

Figure 3.5   Labeled statement syntax.

The **goto** statement uses the first form of the labeled statement, which includes an identifier; the **switch** statement uses the second and third forms of the labeled statement, which use the **case** and **default** keywords. Identifiers used as labels are distinct from other program identifiers; you can have a variable, for example, that has the same name as a label. When you label a statement, the label is visible only within the function in which the labeled statement appears. You can place a **goto** statement that refers to a label before or after the labeled statement. The Immediate Solutions section of this chapter describes the operation of jump statements and the **switch** statement.

Immediate Solutions

Selection Statements

Visual C++ provides two selection statements: the **if** and the **switch**. Figure 3.6 shows the syntax of both selection statements. Notice that the **if** statement has two forms: one that includes the keyword **else** and one that does not.

The **if** Statement

The expression used in an **if** statement must have arithmetic, pointer, or class type. If the expression has class type, Visual C++ must be able to convert the class type to arithmetic or pointer type.

In operation, the **if** statement evaluates its expression. If the value of the expression is non-zero, the statement following the expression is executed. If the value of the expression is 0 and the **if** statement includes the **else** keyword, the second statement within the **if** statement is executed.

Notice that the statement included within an **if** statement can be an **if** statement. Such an **if** statement is called a *nested if statement*. In a nested **if** statement, an **else** is matched with the innermost **if**. For example, consider the following code fragment, which includes whitespace that clarifies the meaning of the code:

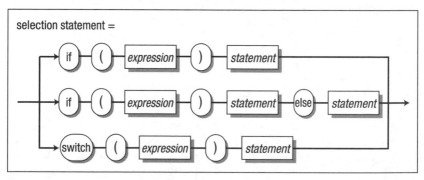

Figure 3.6   Selection statement syntax.

```
c = 0;
if (a == 1)
    if (b == 2)
        c = 1;
    else
        c = 2;
```

The fragment assigns the value 1 to **c** if the value of **a** is 1 and the value of **b** is 2. It assigns the value 2 to **c** if the value of **a** is 1 and the value of **b** is not 2. If the value of **a** is not 1, the initial assignment statement within the fragment assigns the value 0 to **c** and the **if** statement leaves that value intact.

Recall that the compiler generally ignores the use of whitespace. The operation of the following code fragment is identical to that of the earlier example, despite the misleading indentation:

```
c = 0;
if (a == 1)
    if (b == 2)
        c = 1;
else
    c = 2;
```

The **switch** Statement

The **switch** statement tests the value of an expression and transfers control to a statement labeled with a **case** that has a matching value. The expression must have integral or class type. If the expression has class type, Visual C++ must be able to convert the class type to an integral type.

The statement associated with a **switch** statement is generally a compound statement. However, Visual C++ does not require this.

Figure 3.5 (seen earlier) shows the syntax of the **case** label, which consists of the keyword **case**, followed by a constant expression, followed by a colon. Such labels can be used only within the statement associated with a **switch** statement. Within a **switch** statement, no two statements may have **case** labels that have the same value.

Figure 3.5 also shows the syntax of the **default** label. At most, one statement within a **switch** statement may have a **default** label.

In operation, the **switch** statement evaluates its test expression and compares the result to the value of each **case** expression. If one of the **case** expressions has the same value as the test expression, Visual C++ transfers control to the statement associated with that **case** label. If no matching value is found and the **switch** statement includes a statement labeled with **default**, Visual C++ transfers control to that statement; otherwise, Visual C++ executes none of the statements within the **switch**, but transfers control to the next sequential statement following the **switch** statement.

Notice that **case** labels and **default** labels have no effect on the sequential flow of control. For example, a single statement can have multiple **case** labels, in which case it receives control if any of the values of its **case** labels matches the value of the test expression:

```
case 1:
case 2:
case 3:
    printf("The value is 1, 2, or 3.\n");
```

Once Visual C++ transfers control to a statement within a **switch** statement, it executes the statements of the **switch** sequentially until it executes the last statement within the **switch** statement or it encounters a **break** statement. The **break** statement is described in the section "Jump Statements" later in this chapter.

Like **if** statements, **switch** statements can be nested. A **case** or **default** label is associated with the innermost **switch** that contains it.

You can include declaration statements within a **switch** statement. However, you must place declarations that assign an initial value to a program object within an inner block. Otherwise, Visual C++ will flag the declaration as illegal in order to prevent program execution from jumping past the initialization of the object. For example, the following code is legal:

```
int n = 1;
switch (x)
{
case 1:
    {
        int n = 2;
        printf("The value of n is 2.\n");
    }
case 2:
    printf("The value n is 1.\n");
}
```

Iteration Statements

Visual C++ provides three iteration statements: **while**, **do**, and **for**. Iteration statements let you execute program statements repeatedly, based on the value of a test expression. Figure 3.7 summarizes the syntax of the iteration statements.

Notice that each selection statement includes a *statement*; this statement cannot be a declaration, but it can be a compound statement that includes a declaration. Notice also that the **for** statement includes a **for init** statement that consists of an expression statement or declaration statement. As shown in the figure, every **for** statement contains either an expression statement or a declaration statement comprising the **for init** statement part of the **for** statement. Because expression statements and declaration statements end with a semicolon, the **for** statement includes two semicolons within its parenthetical part even though only one appears in the figure.

The **while** Statement

The **while** statement includes a test expression and a statement. The test expression must have integral, pointer, or class type. If it has

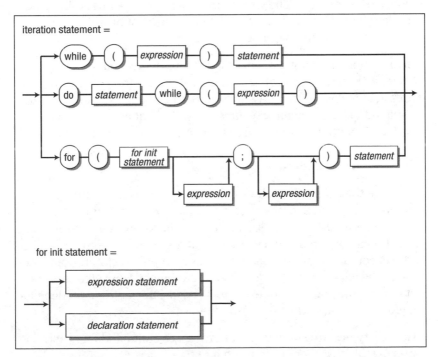

Figure 3.7   Iteration statement syntax.

class type, Visual C++ must be able to convert the class type to an integral or pointer type.

In operation, the **while** statement tests the value of its test expression. If the value of the expression is 0, Visual C++ skips execution of the statement associated with the **while** statement, proceeding to the next sequential statement; otherwise, it executes the statement and then reevaluates the test expression, executing the statement associated with the **while** statement only if the value of the expression is non-zero. Execution of the **while** statement continues until the test expression evaluates to zero.

Here's a typical **while** statement that iterates until input is exhausted:

```
int len = getMoreInput();
while (len)
{
    // Process the input
}
```

The **do** Statement

Like the **while** statement, the **do** statement includes a test expression and a statement. The test expression must have integral, pointer, or class type. If it has class type, Visual C++ must be able to convert the class type to an integral or pointer type.

In operation, the **do** statement first executes its associated statement. Then, it tests the value of its test expression. If the value of the expression is zero, Visual C++ proceeds to the next sequential statement; otherwise, it again executes the statement associated with the **while**. Execution of the **while** statement continues, first executing the statement and then evaluating the test expression, until the test expression evaluates to zero.

Because the **do** statement evaluates its test expression after executing its associated statement, it is termed a *post-test* iteration statement. The **while** statement and the **for** statement are both *pre-test* iteration statements because they evaluate their test expression before executing their associated statement. A post-test iteration statement always executes its associated statement; a pre-test iteration statement may or may not execute its associated statement, depending on the value of the test expression.

Here's a typical **do** statement that processes command lines until the user signals that there is no more input:

```
cmdline = getCommand();
do
{
    doCommand(cmdline);
    cmdline = getCommand();
} while (cmdline);
```

The **for** Statement

The **for** statement is a sophisticated iteration statement that extends the capabilities of the **while** statement. It includes a **for init** statement, two optional expressions, and a statement. The **for init** statement may be an expression statement or a declaration statement. Because an expression statement may be a null statement, you can write a **for** that includes within its parenthetical part only the two semicolons.

The first of the two optional expressions is called the *test expression,* and the second is called the *update expression.* The test expression must have arithmetic, pointer, or class type. If it has class type, Visual C++ must be able to convert the class type to arithmetic or pointer type.

In operation, the **for** statement first executes the **for init** statement. It then evaluates the test expression. If the test expression evaluates to zero, Visual C++ transfers control to the next sequential statement following the **for** statement. Otherwise, it executes the statement associated with the **for** statement, which is generally a compound statement. Following execution of the compound statement, Visual C++ evaluates the update expression of the **for** statement and then re-evaluates the test expression. As before, if the test expression evaluates to 0, Visual C++ transfers control to the next sequential statement following the **for** statement. Otherwise, Visual C++ continues executing the statement associated with the **for** statement, the update expression, and the test expression until the test expression evaluates to zero.

Here's a typical **for** statement:

```
sum = 0;
for (int i = 1; i <= 100; i++)
    sum += i;
```

This **for** statement sums the numbers from 1 to 100. It's not necessary to define the loop variable within the **for** statement. The preceding example can also be written like this:

```
sum = 0;
int i;
for (i = 1; i <= 100; i++)
    sum += i;
```

If you define a name within the **for init** statement, the scope of the name is not limited to the **for** statement; the scope of the name extends to the end of the block containing the **for** statement.

If you omit the test expression, its value is taken as 1 and the **for** statement will iterate until a jump statement (such as a **break**) transfers control. Omitting both the test expression and the update expression specifies an infinite loop:

```
for (;;)
{
    // statements executed until control transferred
    // out of the for statement
}
```

Jump Statements

Visual C++ provides four jump statements: **break**, **continue**, **return**, and **goto**. Figure 3.8 summarizes the syntax of the jump statements.

The **break** Statement

You can use the **break** statement in an iteration statement or a **switch** statement. The **break** statement terminates execution of the innermost enclosing iteration statement or **break** statement and transfers control to the next sequential statement.

The **break** statement is especially useful for writing loops that have multiple exit conditions. For example, you can write a **while** loop like this:

```
while (1)
{
    if (/* condition #1 */) break;
    if (/* condition #2 */) break;
    if (/* condition #3 */) break;
    // other loop statements
}
```

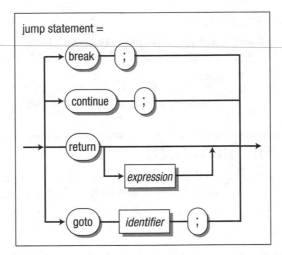

jump statement =

break ;

continue ;

return

expression

goto *identifier* ;

Figure 3.8   Jump statement syntax.

By setting the test expression to a non-zero value (1), this code causes the **while** to be executed indefinitely. The loop will terminate when any of the test expressions of its three **if** statements evaluates to a non-zero value.

The **continue** Statement

You can use a **continue** statement within an iteration statement. Unlike **break**, **continue** cannot be used within a **switch** statement. Execution of a **continue** statement causes an iteration statement to terminate execution of its associated statement and evaluate its test expression. In effect, the **continue** statement transfers control to the end of the loop.

The **return** Statement

You can use the **return** statement to cause a function to return to its caller. If the function was declared as returning a value, you must use the optional expression within the **return** statement to specify the value that the function returns to its caller. If the function was not declared as returning a value, was declared as returning type **void**, or is a constructor or destructor, you may not include an expression in the **return** statement.

If the expression is present, it must have a type compatible with that declared for the function. If a function is not declared as returning a value, it does need to contain a **return** statement. Executing the last sequential statement of the function returns control to the function's caller.

The **goto** Statement

The **goto** statement transfers control to the statement having a matching identifier. The identifier must be associated with a statement in the current function.

Declaration Statement

Figure 3.2 summarized the syntax of the Visual C++ declaration statement, which consists simply of a declaration. Because a declaration ends with a semicolon, a declaration statement always ends with a semicolon.

A declaration statement introduces a new name into the current scope. The name may refer to a type (**class**, **struct**, **union**, **enum**, **typedef**, or pointer-to-member), an object, or a function.

You can declare objects with either automatic or static storage class. An object declared using the **auto** or **register** keyword has automatic storage. An object declared using the **static** or **extern** keyword has static storage. An object declared without using the **auto**, **register**, **static**, or **extern** keyword has automatic storage if it's a local object and static storage if it's a global object (an object declared at file scope, outside all functions).

Name Hiding

If the name has already been declared in an outer block, the inner declaration hides the outer one. Within the current block, the name refers to the type, object, or function declared in the inner block. Following the inner block, the name resumes its original meaning. Visual C++ does not allow you to declare the same name more than once within a single block.

Declaring Automatic Objects

Each time Visual C++ executes the definition of an automatic object, it initializes the object. When Visual C++ exits the scope enclosing the definition, it destroys the object. As a consequence, objects that are defined within a loop are initialized and destroyed once per iteration of the loop. When Visual C++ transfers control out of a block, it destroys any automatic objects declared in the block. Similarly, when Visual C++ transfers control to a point prior to a declaration, it destroys the declared object.

A transfer of control that bypasses a declaration that includes an initializer is illegal, unless the declaration is enclosed within an inner block.

Declaring Static Objects

Visual C++ initializes global objects at program startup. It initializes local objects with static storage the first time it executes their declarations. If a static object is initialized using a nonconstant expression, Visual C++ performs a default initialization before its block is entered. The default initialization assigns the value zero to the object. Visual C++ calls a local object's destructor if, and only if, the local object was constructed: If the flow of program execution bypasses an object's declaration, Visual C++ will not invoke the object's destructor. When Visual C++ calls an object's destructor, it does so as part of the termination specified by **atexit**.

Related solution:	*Found on page:*
atexit	139

Function Definitions

Chapter 1 briefly described the syntax of function declarations. A function definition differs from a function declaration only in that it includes a *function body*, which takes the form of a compound statement. Figure 3.9 summarizes the syntax of the function definition.

The *decl specifiers* specify the function return type. They can also specify that the function is a friend, inline, or virtual function. The *dname* specifies the name of the function. The *cv qualifier list* is used only in class member functions. The *ctor initializer* specifies initialization of base classes and contained objects; it is used only in constructors.

Figure 3.10 shows the syntax of the argument declaration list. To provide a default value for an argument, you use the = *expression* syntax. For example, to declare a function that takes two optional arguments, you might write the declaration:

```
sum(int = 0, int = 0);
```

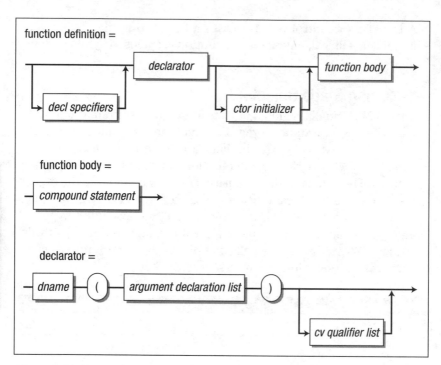

Figure 3.9   Function definition syntax.

You can call this function in any of these ways:

```
sum(1, 2);     sum(1);     sum();
```

The last two calls are equivalent to **sum(1, 0)** and **sum(0, 0)**, respectively.

To declare a function that has a variable number of arguments, you use ellipses (...) in the argument list.

Related solutions:	Found on page:
Virtual Functions	71
Constructors	74
Access To Members	79
Friends	81
stdlib.h And **cstdlib**	136

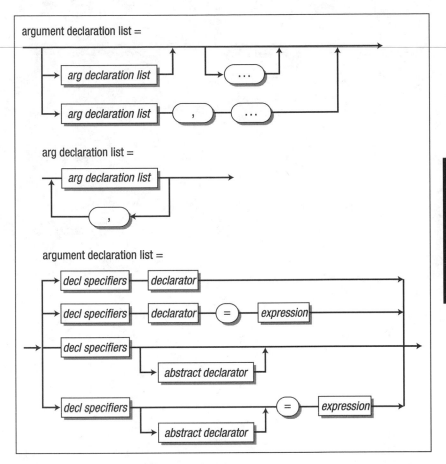

Figure 3.10   Argument declaration list syntax.

Classes, Inheritance, And Overloading

In Brief

Defining Classes

Visual C++ lets you define classes, which are essentially user-defined types that include both data (variables) and operations (functions). As Chapter 1 described, Visual C++ provides three kinds of class types: classes, structures, and unions. The variables defined in a class are called *data members*, and the functions defined in a class are called *member functions*. Data members and member functions are collectively called *members*. A class can contain two special kinds of member functions: *constructors*—which initialize an object of the class type—and *destructors*—which destroy an object of the class type, freeing its dynamically allocated memory. A destructor can also close open files or perform other operations that safeguard the integrity of a system.

Specifying Access To Members

Visual C++ lets you derive new classes from existing ones by using *inheritance*. An original class is called a *base class*, and the new classes are called *derived classes*. A derived class inherits the members possessed by its base classes. By using *multiple inheritance*, you can derive a new class from several base classes. A derived class can define a member function already defined by its base class. When you access a member function using a pointer or reference to a derived class, the definition in the derived class *overrides* that in the base class and Visual C++ uses the member function defined in the derived class. However, when you access a member function using a pointer or reference to the base class, Visual C++ generally uses the member function defined in the base class. By declaring a member function of a base class as *virtual*, you can cause Visual C++ to use the member function definition in a derived class, regardless of whether access is via a pointer or reference to the base class or derived class.

Visual C++ also lets you define *abstract classes*, which cannot be instantiated. However, you can use pointers and references to abstract classes, and you can derive nonabstract classes (*concrete classes*) from an abstract class. Abstract classes let you express general concepts—such as a tree—that can only be realized concretely as a more specific concept—such as an oak, an elm, or a maple. An abstract class contains at least one *pure virtual function*, a virtual member function declared without a function body, using a special syntax. A class derived from an abstract class must implement any pure virtual functions defined in the base class, or the derived class is abstract.

Visual C++ lets you specify the access granted to members as public, private, or protected. By restricting access to members, you can prevent yourself and others from using the members in unintended ways. However, you and others can circumvent these restrictions by casting the type of an object to a type that permits more general access. Visual C++ lets you grant special access to members of a class by specifying the **friend** keyword. A class can define friend functions that access its protected and private members. A class can also define other classes as friends, allowing their member functions to access the class's protected and private members.

Overloading Functions

When you provide more than one definition of a function or operator within a single scope, the function or operator is *overloaded*. Visual C++ chooses which definition to use by examining the types of the arguments provided with a function or operator call. Therefore, the definitions of an overloaded function must have different argument lists, in terms of the number or types of the arguments.

Immediate Solutions

Classes

A *class* is a user-defined type that specifies the data and operations provided by the type. The name of a class must be unique within its scope. Figure 4.1 presents the syntax of a class specifier. A class specifier is considered to define a class even if it does not fully define the member functions of the class. You can create class objects and generally use them in the same ways as non-class objects; for example, you can assign them, you can pass them as arguments to functions, and functions can return them as values.

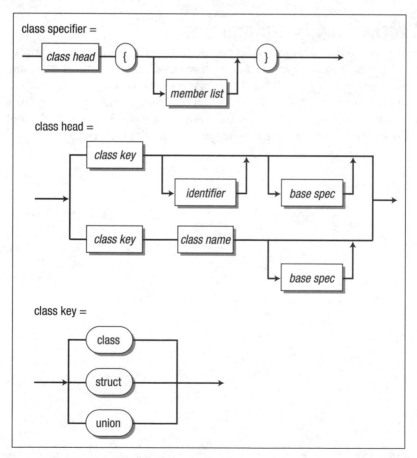

Figure 4.1   Class specifier syntax.

A *structure* is a class type declared by using the **struct** keyword; its members and base classes have public access by default. A *union* is a class type declared by using the **union** keyword; its members have public access by default. A union can hold only one of its members at a time.

Class Names

When you declare a class, you introduce a new name into the current scope. The new name hides the declaration of any other class, object, or function having the same name. Similarly, when you declare a variable or function that has the same name as a previously declared class, the declaration of the class becomes hidden. However, you can refer to the class by using an elaborated type specifier. Figure 4.2 shows the syntax of an elaborated type specifier. Here's a short example that shows how to use one:

```
class x {          // defines a class named x
  // ...
};

x theX;            // defines an object of type x

int x(class x*);   // defines x as a function

void demo()
{
    class x* p;    // refers explicitly to the class x
    // ...
    x(p);          // refers to the function x
    // ...
}
```

You can also use an elaborated type specifier to introduce a class name without defining the class. This lets you define classes that refer to one another.

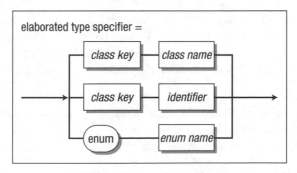

Figure 4.2   Elaborated type specifier syntax.

```
class total;  // specifies that total refers to a class

class entry {
    // ...
      total sum(total&, entry&);
};

class total {
// ...
      total sum(total&, entry&);
};
```

Class Members

A class member may be a data member, function member, class, enumeration, bit-field, friend, or type name. Figure 4.3 presents the syntax of a member list, which declares one or more members. A member list cannot define a single member more than once; however, several members can have the same name if their types are sufficiently different (for example, a data member and a member function). The member list of a class must define all the members of the class.

Class members are subject to several important restrictions:

- A member declarator cannot include an initializer; members must be initialized by means of a constructor member function. Members must not be declared **auto**, **extern**, or **register**.

- A class **x** cannot contain a member that has the type **x**; however, it may contain members that have type ***x** or **&x**. A function member that has the same name as its class is a constructor. A class cannot contain a static data member, enumerator, member of an anonymous union, or nested type that has the same name as the class.

- When you declare a nonstatic member that has array type, you must generally specify all dimensions of the array. However, if you compile your program without using the ANSI-compatibility option (**/Za**), Visual C++ permits you to declare an unsized array as the last member in a class member list. This Microsoft extension is not generally supported by other C++ compilers.

When you declare nonstatic class members without an intervening access specifier, Visual C++ allocates them to successively higher memory addresses. Visual C++ does not guarantee the order of allocation of members separated by an access specifier. Members with-

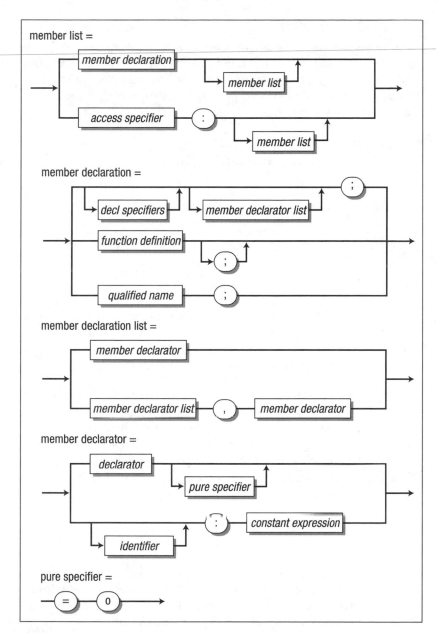

Figure 4.3   Member list syntax.

out an intervening access specifier may not be stored adjacently: The compiler may introduce padding bytes to ensure appropriate alignment of data. The Visual C++ compiler lets you specify alignment options by means of the **/Zp** compiler option and the **pack** pragma.

Member Functions

A function declared as a member is called a *member function* (unless
the declaration includes the **friend** keyword, in which case the function is called a *friend function*). To invoke a member function, you
use the class member syntax. For example, suppose a class defines a
member function like this:

```
class theClass {
  void theFunction(int argument);
};
```

To call the member function, you might use code like this:

```
int someFunction(theClass x)
{
    x.theFunction(0);
}
```

The definition of a member function has class scope, so the member
function can use the names of members of its class. However, a static
member function can use only the names of static members, enumerators, and nested types of its class.

A member function defined within its class declaration is implicitly
inline. You can also declare member functions within their class and
define them outside their class, at file scope. To define a member
function outside its class, you can use the scope resolution operator,
preceded by the class name. For example, you could define the member function **theFunction** outside the class **theClass** by writing a
definition like this:

```
int theClass::theFunction(int argument) {
  // ...
}
```

You can explicitly specify the keyword **inline** for such a function. In
addition, you can declare a member function more than once, but
you must define each member function exactly once.

In a nonstatic member function, the keyword **this** refers to a pointer
to the object through which the function was called. Each call of a
nonstatic member function includes the **this** pointer as an implicit
argument. The **this** pointer has the type **X *const**, where **X** is the
type of the object through which the function was called. Nonstatic

member functions perform operations on objects of the associated class type; calling a nonstatic member function via an object of a different type yields undefined results.

Static Members

A distinct copy of a nonstatic data member exists for each object of a class. However, all objects of a class share a single copy of each static data member of the class. A static data member is a separate object; if its class is global, a static data member has external linkage.

Because a static data member is a separate object, declaring a static data member in a class does not define the data member: You must specify a definition of the static data member elsewhere in your program.

A static member function does not receive an implicit **this** pointer. Therefore, it can access nonstatic members of its class only by means of a pointer or reference to an object of the class type. You cannot specify the **virtual** keyword in the declaration of a static member function, and you cannot define static and nonstatic member functions with the same name and argument types.

If a local class has static members, they have no linkage and must be defined inside the class declaration. Consequently, a local class cannot have a static data member.

You can refer to a static member **m** of a class **C** by using the syntax **C::m**. The static member exists even if no objects of the class have been created.

Visual C++ initializes static members of a global class in the same way it initializes global objects: You must initialize static members at file scope.

Unions

A union is an object large enough to contain the largest of its member objects and that stores all its member objects at offset zero. Consequently, a union can contain only one of its member objects at any time. A union can include member functions, but it cannot include virtual functions. You cannot derive a union from a base class, nor can you use a union to derive a new class.

A union cannot include an object whose class defines a constructor, destructor, or user-defined assignment operator. A union must have only nonstatic data members.

You can define a so-called *anonymous union* like this:

```
union { /* members go here */ } ;
```

If you declare objects or pointers for a union, it is not an anonymous union.

An anonymous union defines an unnamed object. The names of its members must be distinct from other names in the scope of declaration, because the usual member access syntax cannot be employed with an anonymous union. You refer to the members of an anonymous union as though they were ordinary variables.

A global anonymous union must be declared static. An anonymous union cannot have private members, protected members, or function members.

Bit-Fields

A *bit-field* is a data member of integral type that occupies less space than the specified type. A constant expression specifies the number of bits the data member occupies. For example, here's a structure that includes two bit-fields:

```
struct mask {
    unsigned field1:  8;
    unsigned       :  0;
    unsigned field2: 24;
};
```

The bit-field named **field1** occupies 8 bits, and the bit-field named **field2** occupies 24 bits. The unnamed bit-field between them causes **field12** to be aligned on a boundary appropriate for an **unsigned int**. You cannot apply the address-of operator **&** to a bit-field.

Nested Class Declarations

A class declared within another class is called a *nested class*. The name of a nested class is local to its enclosing class and is available for use only within the scope of the enclosing class. To refer to a nested class outside its enclosing class, you must use a fully qualified name. Here's an example of a nested class declaration:

```
class outer {
  class inner {
     // members define here
  };
};
```

Defining a nested class does not automatically create objects of the nested type. The nested class can use type names, static members, and enumerators of the enclosing class. To refer to other sorts of names requires an explicit pointer, reference, or object name. Member functions of a nested class are granted no special access to members of the enclosing class, and member functions of an enclosing class are granted no special access to members of the nested class.

Local Class Declarations

A class declared within a function definition is called a *local class*. The name of a local class is local to its enclosing function. A local class can use only type names, static members, **extern** variables and functions, and enumerators from its enclosing scope. An enclosing function is granted no special access to members of a local class. You must define members of a local class within their class definition; consequently, a local class cannot have static data members.

Inheritance

Visual C++ lets you derive new classes from existing ones by using the facility known as *inheritance*. To specify that a new class derives from an existing class (or classes), you use the syntax shown in Figure 4.4. For example, suppose you have an existing class named **Person**. To derive a new class named **Reader** from the base class **Person**, you might write something like this:

```
class Person;
class Reader : public Person {
    // members defined here
}
```

You can refer to members of the base class as if they were members of the derived class: The derived class is said to *inherit* the members of its base class. If you need to refer explicitly to a base class member, you can use the scope resolution operator (::). For instance, by using the scope resolution operator, you can refer to a name that the derived class redefines.

You can derive further classes from a derived class. A class is called a *direct base* if it appears in the base spec of a derived class. A class is called an *indirect base* if it is a base class of one of the classes that appear in the base spec.

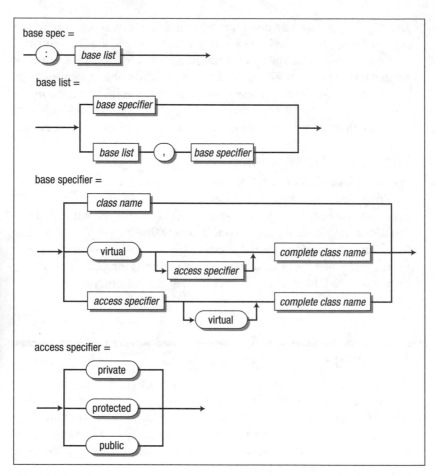

Figure 4.4   Base spec syntax.

Visual C++ may implicitly convert a pointer (or reference) to a derived class to a pointer (or reference) to an accessible unambiguous base class.

Multiple Inheritance

You can derive a class from more than one base class by using *multiple inheritance*. For example, here's a derived class with two base classes:

```
class LandVehicle;
class WaterVehicle;
class AmphibiousVehicle : public LandVehicle,
  public WaterVehicle {
    // members defined here
}
```

When the base classes of a derived class share a common base class, the derived class will contain multiple subobjects of the common base class type. To prevent this, you can specify that derivation is virtual; every base class that specifies a base class as virtual shares a single copy of the virtual base class. For example, consider the following declarations:

```
class Vehicle;
class LandVehicle  : virtual public Vehicle;
class WaterVehicle : virtual public Vehicle;
class AmphibiousVehicle : public LandVehicle,
  public WaterVehicle {
    // members defined here
}
```

Here, an **AmphibiousVehicle** object will contain a single **Vehicle** subobject.

A reference to a base class member is ambiguous if it refers to more than one function, object, type, or enumerator. Visual C++ must be able to access base class members unambiguously. Because Visual C++ checks for ambiguity before it applies access control, you cannot use restricted access to disambiguate reference to a base class member. Instead, you must use a qualified name. For example, suppose that a class is multiply derived from two base classes, each of which defines a function with the same name:

```
class Base1 {
    void f();
};

class Base2 {
    void f();
};

class Derived : public Base1, public Base2 {
    void f() { Base1::f(); Base2::f(); }
};
```

By explicitly specifying the name of the class that defines the member function, the example code avoids ambiguity.

When you use the **virtual** keyword to specify virtual inheritance, one sort of potential ambiguity is eliminated. Consider the following example:

```
class M { public: void f(); };
class A: public virtual M { public: void f(); };
class B: public virtual M { };
class C: public A, public B { void g(); };

void C::g()
{
    f();
}
```

If the keyword **virtual** had not been used, the reference to **f( )** within the member function **C::g( )** would be ambiguous, because it might refer to a member of **M** or a member of **A**. However, when a class **A** has **M** as its base (as in the example), the name **A::f( )** is said to *dominate* the name **M::f( )**. Because only one subobject exists, no ambiguity arises. This principle applies to names generally, not merely to names of member functions.

A conversion from a pointer (or reference) to a derived class to a pointer (or reference) to one of its base classes must refer unambiguously to the object that represents the base class. For example:

```
class Base1 { };
class Base2 { };
class A: public Base2, public virtual Base1 { };
class B: public Base2, public virtual Base1 { };
class C: public A, public B { };

void f()
{
    C c;
    A* pa = &c;
    Base2* pbase2 = &c;  // Error
    Base1* pbase1 = &c;
}
```

The definition of the variable **pbase2** is erroneous, because it's unclear whether it references **A**'s **Base2** or **B**'s **Base2**. You could eliminate the ambiguity by writing

```
Base2* pbase2 = (&A) &c;  // Cast to reference to A
```

or:

```
Base2* pbase2 = (&B) &c;  // Cast to reference to B
```

Virtual Functions

Suppose a class **Parent** contains a virtual function **f** and that a class **Child** derived from it contains a function named **f** of the same type and arguments. The function **f** in the derived class is said to *override* the identically named function in the base class. If the function **f** is called on an object of type **Child**, the member function **Child::f( )** is executed, even if access reference takes the form of a pointer or reference to **Parent**. For example:

```
class Parent {
    virtual void vf();
    void f();
};
class Child : public Parent {
    void vf();
    void f();
};
void g()
{
    Child c;
    Child* pc  = &c;
    Parent* pp = &c;
    pc->vf();  // calls Child class member function
    pp->vf();  // calls Child class member function
    pc->f();   // calls Child class member function
    pp->f();   // calls Parent class member function
}
```

When calling a nonvirtual member function, the form of the reference determines the meaning of the call. When calling a virtual member function, the type of the pointer or reference that denotes the object determines the meaning of the call.

An overriding function is implicitly virtual; the keyword **virtual** can, but need not, be specified. If you don't want to define a virtual function in a base class, you can specify that the function is a pure virtual function. Explicit qualification of a function name by means of the scope operator can suppress a virtual call. In the example given earlier, the line

```
pp->Parent::vf();
```

would invoke the function **vf** in the **Parent** class.

Virtual functions are subject to the following restrictions:

- A derived class function cannot differ from a base class virtual function in only its return type. If the return type differs, the number or types of arguments must also differ.

- A virtual function cannot be a global function.

- A virtual function cannot be static.

Abstract Classes

Abstract classes are classes that contain at least one pure virtual function. The result of calling a pure virtual function is undefined. An abstract class cannot be used to create objects, except objects of a nonabstract class derived from it. A class derived from an abstract class is implicitly abstract unless it implements all pure virtual functions defined in the base class.

You cannot use an abstract class as an argument, a function return type, or the type of an explicit conversion. However, a pointer or reference to an abstract class may serve in all of these roles.

Scope Rules

All names that appear in C++ programs are subject to a set of rules governing scope. These rules distinguish legal and illegal uses of names and establish the meaning of legal uses:

- A name must be unambiguous within its scope. However, function names can be overloaded.

- Access rules cannot disambiguate a name. Names must be unambiguous even if access specifiers prevent access to them.

- A name prefixed by the unary scope operator (::) and used at file scope refers to a global object, function, or enumerator, unless the name is qualified by the binary scope operator (::), or a member operator (-> or .).

- Any name specified after **X::**, **x.**, or **p->** must be a member of class **X** or a member of a base class of **X** (supposing that **X** is the type of an object [or reference to an object] **x** and that **p** is a pointer to an object of type **X**).

- Supposing that a name **x** is used in a function that is not a class member, if **x** is not qualified by the unary scope operator, the binary scope operator, or a member operator, it must be one of the following:

- Declared in the block in which it occurs.

- Declared in an enclosing block.

- A global name. Such a name is known as a *local name* and hides declarations of the same name in enclosing blocks and global names.

- Supposing that a name **x** is used in a function that is a nonstatic member of class **X**, if **x** is not qualified by the unary scope operator, the binary scope operator, or a member operator, it must be one of the following:

  - Declared in the block in which it occurs.

  - Declared in an enclosing block.

  - A member of class **X** or a base class of class **X**.

  - A global name.

- Supposing that a name **x** is used in a function that is a static member of class **X**, if **x** is not qualified by the unary scope operator, the binary scope operator, or a member operator, it must be one of the following:

  - Declared in the block in which it occurs.

  - Declared in an enclosing block.

  - A static member of class **X** or a base class of class **X**.

  - A global name.

- Within a function definition, the scope of a function argument is the outermost block of the function. Arguments within a function declaration that is not a definition are local to the definition and disappear immediately thereafter. A default argument has a scope determined by its point of declaration but may not access local variables or nonstatic members. Default arguments are evaluated at the point of call.

- Visual C++ evaluates constructor initializers in the outermost block of the associated constructor. Therefore, a constructor initializer can refer to the constructor's arguments.

Special Member Functions

A class can have one or more special member functions that govern the operator of objects of their class. Visual C++ invokes these special member functions implicitly in a variety of contexts. The special member functions include constructors (invoked by the **new** operator), destructors (invoked by the **delete** operator), and conversions (invoked during expression evaluation). When Visual C++ creates a temporary object, it calls the appropriate constructor. Visual C++ ensures that temporary objects are destroyed and calls the appropriate destructor when it destroys a temporary object.

Constructors

A constructor is a member function that has the same name as its class. Visual C++ uses a constructor to create and initialize values of its class type. Although Visual C++ invokes a constructor for **const** and **volatile** objects, you cannot declare a **const** or **volatile** constructor, nor can you declare a virtual or static constructor.

Unlike other member functions, constructors are not inherited by derived classes. Instead, Visual C++ generates a *default constructor* for any class that lacks an explicit constructor. A default constructor can be called without specifying any arguments and has public access.

A *copy constructor* for a class **X** copies an object of class **X**. A copy constructor for class **X** takes a single argument of type **X&** (and any number of default arguments). If you declare no copy constructor, Visual C++ generates a default public copy constructor.

When a class has base classes or members that have constructors, Visual C++ calls those constructors before it calls the constructor for the derived class. This way, Visual C++ creates and initializes subobjects that may be needed to initialize the object of derived type. Visual C++ calls the constructors for base classes before it calls the constructors for members.

If a class has a constructor, you cannot specify objects of that class as members of a union. You cannot specify a return type for a constructor, and you cannot take the address of a constructor.

When you invoke the **new** operator to create an object, the operator attempts to allocate storage space for the object by invoking the **operator::new( )** function, if such a function exists. If storage cannot be allocated, the **new** operator returns the value 0.

If you define an operator function **X::operator new( )** for a class **X**, the function is implicitly static. The first argument of the function must have type **size_t**, an integral type defined in the header file **stddef.h**. The value of this argument specifies the size in bytes of the allocated object.

Conversions

By specifying a *user-defined conversion,* you can direct the actions taken by Visual C++ when it converts the type of an object. You can specify user-defined conversions by means of a constructor or conversion function.

A constructor that accepts a single argument defines a conversion from the type of its argument to the type of its class. For example, here's a simple class that defines conversions from **int** and **long**:

```
class X {
  public:
    X(int);
    X(long);
    // ...
};
```

Figure 4.5 shows the syntax of a conversion function name, which begins with the keyword **operator** and specifies a conversion to the type specified by the conversion type name. A member function named using a conversion function name is called a *conversion function.* You cannot declare classes, enumerations, or **typedefs** in the type specifier list of a conversion type name.

Conversion functions are more powerful than constructors because a conversion function can define a conversion from a class type to a basic type or a conversion from one class type to another. Moreover, you can declare virtual conversion functions. A conversion function

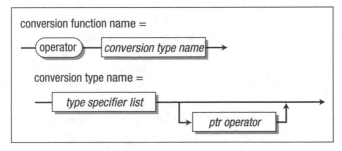

Figure 4.5   Conversion function name syntax.

in a derived class does not hide a conversion function in a base class unless both functions convert to the same type. Here's a simple example of a class that includes a conversion function:

```
class X {
  public:
    operator int();
    operator long();
};
```

Destructors

A destructor for class **X** is a member function of **X** that has the name **~X**. Visual C++ uses a destructor to destroy an object immediately before destroying the object containing it. Destructors take no arguments. Like constructors, destructors have no return type, and you cannot take the address of a destructor. Although Visual C++ can invoke a destructor on **const** and **volatile** objects, you cannot declare a destructor as **const** or **volatile**, nor can you declare a destructor as static. You can, and generally should, declare a virtual destructor. An object of a class with a destructor cannot be a member of a union.

Derived classes do not inherit destructors from their base classes. If you specify no destructor for a class that has a base class or member with a destructor, Visual C++ generates a *default destructor*. The default destructor, which has public access, calls the destructors of the bases and members of the derived class.

Several rules govern the order in which destructors execute:

• Visual C++ executes the destructor of an object before it executes the destructors of member objects.

• Visual C++ executes the destructors for nonvirtual base classes before it executes destructors for virtual base classes.

• Visual C++ executes destructors for nonvirtual base classes in reverse order of their declaration.

• Visual C++ executes destructors for virtual base classes in reverse order of their appearance in the inheritance graph. Consult the Visual C++ documentation for details.

Destructors can be invoked implicitly or explicitly. Visual C++ invokes a destructor:

• When an **auto** or temporary object goes out of scope

• When the program terminates, at which point static objects are destroyed

- When it evaluates an expression including the **delete** operator

You can invoke a destructor for any type name; if no destructor exists, Visual C++ ignores the invocation. This lets you write code such as this:

```
int *p;
p->int::~int();
```

When Visual C++ executes a destructor, the destructor frees allocated storage by calling the **operator delete( )** function, if such a function exists. If you define a function named **X::operator delete( )** within a class **X**, the function is implicitly static. The first argument of the **operator delete( )** function holds a reference to the object whose storage is being freed; the argument must have type **void***. You can declare a second argument of type **size_t** that indicates the size of the object being deleted.

Initialization

Unless an object of a class that includes a constructor has a default constructor, the object must be initialized. When an object's class includes a constructor, you can initialize the object by specifying a parenthesized expression list that Visual C++ uses as the argument list for the constructor. For example, here's a simple class that includes a constructor:

```
class X {
  public:
    X();
    X(int, long);
};
```

You could initialize objects of class **X** by defining them using statements such as these:

```
X a(1, 2);  // Calls constructor using specified arguments
X b = a;    // Initializes b by using copy constructor
X c;        // Calls X()
```

When passing an argument or function return value, Visual C++ implicitly invokes a copy constructor; when evaluating an initializer, Visual C++ implicitly invokes an ordinary constructor.

An object of class **M** can be a member of class **X** only if it meets one of the following criteria:

- The class **M** has no constructor
- The class **M** has a default constructor
- The class **X** has at least one constructor and every such constructor specifies a constructor initializer for the member of type **M**

Figure 4.6 shows the syntax of a constructor initializer, which provides an argument list for initializing the named nonstatic member or base class object. A constructor initializer first initializes all the specified base class objects in the order declared within the class (not the order declared within the constructor initialized), then it initializes the members in the order declared within the class. Finally, the body of the constructor executes. Here's a simple example of a constructor initializer:

```
class Parent {
  public:
    Parent(int);
    int age;
};

class Child: public Parent {
  public:
    Child(): Parent(1), age(25)
    {
        // ...
    }
};
```

Copying Class Objects

You can copy a class object either by means of assignment or initialization, which includes function argument passing and function value return. Assignment is implemented via the assignment operator, and initialization is implemented by means of the copy constructor. You can define member functions for either or both of these operations. If you define no member function for the assignment operator, Visual C++ defines a default assignment operator that performs memberwise assignment. Similarly, if you define no copy constructor, Visual C++ defines a default copy constructor that performs memberwise initialization.

For a class **X**, the generated assignment operator has the form **X& X::operator=(X&)** unless all the bases and members of **X** have assignment operators that accept **const** arguments. In that case, the operator has the form **X& X::operator(const X&)**.

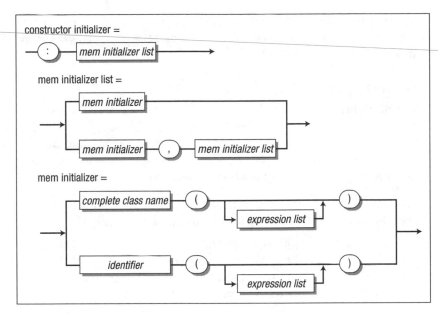

Figure 4.6   Constructor initializer syntax.

Similarly, for a class **X**, the generated copy constructor has the form
X::X(X&) unless all the bases and members of **X** have copy constructors that accept **const** arguments. In that case, the copy constructor has the form **X::X(const X&)**.

Access To Members

When you declare a function member, data member, member constant, or nested (member) type, you can control access to the member by specifying the keyword **public**, **private**, or **protected**. Access
to a private member is highly restricted, whereas access to a public
member is universal:

- A private member can be accessed only by member functions and
  friends (either functions or classes) of the class that defines it.

- A protected member can be accessed only by member functions
  and friends of the class that defines it and by member functions
  and friends of classes derived from the class that defines it.

- A public member can be accessed by any function.

Members of a class defined by using the keyword **class** are private by default; members of a class defined by using the keyword **struct** or **union** are public by default.

Access Specifiers

Recall Figure 4.3, which shows that a member declaration may be preceded by an access specifier. An access specifier applies to all the members that follow it until the end of the class or until another access specifier occurs. You can include access specifiers in any order, and you can include as many access specifiers as you like.

When you derive a class from a base class, you can include an access specifier that controls access to the inherited members:

- When you use the **public** access specifier to derive the class, the **public** members of the base class are **public** members of the derived class and the **protected** members of the base class are **protected** members of the derived class.

- When you use the **private** access specifier to derive the class, the **public** and **protected** members of the base class are **private** members of the derived class. The **private** members of the base class cannot be accessed unless **friend** declarations provide special access.

If you derive a class without using an access specifier, the derivation is considered public if the derived class is declared as a **struct** or **union** and considered private if the derived class is declared as a **class**.

Access to a static member of a class is controlled by the access specifier associated with the member; specifying the base class as private does not affect access to static members of the base class.

Access Declarations

You can tailor access to a member of a base class by specifying the qualified name of the member in an *access declaration*. Here's a short example:

```
class Parent {
  public:
    int x;
  private:
    int y;
};
```

```
class Child : private Parent {
{
    public:
        Parent::y;  // Tailors access to Parent::y
};
```

However, you cannot use an access declaration to restrict access to an accessible member of a base class; nor can you use an access declaration to enable access to an inaccessible member of a base class. If you specify an access declaration for an overloaded function, the declaration applies to all functions of the name in the base class.

The declaration of a virtual function determines its access; access to a virtual function is not affected by more or less stringent access rules associated with an overriding function. If, because of multiple inheritance, a name can be reached multiple ways along an inheritance graph, the permitted access is that of the path that gives most access.

Friends

A *friend function* is a function that is not a member of a class but nevertheless can access the **private** and **protected** members of the class. Despite its special access privileges, the name of a friend function is not in the scope of the class and cannot be called using the member operators with a reference or pointer to an object of the class type.

When you declare a function as a friend, only the function specified by the argument types within the declaration becomes a friend. Consider, for example:

```
class Gregarious {
    friend orfoe(int);
    orfoe(long);
    // ...
};
```

Here, only the **orfoe( )** member function taking an **int** argument has friend access privileges.

If you want to specify all the functions of a class **X** as friends of a class **Y**, you can use an elaborated type specifier:

```
class Y {
    friend class X;
    // ...
};
```

Friendship is not affected by access specifiers and is not inherited; nor is friendship transitive. If class **B** is a friend of class **A**, and class **C** is a friend of class **B**, class **C** is not thereby a friend of class **A**.

Like member functions of a derived class, friends can access a protected static member of a base class.

Overloading

An *overloaded function* is a function that has multiple declarations. When Visual C++ invokes an overloaded function, it selects the function definition by comparing the types of the actual arguments of the function with the types of the formal arguments. Because Visual C++ initializes formal arguments with the values of the actual arguments, arguments of type **X** and type **X&** are indistinguishable. Consequently, you cannot overload a function by defining argument types that differ from those of another function only in that the overloading function accepts type **X**, whereas the overloaded function accepts type **X&**.

Similarly, you cannot overload a function by defining argument types that differ from those of another function only in that the overloading function accepts an argument that is **const** or **volatile**, whereas the overloaded function accepts a non-**const** or non-**volatile** argument. However, because the types **X&**, **const X&**, and **volatile X&** are distinguishable, you can specify functions that differ only in that respect.

Likewise, you can specify functions that differ in respect of argument types **X***, **const X***, and **volatile X***. You cannot overload a function by giving it a different return type; nor can you overload a nonstatic function by defining a static function or a static function by defining a nonstatic function. The array **[]** argument type is considered identical to the pointer * argument type for purposes of distinguishing overloaded functions.

Because a **typedef** is merely a synonym for a type, arguments that have the same underlying type are considered to have the same type, even if you specify their types by means of distinct **typedef**s. Enumeration types, by contrast, are distinct types. Argument types that have different enumeration types can be used to distinguish overloaded functions.

Declaration And Argument Matching

If two function declarations having the same name and argument types occur within the same scope, they refer to the same function. Note, however, that a base class and a derived class define distinct scopes; so, a function member of a derived class is not in the same scope as an identically named function in a base class.

When Visual C++ calls a function, it chooses (from among all functions by that name within scope) the function whose formal argument types best match those of the actual arguments. When necessary and possible, Visual C++ applies conversions to convert the type of an actual argument to that of the corresponding formal argument. The selected function must be a strictly better match for at least one argument than every other candidate function; otherwise, the call is illegal. Several special rules apply to this determination:

- A function with n default arguments is treated as $n+1$ functions with different numbers of arguments.

- A nonstatic member function is treated as having an extra argument (the implicit **this** pointer) that specifies the object for which it is called. The extra argument can be matched by either an object or pointer specified in the member call notation or by the first operand of an overloaded operator.

- An ellipsis as a formal argument matches an actual argument of any type.

For any actual argument, Visual C++ will consider no sequence of conversions that involves more than one user-defined conversion. Visual C++ considers only the shortest-possible sequences of conversion. For example, Visual C++ will not consider the sequence **int->float->long**, when the sequence **int->long** is possible. Table 4.1 shows several conversions that Visual C++ considers trivial and therefore do not affect which of two conversion sequences it considers better.

Visual C++ classifies sequences of conversions by following these rules:

1. *Exact match*—Visual C++ considers an actual argument type that can be converted into the corresponding formal argument type by means of zero or more trivial conversions to be an exact match. Of exact matches, Visual C++ considers those that do not convert **X*** to **const X***, **X*** to **volatile X***, **X&** to **const X&**, or **X&** to volatile **X&** superior to others.

Table 4.1   Trivial conversion sequences.

From	To
T	T&
T&	T
T[ ]	T*
T(*args*)	(*T)(*args*)
T	const T
T	volatile T
T*	const T*
T*	volatile T*

2. *Match with promotions*—If Rule 1 does not apply, Visual C++ considers conversions that contain only integral promotions, conversions from **float** to **double**, and trivial conversions superior to others.

3. *Match with standard conversions*—If Rules 1 and 2 do not apply, Visual C++ considers conversions involving only standard and trivial conversions superior to others.

4. *Match with user-defined conversions*—If none of Rules 1 through 3 apply, Visual C++ considers conversions that involve only user-defined conversions, standard conversions, and trivial conversions superior to others.

5. *Match with ellipsis*—Visual C++ considers conversions that involve matches with an ellipsis inferior to others.

Overloaded Functions And Operators

If you use a function name without arguments, Visual C++ selects the unique function that exactly matches the target, which may be:

- An object being initialized
- The left side of an assignment expression
- A formal argument of a function or user-defined operator
- A function return type

Consider the following example:

```
int f(int);
int f(float);
int (*pfint) (int) = &f;
int (*pffloat) (float) + &f;
```

In each of these declarations, Visual C++ can determine which function the pointer references by examining the type of the target. If Visual C++ cannot make this determination, the function reference fails.

You can overload an operator by defining a function that has an operator function name, the syntax of which is shown in Figure 4.7. You can overload both the unary and binary forms of the **+ - *** and **&** operators. However, you cannot overload any of the following operators: member (.), pointer to member (.*), scope resolution (::), or conditional (?:).

Operator functions except **operator=** are inherited by derived classes. An overloaded operator cannot have default arguments.

A unary prefix operator function (**@**) can be defined by a nonstatic member function that takes no arguments or by a nonmember function taking one argument, and can be interpreted as either **x.operator@** or **operator@(x)**, respectively. If you define both forms, argument matching determines which interpretation applies.

A binary operator can be defined as a nonstatic member function that takes one argument or by a nonmember function that takes two arguments. For a binary operator **@**, Visual C++ interprets the former form as **x.operator@(y)** or **operator@(x, y)**. If you define both forms, argument matching determines which interpretation applies.

The assignment operator must be a nonstatic member function and is not inherited by a derived class.

Visual C++ considers a function call a binary operator, for which the first operand denotes the function and the second operand—which

4. Classes, Inheritance, And Overloading

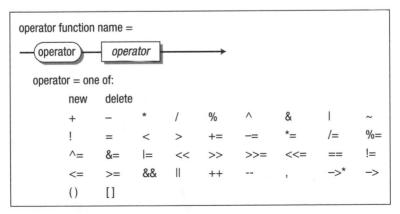

Figure 4.7   Operator function name syntax.

may be empty—is an expression list that contains the actual arguments. The name of the defining operator function is **operator( )**.

Visual C++ considers a subscript a binary operator, for which the first operand denotes a pointer and the second operand denotes an offset applied to the pointer. The name of the defining operator function is **operator[ ]**.

Visual C++ considers class member access a unary operator, whose operand denotes an object or reference of class type. The name of the defining operator function is **operator->**.

Visual C++ considers the prefix increment and decrement operators as unary operators, whose operand denotes an object of some class. It considers the postfix increment and decrement operators as binary operators, for which the first operand denotes an object of some class. The second operand must be of type **int** and will be called with an actual argument value of 0.

Advanced Features And Facilities

In Brief

Handling Expressions

Visual C++ provides advanced features and facilities that help you write robust classes and programs that are reusable and portable:

- *Exception handling* lets your program detect and recover from errors and exceptions.
- *Templates* let you write highly general, parameterized classes that you can reuse in a variety of contexts.
- *The preprocessor* lets you write a single source file that you can compile on a variety of platforms and environments.

The Visual C++ exception handling facility includes three main elements:

- A special kind of statement, the **try** block
- A special kind of expression, the **throw** expression
- An exception specification, which you can add to a function definition to specify the exceptions the function might throw

To use exception handling, you enclose code that might generate an error or exception within a **try** block that specifies one or more *handlers*, special compound statements that execute when an error or exception of a particular kind occurs. The **throw** expression lets you programmatically raise exceptions. It helps you handle exceptions centrally and is also useful for program testing.

Using Templates

When you define a class, you specify the types of its members. By defining a template, you can define class member types parametrically. Each time you use the template, you specify the actual types that Visual C++ should substitute for the formal types given in the template definition.

A template resembles a factory for defining members of a family of related classes. Templates are especially useful when you're working with *collection classes*, classes that model data structures such as the linked list. Without templates, it's cumbersome to create type-safe collection classes that accept only elements that have a specified type, because you must define a distinct class for each type of element. Templates let you create a single type-safe parameterized class that you can instantiate for a variety of element types.

Writing Portable Programs

Differences among platforms often make it impossible to write a single C++ program that functions identically on each platform. However, having separate source files for each platform complicates program maintenance, because changes must be applied separately to each source file. The C++ preprocessor lets you maintain a single source file that you can compile on a variety of platforms. Before Visual C++ compiles a source file, it passes the source text through the preprocessor, which can modify the source text conditionally. By controlling the preprocessor via directives, you can cause the compiler to see different versions of your program, all of which are stored in a single file.

5. Advanced Features And Facilities

Immediate Solutions

Exceptions

To handle exceptions thrown by program statements, you must embed the statements within a **try** block. Figure 5.1 shows the syntax of the **try** block. The most salient feature of a **try** block is its exception declaration, which specifies which kinds of exceptions are caught and processed. C++ represents exceptions as objects, the type of which indicates the kind of exception. A **try** block catches only those exceptions that have a type matching an entry in the **try** block's exception declaration. Visual C++ checks the handlers in the order of their appearance. To specify that a **try** block should catch all

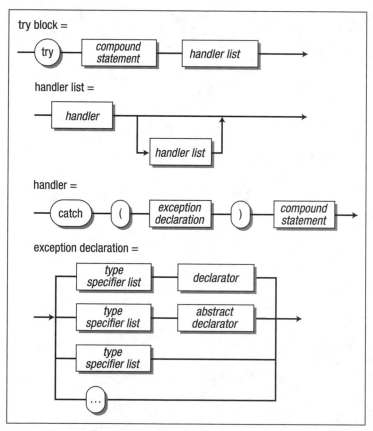

Figure 5.1   Try block syntax.

exceptions regardless of type, you specify an ellipsis in the exception declaration; such a handler must be the last handler within its **try** block.

When an exception occurs and Visual C++ cannot find an exception declaration entry that has a type matching the exception, Visual C++ calls the **terminate** runtime function. The default action of the **terminate** function is to abort the program; however, you can redefine the **terminate** function as described in the upcoming section "Special Functions."

Here's a simple example of a **try** block:

```
int main()
{
    try
    {
        // "risky" statements go here
    }
    catch (char* p)
    {
        // handler statements go here
    }
}
```

When an exception is thrown and its type matches that of an entry in the exception declaration, Visual C++ uses the value of the exception object to initialize the formal argument corresponding to the entry. In the example, the formal argument **p** would be initialized to the value of the exception object. If you're not interested in the value of the exception object, you can specify an abstract declarator that names no formal argument.

A program can contain multiple **try** blocks. You can nest **try** blocks by placing one inside another. And, a statement within a **try** block can invoke a function that contains a **try** block. When an exception is thrown, Visual C++ transfers control to the most recently entered active (that is, not yet exited) **try** block having a matching appropriate type.

When Visual C++ transfers control to a handler, it destroys all automatic objects created since it entered the handler's **try** block. Visual C++ invokes the destructor of each such object, unless the object was only partially constructed when the exception occurred. In that case, Visual C++ invokes the destructors only for the fully constructed subobjects of the partially constructed object. The process of calling the destructors is referred to as *unwinding the stack*.

Throwing An Exception

You can throw an exception of any type by executing a **throw** expression, the syntax of which is shown in Figure 5.2. The operation of a **throw** expression resembles that of the **return** statement. The type of the object returned, if any, denotes the kind of exception. A **throw** expression that has no operand rethrows the current exception; thus, a **throw** expression that has no operand can appear only in a handler or a function called from a handler.

Here's a simple example of an exception and a matching handler:

```
class MyException {
  public:
    char* exceptionText() {
        return "MyException was thrown.";
    }
};

int main()
{
    try
    {
        throw MyException();
    }
    catch (MyException x)
    {
        cout << x.exceptionText();
    }
    return 0;
}
```

When Visual C++ evaluates the **throw** expression, it throws an exception, which is caught by the matching handler of the **try** block. Visual C++ initializes the formal argument to the value of the **MyException** object provided as an operand within the **throw** expression. The handler invokes the **exceptionText** member function

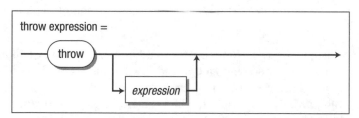

*Figure 5.2   **Throw expression syntax.***

on its formal argument and displays the return value, an explanation of the cause of the exception.

When searching for an exception declaration entry that has a type matching that of an exception, Visual C++ does not require an exact match. For a handler having type **T**, **const T**, **T&**, or **const T&**, and an expression type **E**, Visual C++ considers the types **T** and **E** as matching if one of the following criterion is met:

- Types **T** and **E** are the same type
- Type **T** is a public base class of derived class **E**
- Types **T** and **E** are pointer types and type **E** can be converted to type **T** by a standard pointer conversion

Because Visual C++ checks handlers in the order of their appearance, it is an error to specify a handler for a base class ahead of the handler for its derived class, because that would prevent the handler for the derived class from executing.

Specifying Exceptions

You can specify the exceptions that a function might throw by including an exception specification following the function's declarator. Figure 5.3 shows the syntax of such an exception specification. If a function attempts to throw an exception not listed in its exception specification, Visual C++ invokes the **unexpected( )** function, which is described in the upcoming section "Special Functions."

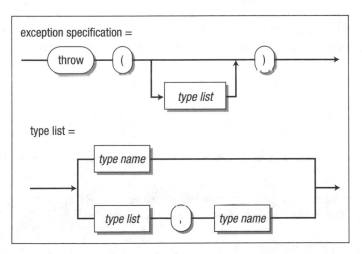

Figure 5.3   Exception specification syntax.

Visual C++ checks for unexpected exceptions when exceptions are thrown, not at compile time. A function that has no exception specification can throw any exception; a function that has an empty exception specification cannot throw any exception. Based on the rules for matching exception types, a function that is specified as throwing an exception of type **X** can throw an exception of any class derived from **X**.

Special Functions

Visual C++ provides the **terminate( )** and **unexpected( )** functions for dealing with errors that occur during exception handling.

During exception handling, Visual C++ calls the **terminate( )** function when one of the following criterion is met:

- Visual C++ cannot find a handler that matches a thrown exception
- The stack has become corrupted
- A destructor invoked while unwinding the stack throws an exception

The default action of the **terminate( )** function is to call the **abort( )** function, which terminates the program. However, you can use the **set_terminate( )** function to specify the function that **terminate( )** calls before it terminates the program.

When Visual C++ finds that a function has thrown an exception not listed in the function's exception specification, Visual C++ invokes the **unexpected( )** function. The default action of the **unexpected( )** function is to call the **terminate( )** function, which terminates the program. However, you can use the **set_unexpected( )** function to specify a function that Visual C++ calls in place of the **unexpected( )** function.

Templates

Templates are of two varieties: class templates and function templates. The following Immediate Solutions discuss each.

Class Templates

By writing a single class template, you can easily write definitions for an entire family of related classes. For example, suppose you want to create a class that functions as a stack, allowing you to push and pop elements of another class. You could define a class named **Stack** with **push()** and **pop()** member functions that accept arguments having the type **void***. However, such member functions would accept arguments that point to a variety of types. If you want several **Stack** objects, with each accepting a distinct element type (and only that type), you must write several classes rather than a single class. For example, you might have classes such as **StackChar**, **StackInt**, and **StackFloat**.

Class templates let you write a single parametric definition that you can use to define classes quickly and easily. Figure 5.4 shows the syntax of a template declaration. Template declarations must be in file scope (global). The keyword **template** and the associated template argument list distinguish the template declaration from an ordinary declaration. The declaration part of the template declaration must declare or define a function or a class. This section focuses on using templates to declare or define classes; the next section focuses on using templates to declare or define functions.

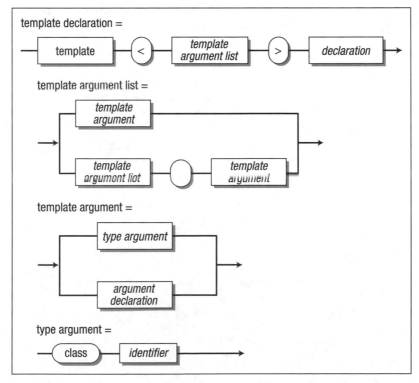

Figure 5.4   Template declaration syntax.

Here's a simple example of a template declaration:

```
template<class T> class Stack {
    T* theStack;
    int theStackSize;
  public:
    void push(T);
    T pop();
};
```

Notice how the name **T**, a type name within the template argument list, is used throughout the template as though it were a type name.

To use the class template to define a class, you define a template class, using the syntax shown in Figure 5.5. Each class template name must be unique and cannot refer to a class, function, object, value, or type of the same name in the scope of the class template.

A template arg can be a type name or an expression, which must be a constant expression, the address of an object or function with external linkage, or the address of a class member. If the template arg is an expression, its type must exactly match that of the corresponding type argument in the template declaration.

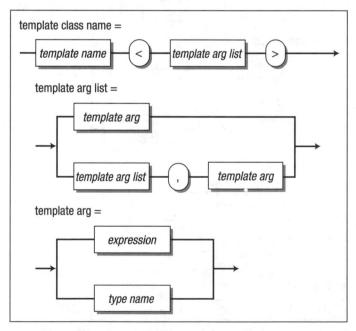

Figure 5.5   Template class syntax.

Here's an example of several template classes based on the template declaration given earlier:

```
Stack<char>  theCharStack;
Stack<int>   theIntStack;
Stack<float> theFloatStack;
```

Visual C++ generates a class definition from each template class. Visual C++ considers two identical template class names to refer to the same class if their arguments have identical values.

Function Templates

You can use a function template to specify a parametric function declaration or definition. For example, you could define a set of functions that display the contents of various types of stacks by writing:

```
template<class T> void dumpStack(Stack<T>);
```

The template args of a function template must be type arguments; they cannot be expressions. A function generated from such a function template is called a *template function*. The same term applies to functions that have a type matching that of the function template, even if they are not specified by means of a function template.

To call a function generated from a function template, Visual C++ follows these three steps:

1. Visual C++ attempts to find a function that has argument types that exactly match the types of the actual function arguments. If Visual C++ finds such a function, it calls the function.

2. If no matching function is found, Visual C++ attempts to find a function template whose template args have types exactly matching those of the actual function arguments. If Visual C++ finds such a template, it generates and calls the function.

3. If no matching function or function template is found, Visual C++ uses the ordinary rules for resolving a call of an overloaded function.

A member function of a template class is implicitly a template function. The template arguments of the class are its template arguments. However, a friend function of a template is not implicitly a template function.

When Visual C++ generates a template class or function, it provides each template class or function with its own copies of any static members or variables.

Template Declarations And Definitions

You can declare a template with a given name more than once, but you must provide exactly one definition of the template. Each use of a template class name is a declaration of that name. Calling a function template constitutes a declaration of the template function, as does taking the address of a function template.

The Preprocessor

Before the Visual C++ compiler compiles a source file, it preprocesses the contents of the file. Lines that begin with number sign (#) specify directives that control the operation of the preprocessor. Such lines can be preceded by spaces or horizontal tab characters.

You can write a preprocessor directive that extends across multiple lines by following each line other than the last with a backslash character (\), which must immediately precede the new-line character that ends the line.

The preprocessor operates on tokens, which may be a C++ language token, a file name, or any single non-whitespace character.

The preprocessor performs the following steps:

1. The preprocessor translates any system-dependent characters in the source text. For example, it inserts new-line characters to replace any system-dependent end-of-line characters and replaces trigraphs with their single-character equivalents (see the next section).

2. The processor deletes each backslash character that is immediately followed by a new-line, appending the following source line to the line containing the backslash/new-line sequence.

3. The preprocessor parses the source text into tokens and sequences of whitespace. It replaces each comment with a single whitespace.

4. The preprocessor expands all macros and executes all directives.

5. The preprocessor concatenates adjacent string literals.

Trigraphs

To accommodate computer systems that do not support the full ASCII character set, the C++ preprocessor lets you specify certain delimiters using three-character sequences known as *trigraphs*. The preprocessor substitutes each trigraph with an equivalent single-character token. Table 5.1 summarizes each trigraph and its meaning.

Writing Macros

The **define** preprocessor directive defines a macro that instructs the preprocessor to replace subsequent instances of the specified identifier with a specified sequence of tokens. Figure 5.6 shows the syntax of the macro definition syntax. For example, consider the following macro definition:

```
#define hex 16
```

This macro causes subsequent occurrences of the token **hex** to be replaced by 16. For example, the declaration

```
int bits[hex];
```

becomes:

```
int bits[16];
```

A macro definition can include a list of formal arguments. When such a macro is invoked, the value of each actual argument replaces that of the corresponding formal argument in the macro definition. For example, consider the following macro definition:

```
#define shift(len)    >> len
```

Table 5.1   C++ trigraphs.

Trigraph	Equivalent Character
??=	#
??/	\
??'	^
??(	[
??)	]
??!		
??<	{
??>	}
??-	~

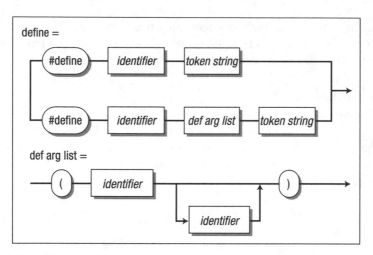

Figure 5.6   Macro definition syntax.

This macro causes the line

```
y = x shift(2);
```

to be interpreted as:

```
y = x >> 2;
```

You can cause the preprocessor to forget a macro definition by using a macro *un-definition*. The syntax of the macro un-definition is shown in Figure 5.7. If the specified identifier is not currently defined, the preprocessor ignores the un-definition.

As described in a following section, the preprocessor automatically substitutes the identifier __**LINE**__ with the current line number of the source file. You can set the line number to a specified value by using the **#line** directive, the syntax of which is shown in Figure 5.8. If you specify a file name, the preprocessor also sets the identifier __**FILE**__ to the specified value.

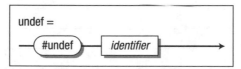

Figure 5.7   Macro un-definition syntax.

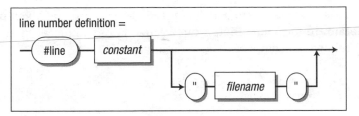

Figure 5.8   Line number definition syntax.

Operators And Directives

Visual C++ provides operators that let you manipulate source text. Table 5.2 summarizes these operators.

The stringizing operator causes its arguments to be enclosed in double quotation marks. To see how it can be used, consider the following example:

```
#define rootdir "/usr/" #userid "/public_html/"
```

The macro defines an identifier, **rootdir**, which receives a value that includes the string literal **"/usr/"**, the value of the identifier **userid**, and the string literal **"/public_html/"**. The stringizing operator causes the value of the identifier **userid** to be enclosed in double quotation marks. When the preprocessor performs its final phase, in which it concatenates adjacent string literals, the two string literals and the value of **userid** will be concatenated as a single string literal that becomes the value of **rootdir**.

A number sign (**#**) that appears on a line by itself is interpreted as a null preprocessor directive, which has no effect.

When the preprocessor encounters the token-pasting operator, it concatenates the preceding and following tokens, forming a single token. Because the preprocessor scans the result of a macro replacement

Table 5.2   Preprocessor operators.

Operator	Function
#	Stringizing operator: Causes the corresponding actual argument to be enclosed in double quotation marks.
##	Token-pasting operator: Allows tokens used as actual arguments to be concatenated to form other tokens.
defined	Defined operator: Simplifies the writing of compound expressions in certain macro directives.

for additional macros that it can replace, you can use the token-paste operator to form identifiers from tokens. For example, assume that the following macros have been defined as shown:

```
#define paste(x)        x ## town
#define hometown scottsdale
```

Then, the call **paste(home)** will have the value **scottsdale**, not the value **hometown**.

The **defined** operator can be used either of two ways:

```
defined identifier
```

or:

```
defined(identifier)
```

Both forms have the same result: If the specified identifier has been defined (and not later undefined), the operator returns the value 1; otherwise, it returns 0. You can also specify the form:

```
!defined identifier
```

This form yields the value 1 if the specified identifier is currently un-defined and the value 0 otherwise.

In addition to the standard C++ operators, Visual C++ defines a Microsoft-specific *charizing* operator (**#@**), which causes its arguments to be enclosed in single quotes and treated as a character literal.

Including Files

The **include** directive, the syntax of which is shown in Figure 5.9, causes the preprocessor to open the named file and replace the current line of the source text by the contents of the file. The two forms of the **include** directive search differently for the named file. The manner of the search is implementation-dependent.

If you specify the quoted form, the Visual C++ preprocessor looks for the file in the same directory of the source file that contains the **#include** statement, and then in the directories of whatever files that include (**#include**) that file. The preprocessor then searches along the path specified by the **/I** compiler option, then along paths specified by the **INCLUDE** environment variable. If you specify the form

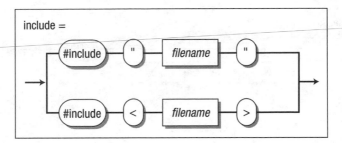

Figure 5.9   File include syntax.

that includes angle brackets (**<>**), the preprocessor searches for include files first along the path specified by the **/I** compiler option,
then along the path specified by the **INCLUDE** environment variable.

Conditional Compilation

The preprocessor can conditionally process lines of source text. Figure 5.10 shows the syntax of the conditional macro definition, which
supports this feature. When the preprocessor encounters a conditional
macro definition, it evaluates the constant expressions in the **#if** and
#elifs in the order in which they appear, until an expression evaluates to a non-zero value. Statements that follow a line whose expression evaluates to zero are not compiled and preprocessor directives
following such a line have no effect.

The conditional macro line

```
#ifdef identifier
```

is equivalent to the line:

```
#if defined identifier
```

The conditional macro line

```
#ifndef identifier
```

is equivalent to the line:

```
#if !defined identifier
```

You can nest conditional macro definitions to a maximum depth im-
posed by the implementation.

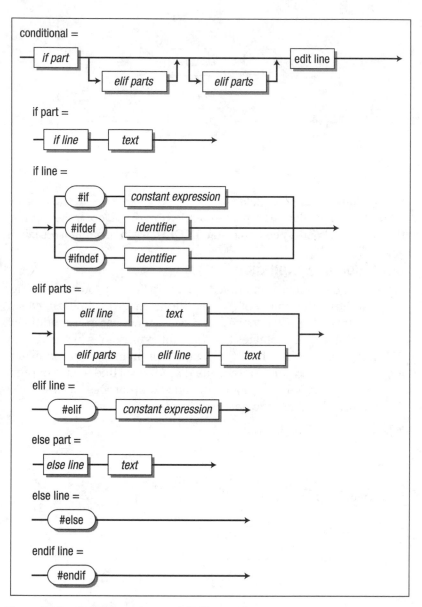

Figure 5.10   Conditional macro definition syntax.

Predefined Macros

Visual C++ predefines a set of standard C++ macros, which are summarized in Table 5.3. Visual C++ also defines a set of Microsoft-specific macros, which are summarized in Table 5.4.

Table 5.3   Predefined C++ macros.

Macro	Description
__DATE__	Contains the compilation date of the current source file. The date is a string literal of the form *Mmm dd yyyy*.
__FILE__	Contains the name of the current source file, surrounded by double quotation marks.
__LINE__	Contains the line number in the current source file.
__STDC__	Indicates whether the compiler fully conforms to the ANSI C standard. Defined as the integer constant 1 only if the **/Za** compiler option was specified; otherwise, the macro is undefined.
__TIME__	Contains the most recent compilation time of the current source file. The time is a string literal of the form *hh:mm:ss*.
__TIMESTAMP__	Contains the date and time of the last modification of the current source file, expressed as a string literal in the form *Ddd Mmm Date hh:mm:ss yyyy*, where *Ddd* is the abbreviated day of the week and *Date* is an integer from 1 to 31.

Table 5.4   Microsoft-specific Predefined C++ macros.

Macro	Description
_CHAR_UNSIGNED	Indicates that the default char type is unsigned. Defined when **/J** is specified.
__cplusplus	Indicates that the compiler is compiling a C++ program.
_CPPRTTI	Indicates the **/GR** compiler option (Enable Runtime Type Information) was specified.
_CPPUNWIND	Indicates that **/GX** compiler option (Enable Exception Handling) was specified.
_DLL	Indicates that **/MD** or **/MDd** compiler option (Multithread DLL) was specified.
_M_ALPHA	Defined as 1 by the DEC ALPHA compiler; not defined if another compiler is used.
_M_IX86	Defined by compilers for x86 processors.
_M_MPPC	Defined by compilers for Power Macintosh platforms.
_M_MRX000	Defined by compilers for MIPS platforms.
_M_PPC	Defined by compilers for PowerPC platforms.
_MFC_VER	Indicates the MFC version. Defined as 0x0421 for Microsoft Foundation Class Library 4.21. Always defined.

(continued)

Table 5.4   Microsoft-specific Predefined C++ macros (continued).

Macro	Description
_MSC_EXTENSIONS	Indicates that the **/Ze** compiler option (use Microsoft extensions) was specified.
_MSC_VER	Indicates the compiler version. Defined as 1200 for Microsoft Visual C++ 6. Always defined.
_MT	Indicates that the **/MD** or **/MDd** compiler option (Multithreaded DLL) or **/MT** or **/MTd** (Multithreaded) compiler option was specified.
_WIN32	Indicates that a Win32 is being compiled. Always defined.

Pragmas

A pragma directive lets you direct the preprocessor in an implementation-dependent way. Figure 5.11 shows the syntax of the pragma directive, and Table 5.5 shows the token strings recognized by Visual C++. For further information on the operation of each pragma directive, consult the Visual C++ documentation.

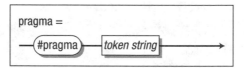

Figure 5.11   Pragma directive syntax.

Table 5.5   Pragma directives.

Pragma	Function
alloc_text	Specifies the name of the code section in which function definitions reside.
auto_inline	Enables or disables automatic inlining of functions.
bss_seg	Specifies the default section for uninitialized data.
check_stack	Enables or disables probes that check the status of the stack.
code_seg	Specifies the name of the default code segment.
comment	Inserts a comment into the object file.
component	Enables or disables collection of browse information from the source file.
const_seg	Specifies the name of the default section for constant data.
data_seg	Specifies the name of the default section for data.

(continued)

Table 5.5   Pragma directives (continued).

Pragma	Function
function	Overrides the effect of the **intrinsic** pragma, forcing generation of function calls rather than inline code for certain library functions.
hdrstop	Controls the precompilation of headers.
include_alias	Specifies an alias for an include file name.
init_seg	Controls the sequence of execution of startup code.
inline_depth	Controls the number of times a series of function calls can be expanded.
inline_recursion	Controls the expansion of recursive functions.
intrinsic	Specifies that certain library functions are to be called inline.
message	Sends a text string to the standard output device.
once	Specifies that the current source file is to be included only once in the current compilation.
optimize	Specifies optimizations performed by the Professional and Enterprise edition compilers.
pack	Specifies alignment of structure and union members.
pointers_to_ members	Specifies the size and interpretation of pointers to members.
setlocale	Specifies the locale (country and language) used to translate wide-character constants and string literals.
vtordisp	Affects the layout of derived classes that inherit from a virtual base class.
warning	Specifies compiler behavior related to warning messages.

5. Advanced Features And Facilities

Part II

The C++ Libraries

General-Purpose Library Components

In Brief

Using Header Files

Visual C++ provides an extensive library of routines that you can incorporate into your programs. To facilitate working with these routines, Visual C++ provides prewritten header files that you can include in your programs by using the preprocessor **include** directive. The header files declare and define global variables, constants, types, functions, and macros required by the library routines.

Namespaces help you use these header files. When your program includes multiple header files that define distinct program objects having the same name, a name conflict arises. Visual C++ lets you define namespaces that alleviate such conflicts. Consider the following code, which defines two distinct classes, each named **Vector**:

```
// Header File #1
class Vector { ... };

// Header File #2
class Vector { ... };
```

Visual C++ cannot compile this code, because the **Vector** class is defined more than once. To alleviate the problem, you can define distinct namespaces that contain the incompatible definitions:

```
// Header File #1
namespace alpha
{
    class Vector { ... };
}

// Header File #2
namespace beta
{
    class Vector { ... };
}
```

Having established distinct namespaces, you can refer to the **Vector** class defined by the first header as **alpha::Vector** and to that defined by the second header as **beta::Vector**.

Some global variables and constants, macros, and functions are Microsoft-specific. Names of Microsoft-specific global variables and constants begin with an underscore character (_); names of Microsoft-specific constants begin with two underscores. By never giving your own program objects names that begin with an underscore, you can avoid conflict with these Microsoft-specific identifiers.

Functions and macros are collectively referred to as *routines*. Many routines defined in the Visual C++ libraries exist as both functions and macros. If your program refers to a routine that exists as both a function and a macro, Visual C++ understands the reference as pertaining to the macro, because macro definitions always follow function definitions in the Visual C++ header files. If you want the reference to pertain to the function, you can use the **#undef** preprocessor directive to undefine the macro name. Alternatively, you can enclose the name of the routine in parentheses; Visual C++ takes such a reference as pertaining to the function.

6. General-Purpose Library Components

Immediate Solutions

stddef.h And cstddef

The **stddef.h** header file defines several program objects of general relevance. The **cstddef** header provides a convenient way to include the **stddef.h** header file and define the contents of that file within the **std** namespace. You must reference the names introduced by **cstddef** by qualifying them using the namespace (**std**) and the scope resolution operator. Alternatively, you can incorporate the members of the **std** namespace into the current namespace by including the following line after the **#include** directives:

```
using namespace std;
```

Variables And Constants

errno

```
extern int errno;
```

The **errno** variable is a global variable that identifies the most recent system call error condition. The header file **errno.h** defines the values that the **errno** variable can assume, as shown in Table 6.1. Some of these values are not returned by 32-bit Windows applications. The **stddef.h** header defines a similar global variable, **_doserrno**, that identifies the most recent error condition associated with an input/output operation.

NULL

The **NULL** constant is a pointer constant that has a unique value that points to no program object.

Types

Table 6.2 shows the major types defined by the **stddef.h** header file.

Table 6.1 **errno** *values.*

Value	Message
E2BIG	Argument list too long
EACCESS	Permission denied
EAGAIN	No more processes or not enough memory or maximum nesting level reached
EBADF	Bad file number
ECHILD	No spawned processes
EDEADLOCK	Resource deadlock would occur
EDOM	Math argument
EEXIST	File exists
EINVAL	Invalid argument
EMFILE	Too many open files
ENOENT	No such file or directory
ENOEXEC	Exec format error
ENOMEM	Not enough memory
ENOSPC	No space left on device
ERANGE	Result too large
EXDEV	Cross-device link

Table 6.2 *Types defined by* **stddef.h.**

Type	Description
ptrdiff_t	The **ptrdiff_t** type represents the result of subtracting two pointers.
size_t	The **size_t** type represents the type returned by the **sizeof** operator. The Visual C++ **sizeof** operator returns its result as a count of bytes. Several Visual C++ header files, other than **stddef.h**, also define the type **size_t**.
wchar_t	The **wchar_t** type represents the type used to store wide characters. The **stdlib.h** header also defines this type.

Routines

offsetof *(ANSI, Win 9x, Win NT)*

This macro returns the offset of a member from the beginning of its structure or class.

```
size_t offsetof(structureName, memberName);
```

6. General-Purpose Library Components

The **offsetof** macro returns the offset in bytes of the specified member from the beginning of the specified data structure, which must contain the member. The return value is not defined for bit fields.

It contains the following parameters:

- *structureName*—The name of the data structure.
- *memberName*—The name of the member of the data structure.

stdio.h And cstdio

The **stdio.h** header file defines many program objects useful for input/output operations. The **cstdio** header provides a convenient way to include the **stdio.h** header file and define the contents of that file within the **std** namespace. You must reference the names introduced by **cstdio** by qualifying them using the namespace (**std**) and the scope resolution operator or by specifying a **using namespace** statement, as explained in the previous section.

Constants

Table 6.3 shows the major constants defined by the **stdio.h** header file.

Table 6.3   Constants defined by stdio.h.

Name	Description
BUFSIZ	Holds the size of the buffer allocated for the **setvbuf** routine.
EOF	Returned by an input/output routine when the routine encounters an end-of-file condition or certain errors. An input/output routine processing a wide stream may return the value **WEOF**.
FILENAME_MAX	Specifies the maximum permissible length of a file name.
FOPEN_MAX	Specifies the maximum number of files that can be open simultaneously.
L_tmpnam	Specifies the length of the temporary file names generated by the **tmpnam** function.
stderr	Points to the standard error stream.
stdin	Points to the standard input stream.
stdout	Points to the standard output stream.
TMP_MAX	Specifies the maximum number of unique file names that the **tmpnam** function can generate.
WEOF	Returned by an input/output routine processing a wide stream when the routine encounters an end-of-file condition or certain errors.

Types

Table 6.4 shows the major types defined by the **stdio.h** header file.

Routines

clearerr (ANSI, Win 9X, Win NT)
This routine resets the error and end-of-file status of a stream.

```
void clearerr(FILE* stream);
```

It contains the following parameter:

- *stream*—The stream whose status is to be reset.

fclose And *_fcloseall (ANSI, Win9X, WinNT)*
The **fclose** routine closes the specified stream and the **_fcloseall** routine closes all open streams.

```
int fclose(FILE* stream);
int _fcloseall(void);
```

fclose returns 0 if it successfully closed the stream. **_fcloseall** returns the number of streams closed. Both routines return **EOF** if an error occurs.

These routines contain the following parameter:

- *stream*—The stream that is to be closed.

_fdopen And *_wfdopen (ANSI, Win 9X, Win NT)*
These routines associate a stream with an open file.

```
FILE* _fdopen(int handle, const char* mode);
FILE* _wfdopen(int handle, const wchar_t* mode);
```

They return a pointer to the open stream if the stream was successfully opened; otherwise, they return **NULL**.

Table 6.4   Major types defined by stdio.h.

Name	Purpose
FILE	Stores information about the current state of an input/output stream.
fpos_t	Used by **fgetpos** and **fsetpos** to uniquely specify a position within a file.

The **_fdopen** and **_wfopen** routines contain the following parameters:

- *handle*—A handle to the open file.
- *mode*—The type of file access desired, specified using a series of characters (see Table 6.5).

feof (ANSI, Win 9X, Win NT)

This routine tests the end-of-file status of a stream.

```
int feof(FILE* stream);
```

feof returns 0 if the specified stream is not at end of file; otherwise, it returns a non-zero value.

It contains the following parameter:

- *stream*—The file whose status is to be tested.

ferror (ANSI, Win 9X, Win NT)

This routine determines the error status of a stream.

```
int ferror(FILE* stream);
```

Table 6.5   File access modes.

Mode	Function
"r"	Read mode: Opens an existing file for reading.
"w"	Write mode: Opens the file for writing and creates the file if it does not exist. If the file exists, its original contents are destroyed.
"a"	Append mode: Opens the file for writing at the end of the file and creates the file if it does not exist. If the file exists, its original contents are retained; new data is written at the end of the file.
"r+"	Opens the file for both reading and writing. The file must exist.
"w+"	Opens the file for both reading and writing. Destroys the original contents of an existing file.
"a+"	Opens the file for both reading and appending. Creates the file if it does not exist.
"t"	Translates CR-LF pairs to LF on input; translates LF to CR-LF on output. Interprets Ctrl+Z as the end-of-file condition on input. (Microsoft extension)
"b"	Suppresses translation of CR-LF and LF.
"c"	Causes the stream buffer contents to be immediately written to disk when **fflush** is called. (Microsoft extension)
"n"	Allows the operating system to determine when the stream buffer contents should be written. (Microsoft extension)

If no error has occurred, **ferror** returns 0; otherwise, it returns a non-zero value.

The **ferror** routine contains the following parameter:

• *stream*—The stream whose error status is to be determined.

fflush *(ANSI, Win 9X, Win NT)*
This routine flushes the contents of a stream's buffers.

```
int fflush(FILE* stream);
```

fflush generally returns 0 if the flush was successful; it returns **EOF** to indicate an error.

It contains the following parameter:

• *stream*—The stream that is to be flushed.

fgetc *And* fgetwc *(ANSI, Win 9X, Win NT)*
_fgetchar *And* _fgetwchar *(Win 9X, Win NT)*
These routines read a character from a specified stream (**fgetc**, **fgetwc**) or from **stdin** (**_fgetchar**, **_fgetwchar**).

```
int fgetc(FILE* stream);
wint_t fgetwc(FILE* stream);
int _fgetchar(void);
wint_t _fgetwchar (void);
```

If the operation was successful, they return the character read; otherwise, they return **EOF** (**fgetc**, **_fgetchar**) or **WEOF** (**fgetwc**, **_fgetwchar**).

They contain the following parameter:

• *stream*—The stream from which the character is to be read.

fgetpos *(ANSI, Win 9X, Win NT)*
This routine returns the file position indicator of the specified stream.

```
int fgetpos(FILE* stream, fpos_t* pos);
```

If successful, **fgetpos** returns 0; otherwise, it returns a non-zero value and sets **errno** to indicate the cause of the error.

It contains the following parameters:

• *stream*—The stream whose file position indicator is to be returned.

• *pos*—A pointer to a buffer that receives the file position indicator.

fgets And fgetws
These routines read a string from a stream.

```
char* fgets(char* string, int n, FILE* stream);
wchar_t* fgetws(wchar_t* string, int n, FILE* stream);
```

They return the string that is read if the operation was successful; otherwise, they return **NULL**.

The **fgets** and **fgetws** routines contain the following parameters:

- *string*—A pointer to a buffer that receives the string.
- *n*—The maximum number of characters to be read.
- *stream*—The stream that is to be read.

_fileno (Win 9X, Win NT)
This routine returns the handle of the file associated with a stream.

```
int _fileno(FILE* stream);
```

_fileno returns the handle of the file if the operation was successful; otherwise, the result is undefined.

It contains the following parameter:

- *stream*—The stream whose handle is to be returned.

_flushall (Win 9X, Win NT)
This routine flushes all open streams.

```
int _flushall(void);
```

_flushall returns the number of open streams.

fopen (ANSI, Win 9X, Win NT)
_wfopen (Win NT)
These routines open a file.

```
FILE* fopen(const char* filename, const char* mode);
FILE* _wfopen(const wchar_t* filename, const wchat_t* mode);
```

They return a pointer to the open stream if the operation was successful; otherwise, they return **NULL**.

The **fopen** and **_wfopen** routines contain the following parameters:

- *filename*—The name of the file to be opened.

- **mode**—The type of file acccss desired, specified using a series of characters (see Table 6.5 earlier in this chapter).

fprintf And *fwprintf (ANSI, Win 9X, Win NT)*
These routines print formatted data to an open stream.

```
int fprintf(FILE* stream, const char* format
  [, argument]...);
int fwprintf(FILE* stream, const wchar_t* format
  [, argument]...);
```

They return the number of characters written if the operation was successful; otherwise, they return a negative value.

They contain the following parameters:

- **stream**—The stream to which the data is to be written.

- **format**—The format-control string (see the description of the **printf** routine later in this chapter).

- **argument**—Optional arguments whose values are printed.

fputc And *fputwc (ANSI, Win 9X, Win NT)*
_fputchar And *_fputwchar (Win 9X, Win NT)*
These routines write a character to the specified stream (**fputc**, **fputwc**) or **stdout** (**_fputchar**, **_fputwchar**).

```
int fputc(int c, FILE* stream);
wint_t fputwc(wint_t c, FILE* stream);
int _fputchar(int c);
wint_t _fputwchar(wint_t c);
```

They return the character written if the operation was successful; otherwise, they return **EOF** (**fputc**, **_fputchar**) or **WEOF** (**fputwc**, **_fputwchar**).

The **fputc**, **fputwc**, **_fputchar**, and **_fputwchar** routines contain the following parameters:

- **c**—The character to be written.

- **stream**—The stream to which the character is to be written.

fputs And *fputws (ANSI, Win 9X, Win NT)*
These routines write a string to a stream.

```
int fputs(const char* string, FILE* stream);
int fputws(const wchar_t string, FILE* stream);
```

They return a nonnegative value if the operation was successful; otherwise, they return **EOF** (**fputs**) or **WEOF**(**fputws**).

The **fputs** and **fputws** routines contain the following parameters:

- *string*—The string to be written.
- *stream*—The stream to which the string is to be written.

fread *(ANSI, Win 9X, Win NT)*
This routine reads data from a stream.

```
size_t fread(void* buffer, size_t size, size_t count,
  FILE* stream);
```

fread returns the number of items actually read. This will be less than *count* if an error occurred or end of file was reached.

It contains the following parameters:

- *buffer*—The buffer that will receive the data that is read.
- *size*—The size (in bytes) of each item to be read.
- *count*—The maximum number of items to be read.
- *stream*—The stream from which data is to be read.

freopen *(ANSI, Win 9X, Win NT)*
_wfreopen *(Win NT)*
These routines reassign a file pointer to a different stream.

```
FILE* freopen(const char* path, const char* mode,
  FILE* stream);
FILE* _wfreopen(const wchar_t* path, const wchar_t* mode,
  FILE* stream);
```

They return a pointer to the opened file if the operation was successful; otherwise, they return **NULL**.

The **freopen** and **_wfreopen** routines contain the following parameters:

- *path*—The path of the file to be opened.
- *mode*—The type of access for which the file is to be opened (see Table 6.5 earlier in this chapter).
- *stream*—A pointer to a **FILE** structure.

NOTE: *If an error occurs, the original file is closed.*

---

fscanf And *fwscanf* *(ANSI, Win 9X, Win NT)*

These routines read formatted data from a stream.

```
int fscanf(FILE* stream, const char* format
  [, argument]...);
int fwscanf(FILE* stream, const wchar_t* format
  [, argument]...);
```

They return the number of fields converted and assigned. If an error occurs, they return the value **EOF** (**fscanf**) or **WEOF** (**fwscanf**).

The **fscanf** and **fwcanf** routines contain the following parameters:

* *stream*—The stream to which the data is to be read.

* *format*—The format-control string (see the description of the **printf** routine later in this chapter).

* *argument*—Optional arguments that receive the values read.

fseek *(ANSI, Win 9X, Win NT)*

This routine moves the file pointer to the specified location.

```
int fseek(FILE* stream, long offset, int origin);
```

If successful, **fseek** returns the value 0; otherwise, it returns a non-zero value.

It contains the following parameters:

* *stream*—The stream whose file position is to be adjusted.

* *offset*—The number of bytes from *origin* to which the file pointer is to be moved.

* *origin*—A value that specifies the point of reference to which the *offset* applies (see Table 6.6).

Table 6.6   *origin* values for *fseek*.

Value	Function
SEEK_CUR	Specifies that an input/output operation begins at the current position of the file pointer.
SEEK_END	Specifies that an input/output operation begins at the end of the file.
SEEK_SET	Specifies that an input/output operation begins at the beginning of the file.

fsetpos *(ANSI, Win 9X, Win NT)*
This routine sets the file position pointer to a previously saved value.

```
int fsetpos(FILE* stream, const fpos_t* pos);
```

fsetpos returns the value 0 if the operation succeeds; otherwise, it returns a non-zero value. If the operation fails, **fsetpos** sets **errno** to indicate the cause of the failure.

It contains the following parameters:

- **stream**—The stream that is to be repositioned.

- **pos**—A file position obtained by using the **fgetpos** routine.

_fsopen *(Win 9X, Win NT)*
_wfsopen *(Win NT)*
These routines open a file for shared access.

```
FILE* _fsopen(const char* filename, const char* mode,
  int shflag);
FILE* _wfsopen(const wchar_t* filename, const wchar_t* mode,
  int shflag);
```

They return a pointer to the opened stream, or **NULL** if an error occurs.

The **_fsopen** and **_wfsopen** routines contain the following parameters:

- **filename**—The file to be opened.

- **mode**—The type of access for which the file is to be opened (see Table 6.5 earlier in this chapter).

- **shflag**—The type of sharing allowed (see Table 6.7).

Table 6.7   shflag values for _fsopen and _wfsopen.

Value	Function
_SH_COMPAT	Sets compatibility mode for 16-bit applications.
_SH_DENYNO	Permits both read and write access by others.
_SH_DENYRD	Denies read access by others.
_SH_DENYRW	Denies read and write access by others.
_SH_DENYWR	Denies write access by others.

ftell *(Win 9X, Win NT)*

This routine gets the current position of the file pointer of the specified stream.

```
long ftell(FILE* stream);
```

ftell returns the current file position, which can be used with **fseek** to reset the file to the current position. If an error occurs, **ftell** returns –1L and sets **errno** to indicate the cause of the error.

It contains the following parameter:

- *stream*—The stream whose file pointer is to be returned.

fwrite *(Win 9X, Win NT)*

This routine writes data to a stream.

```
size_t fwrite(const void* buffer, size_t size, size_t count,
  FILE* stream);
```

fwrite returns the number of items actually written. If an error occurs, this value may be less than *count*.

It contains the following parameters:

- *buffer*—The buffer that holds the data to be written.
- *size*—The size (in bytes) of each item to be written.
- *count*—The maximum number of items to be written.
- *stream*—The stream to which data is to be written.

getc, getwc, getchar, *And* getwchar *(ANSI, Win 9X, Win NT)*

These routines read and return a character from a stream (**getc**, **getwc**) or **stdin** (**getchar**, **getwchar**).

```
int getc(FILE* stream);
wint_t getwc(FILE* stream);
int getchar(void);
wint_t getwchar(void);
```

They return the character read if the operation was successful; they return **EOF** (**getc**, **getchar**) or **WEOF** (**getwc**, **getwchar**) if the operation encountered an end-of-file condition or an error.

They contain the following parameter:

- *stream*—The stream to be read.

gets *And* _getws *(ANSI, Win 9X, Win NT)*
These routines read a line of text from **stdin**.

```
char* gets(char* buffer);
wchar_t* getws(wchart* buffer);
```

They return the argument if the operation was successful; they return **NULL** otherwise.

The **gets** and **getws** routines contain the following parameter:

* **buffer**—The buffer that is to receive the text read.

_getw *(Win 9X, Win NT)*
This routine reads an integer from a stream.

```
int _getw(FILE* stream);
```

_getw returns the integer read if the operation was successful; it returns **EOF** otherwise. You should use the **feof** or **ferror** routine to distinguish an error or end-of-file condition from a legitimate integer value.

It contains the following parameter:

* **stream**—The stream from which the integer is to be read.

_pclose *(Win 9X, Win NT)*
This routine returns the exit status of a command processor and closes the associated pipe.

```
int _pclose(FILE* stream);
```

_pclose returns the exit status of the command processor, or −1 if an error occurs.

It contains the following parameter:

* **stream**—A stream created using **_popen**. The stream receives the output of a command processor.

perror *(ANSI, Win 9X, Win NT)*
_wperror *(Win 9X, Win NT)*
These routines print an error message to **stderr**.

```
void perror(const char* string);
void wperror(const wchar_t* string);
```

They contain the following parameter:

• *string*—The error message to be printed.

_popen *(Win 9X, Win NT)*
_wpopen *(Win NT)*
These routines start a command processor and execute a command.

```
FILE* _popen(const char* command, const char* mode);
FILE* wpopen(const wchart* command, const wchar_t* mode);
```

They return a stream associated with a pipe. The command process uses the pipe as its **stdin** or **stdout**, depending on the value of *mode*. The routines return **NULL** if an error occurs.

The **_popen** and **_wpopen** routines contain the following parameters:

• *command*—The command to be executed.

• *mode*—A character string that specifies the type of access. The values **"r"**, **"w"**, **"b"**, and **"t"** are accepted. See Table 6.5 earlier for a description of each value.

printf And wprintf *(ANSI, Win 9X, Win NT)*
These routines print formatted output to **stdout**.

```
int printf(const char* format, [, argument]...);
int wprintf(const wchar_t* format, [, argument]...);
```

They return the number of characters printed if successful; otherwise, they return a negative value.

The **printf** and **wprintf** routines contain the following parameters:

• *format*—The format-control string containing text—which appears in the output verbatim—and specifications that determine the form in which arguments are printed. Each specification has the form:

```
%[flags][width][.precision][{h|I|I64|L}]type
```

Table 6.8 summarizes the flags, and Table 6.9 summarizes the types. For further information on format specifiers, consult the Visual C++ documentation.

• *argument*—The arguments whose values are to be printed.

Table 6.8   printf flags.

Flag	Meaning
-	Left align.
+	Prefix with sign.
0	Zero pad.
blank	Pad with spaces.
#	With the **o**, **x**, or **X** format, prefix the output with 0, 0x, or 0X. With the **e**, **E**, or **f** format, force a decimal point. With the **g** or **G** format, force a decimal point and do not truncate trailing zeroes.

Table 6.9   printf types.

Character	Type	Format
c	**int**	Single-byte character.
	wint_t	Wide character.
C	**int**	Single-byte character.
	wint_t	Wide character.
d	**int**	Signed decimal integer.
i	**int**	Signed decimal integer.
o	**int**	Unsigned octal integer.
u	**int**	Unsigned decimal integer.
x	**int**	Unsigned hexadecimal integer.
X	**int**	Unsigned hexadecimal integer.
e	**double**	Signed value in exponential format.
E	**double**	Signed value in exponential format.
f	**double**	Signed value in decimal format.
g	**double**	Signed value in exponential or decimal format.
G	**double**	Signed value in exponential or decimal format.
n	Pointer to integer	Stores the number of characters written to the stream buffer in the associated integer argument.
p	Pointer to **void**	Address in segment-offset format.
s	String	A single-byte character string.
S	String	A wide-character string.

putc, putwc, putchar, And putwchar (ANSI, Win 9X, Win NT)

These routines write a character to a stream (**putc**, **putwc**) or **stdout** (**putchar**, **putwchar**).

```
int putc(int c, FILE* stream);
wint_t putwc(wint_t c, FILE* stream);
int putchar(int c);
wint_t putwchar(wint_t c);
```

They return the character written if the operation was successful; otherwise, they return **EOF** (**putc**, **putchar**) or **WEOF** (**putwc**, **putwchar**).

The **putc**, **putwc**, **putchar**, and **putwchar** routines contain the following parameters:

- *c*—The character to be written.
- *stream*—The stream to which the character is to be written.

puts And _putws (ANSI, Win 9X, Win NT)

These routines write a string to **stdout**.

```
int puts(const char* string);
input putws(const wchar_t* string);
```

They return a nonnegative value if the operation was successful; otherwise, they return **EOF** (**puts**) or **WEOF** (**_putws**).

The **puts** and **_putws** routines contain the following parameter:

- *string*—The string to be written.

_putw (Win 9X, Win NT)

This routines writes an integer to a stream.

```
int _putw(int n, FILE* stream);
```

_putw returns the value written, or **EOF** to signify an error.

It contains the following parameters:

- *n*—The integer to be written.
- *stream*—The stream to which the integer is to be written.

6. General-Purpose Library Components

remove *(ANSI, Win 9X, Win NT)*
_wremove *(Win NT)*
These routines delete a file.

```
int remove(const char* path);
int wremove(const wchart* path);
```

They return the value 0 if the operation was successful; otherwise, they return –1. The value of **errno** indicates the cause of the error, if any.

The **remove** and **_wremove** routines contain the following parameter:

• **path**—The path of the file to be deleted.

rename *(ANSI, Win 9X, Win NT)*
_wrename *(Win NT)*
These routines rename a file or directory.

```
int rename(const char* oldname, const char* newname);
int _wrename(const wchart* oldname, const wchar_t* newname);
```

They return the value 0 if the operation was successful; otherwise, they return a non-zero value. The value of **errno** indicates the cause of the error, if any.

The **rename** and **_wrename** routines contain the following parameters:

• **oldname**—The original name of the file or directory.

• **newname**—The new name of the file or directory.

rewind *(ANSI, Win 9X, Win NT)*
This routine positions the file pointer to the beginning of the file.

```
void rewind(FILE* stream);
```

It contains the following parameter:

• **stream**—The file whose pointer is to be repositioned.

_rmtmp *(Win 9X, Win NT)*
This routine removes temporary files.

```
int _rmtmp(void);
```

_rmtmp returns the number of temporary files closed and deleted.

scanf And wscanf *(ANSI, Win 9X, Win NT)*
These routines read formatted data from **stdin**.

```
int scanf(const char*format, [, argument]...);
int wscanf(const wchar_t*format, [, argument]...);
```

They return the number of fields converted and assigned, or **EOF** to indicate an error or end-of-file condition.

The **scanf** and **wscanf** routines contain the following parameters:

- *format*—A format-control string specifying the format of the input (see the description of **printf** earlier in this chapter). The string can contain whitespace characters, non-whitespace characters other than the percent sign (%), and format specifications. Each specification has the form:

```
%[*][width][.precision][{h|I|I64|L}]type
```

For further information on format specifiers, consult the Visual C++ documentation.

- *argument*—The arguments that are to receive the data read.

setbuf *(ANSI, Win 9X, Win NT)*
This routine associates a user-allocated buffer with a stream.

```
void setbuf(FILE* stream, char* buffer);
```

It contains the following parameters:

- *stream*—The stream whose buffer is to be controlled.
- *buffer*—The user-allocated buffer to be associated with the stream.

NOTE: *The **setbuf** routine has been superseded by the **setvbuf** routine.*

_setmaxstdio *(Win 9X, Win NT)*
This routine sets the maximum number of files that can be open simultaneously.

```
int _setmaxstdio(int max);
```

_setmaxstdio returns *max* if successful and –1 otherwise.

6. General-Purpose Library Components

It contains the following parameter:

- *max*—The maximum number of simultaneously open files.

setvbuf *(ANSI, Win 9X, Win NT)*

This routine controls stream buffering.

```
int setvbuf(FILE* stream, char* buffer, int mode,
  size_t size);
```

setvbuf returns the value 0 if successful; otherwise, it returns a non-zero value if an error occurs.

It contains the following parameters:

- *stream*—The stream whose buffer is to be controlled.
- *buffer*—The user-allocated buffer to be associated with the stream.
- *mode*—The buffering mode. Possible values are:

  - **_IOFBF**, which specifies full buffering

  - **_IOLBF**, which specifies full buffering for MS-DOS programs

  - **_IONBF**, which specifies no buffering

- *size*—The buffer size in bytes, which must be greater than 2 and less than 32768.

_snprintf *And* _snwprintf *(Win 9X, Win NT)*

These routines write formatted data to a string.

```
int _snprintf(char* buffer, size_t count,
  const char* format [, argument]...);
int snwprintf(wchar_t* buffer, size_t count,
  const wchar_t* format [, argument]...);
```

They return the number of bytes stored in *buffer*, not counting the terminating null character.

_snprintf and **_snwprintf** contain the following parameters:

- *buffer*—The buffer into which the characters are to be written.
- *count*—The maximum number of characters to be written.
- *format*—The format-control string (see the description of **printf** earlier in this chapter).
- *argument*—The optional arguments whose values are written.

sprintf And swprintf *(ANSI, Win 9X, Win NT)*
These routines write formatted data to a string.

```
int sprintf(char* buffer, const char* format
  [, argument]...);
int swprintf(wchar_t* buffer, const wchar_t* format
  [, argument]...);
```

They return the number of bytes written to **buffer**, not counting the terminating null character.

The **sprintf** and **swprintf** routines contain the following parameters:

- *buffer*—The buffer into which the characters are to be written.

- *format*—The format-control string (see the description of **printf** earlier in the chapter).

- *argument*—The optional arguments whose values are written.

sscanf And swscanf *(ANSI, Win 9X, Win NT)*
These routines read formatted data from a string.

```
int sscanf(const char* buffer, const char* format
  [, argument]...);
int swscanf(const wchar_t* buffer, const wchar_t* format
  [, argument]...);
```

They return the number of fields converted and assigned, or **EOF** if an error occurred.

The **sscanf** and **swscanf** routines contain the following parameters:

- *buffer*—The buffer from which the formatted data is to be read

- *format*—The format-control string (see the description of **scanf** earlier in this chapter).

- *argument*—The optional arguments to which the data read is assigned.

_tempnam, _wtempnam, And _wtmpnam *(Win 9X, Win NT)*
tmpnam *(ANSI, Win 9X, Win NT)*
These routines create temporary file names.

```
char* _tempnam(char* dir, char* prefix);
wchar_t* _wtempnam (wchar_t* dir, wchar_t* prefix);
char* tmpnam(char* string);
wchar_t* _wtmpnam (wchar_t* string);
```

They return a pointer to the name generated, or **NULL** if an error occurred.

The **_tempnam**, **_wtempnam**, **_wtmpnam**, and **tmpnam** routines contain the following parameters:

- *dir*—The directory to be used if the **TMP** directory is not available.

- *prefix*—The file name prefix; all file names share the prefix.

- *string*—The buffer that receives the temporary name.

tmpfile (ANSI, Win 9X, Win NT)
This routine creates a temporary file.

```
FILE* tmpfile(void);
```

tmpfile returns a stream pointer to the created temporary file, or **NULL** if an error occurred.

ungetc And ungetwc (ANSI, Win 9X, Win NT)
These routines push a character back onto a stream.

```
int ungetc(int c, FILE* stream);
int ungetwc(wint_t c, FILE* stream);
```

They return the value of *c* if successful; otherwise, they return the value **EOF** (**ungetc**) or **WEOF** (**ungetwc**).

The **ungetc** and **ungetwc** routines contain the following parameters:

- *c*—The character to be pushed back onto the stream.

- *stream*—The stream to receive the character.

vfprintf (ANSI, Win 9X)
vfwprintf (ANSI, Win 9X, Win NT)
These routines write formatted output to a stream.

```
int vfprintf(FILE* stream, const char* format,
  va_list argptr);
int vfwprintf(FILE* stream, const wchar_t* format,
  va_list argptr);
```

They return the number of characters written—not including the terminating null character—or a negative value if an error occurs.

The **vfprintf** and **vfwprintf** routines contain the following parameters:

- *stream*—The stream to which data is to be written.
- *format*—The format-control string (see the description of **printf** earlier in this chapter).
- *argptr*—The pointer to a list of arguments.

vprintf (ANSI, Win 9X, Win NT)
vwprintf (ANSI, Win 9X, Win NT)
These routines write formatted output to **stdout**.

```
int vprintf(const char* format, va_list argptr);
int vwprintf(const wchar_t* format, va_list argptr);
```

They return the number of characters written—not including the terminating null character—or a negative value if an error occurs.

The **vprintf** and **vwprintf** routines contain the following parameters:

- *format*—The format-control string (see the description of **printf** earlier in this chapter).
- *argptr*—The pointer to a list of arguments.

_vsnprintf (Win 9X, Win NT)
_vsnwprintf (Win 9X, Win NT)
These routines write formatted output to a buffer.

```
int _vsnprintf(char* buffer, size_t count,
  const char* format, va_list argptr);
int _vsnwprintf(wchar_t* buffer, size_t count,
  const wchar_t* format, va_list argptr);
```

They return the number of characters written—not including the terminating null character—or a negative value if an error occurs.

The **vsnprintf** and **vsnwprintf** routines contain the following parameters:

- *buffer*—The buffer to which data is to be written.
- *count*—The maximum number of characters to be written.
- *format*—The format-control string (see the description of **printf** earlier in this chapter).
- *argptr*—The pointer to a list of arguments.

6. General-Purpose Library Components

***vsprintf** (ANSI, Win 9X, Win NT)*
***vswprintf** (ANSI, Win 9X, Win NT)*
These routines write formatted output to a buffer.

```
int vsprintf(char* buffer, const char* format,
  va_list argptr);
int vswprintf(wchar_t* buffer, const wchar_t* format,
  va_list argptr);
```

Each returns the number of characters written—not including the terminating null character—or a negative value if an error occurs.

The **vsprintf** and **vswprintf** routines contain the following parameters:

- ***buffer***—The buffer to which data is to be written.

- ***format***—The format-control string (see the description of **printf** earlier in the chapter).

- ***argptr***—The pointer to a list of arguments.

stdlib.h And cstdlib

The **stdlib.h** header file defines many program objects useful for a variety of operations. The **cstdlib** header provides a convenient way to include the **stdlib.h** header file and define the contents of that file within the **std** namespace. You must reference the names introduced by **cstdlib** by qualifying them using the namespace (**std**) and the scope resolution operator or by specifying a **using namespace** statement, as explained in the In Brief section.

Variables And Constants

Table 6.10 summarizes the constants defined in the **stdlib.h** header file. Most of these constants hold information about the maximum length of the components of a path.

The **stdlib.h** header also defines several variables.

_doserrno Variable
```
extern int _doserrno;
```

The **_doserrno** variable holds an error code that indicates the most recent input/output error.

*Table 6.10 Constants defined in **stdlib.h.***

Name	Description
EXIT_SUCCESS and **EXIT_FAILURE**	Used as arguments of the **exit** and **_exit** routines and as return values of the **atexit** and **_onexit** routines.
_MAX_DIR	Holds the maximum length of the directory component of a path.
MAX_DRIVE	Holds the maximum length of the drive component of a path.
_MAX_EXT	Holds the maximum length of the extension component of a path.
_MAX_FNAME	Holds the maximum length of the file name component of a path.
_MAX_PATH	Holds the maximum length of the full path.
MB_CUR_MAX	Holds the maximum number of bytes in a multibyte character.
RAND_MAX	Holds the maximum value that can be returned by the **rand** routine.

_environ And _wenviron Variables

```
extern char** _environ;
extern wchar_t** _wenviron;
```

The **_environ** variable points to an array of pointers to the character strings that compose the process environment. The **_wenviron** variable is a wide-character version of **_environ** that can be used by a program that uses the **wmain** function; it has the value **NULL** for programs that use the ordinary **main** function.

_fileinfo Variable

```
extern int _fileinfo;
```

The **_fileinfo** variable determines whether information about open files is passed to new processes by routines such as **_spawn**. If **_fileinfo** is 0 (the default), the information is not passed; otherwise, the information is passed.

_fmode Variable

```
extern int _fmode;
```

The **_fmode** variable sets the default file-translation mode. The default value, **_O_TEXT**, specifies text-mode translation; the value **_O_BINARY** specifies binary-mode translation.

_osver, _winmajor, _winminor, And _winver *Variables*

```
extern unsigned int _osver;
extern unsigned int _winmajor;
extern unsigned int _winminor;
extern unsigned int _winver;
```

The **_osver**, **_winmajor**, and **_winminor** variables specify the operating system version and the major and minor versions of Microsoft Windows. The **_winver** variable specifies the major version of Microsoft Windows in its high-order byte and the minor version of Microsoft Windows in its low-order byte.

_pgmptr And _wpgmptr *Variables*

```
extern char* _pgmptr;
extern wchar_t* _wpgmptr;
```

The **_pgmptr** variable holds the full path of an executable file run by the command interpreter in a program using **main**. When a program is run from the command line, the **_pgmptr** variable may hold the program name, the program file name, a relative path, or an absolute path. The **_wpgmptr** variable performs the identical function in a program using **wmain**.

_sys_errlist[ ] *Variable*

```
extern char* _sys_errlist[];
```

The **_sys_errlist[]** variable holds an array of standard error messages. The messages are ordered so that the index of a message corresponds to the value of **errno** that the message describes.

_sys_nerr *Variable*

```
extern int _sys_nerr;
```

The **_sys_nerr** variable holds the number of entries in the **_sys_errlist** array.

Types

Table 6.11 shows the major types defined by the **stdlib.h** header file.

*Table 6.11   Types defined in **stdlib.h**.*

Name	Description
div_t	Stores values returned by the **div** routine.
ldiv_t	Stores values returned by the **ldiv** routine.
_onexit_t	Stores values returned by the **_onexit** routine.

Routines

abort (ANSI, Win 9X, Win NT)
This routine aborts the current process.

```
void abort(void);
```

atexit (ANSI, Win 9X, Win NT)
This routine executes the specified function at termination.

```
int atexit(void (__cdecl* func) (void));
```

atexit returns the value 0 if successful; otherwise, it returns a non-zero value.

It contains the following parameter:

• *func*—The function to be called on termination.

atof, atoi, And atol (ANSI, Win 9X, Win NT)
_atoi64 (Win 9X, Win NT)
These routines convert strings to double (**atof**), integer (**atoi**, **_atoi64**), or long (**atol**).

```
double atof(const char* string);
int atoi(const char* string);
__int64 _atoi64(const char* string);
long atol(const char* string);
```

They return the numeric value contained in **string**. If an error occurred, the value is 0 unless overflow occurred; in that case, the return value is undefined.

The **atof**, **atoi**, **atol**, and **_atoi64** routines contain the following parameter:

• *string*—The string that contains the text to be converted to a number.

6. General-Purpose Library Components

bsearch *(ANSI, Win 9X, Win NT)*
This routine searches a sorted array using a binary search.

```
void* bsearch(const void* key, const void* base, size_t num,
  size_t width,
  int(__cdecl* y) (const void* x1, const void* x2));
```

bsearch returns a pointer to the element of the array **base** that has the key value **key**, or **NULL** if no such element exists.

It contains the following parameters:

- **key**—The key value for which to search.
- **base**—The base of the array to be searched.
- **num**—The number of elements in the array.
- **width**—The width of each array element.
- **y**—A function that compares two elements, **x1** and **x2**.
- **x1**—The pointer to the key for the search.
- **x2**—The pointer to the array element to be compared with the key.

calloc *(ANSI, Win 9X, Win NT)*
This routine allocates an array and initializes its elements to 0.

```
void* calloc(size_t num, size_t size);
```

calloc returns a pointer to the allocated memory.

It contains the following parameters:

- **num**—The number of elements to be allocated.
- **size**—The length in bytes of each element.

div *(ANSI, Win 9X, Win NT)*
This routine divides two integer values.

```
div_t div(int numerator, int denominator);
```

div returns a structure of type **div_t**, which contains the quotient and remainder.

It contains the following parameters:

- **numerator**—The numerator.
- **denominator**—The denominator.

_ecvt *(Win 9X, Win NT)*
This routine converts a double number to a string.

```
char* _ecvt(double value, int count, int* dec, int* sign);
```

_ecvt returns a pointer to a string of digits.

It contains the following parameters:

- *value*—The number to be converted.
- *count*—The maximum number of digits to be converted.
- *dec*—The implied decimal point position.
- *sign*—The sign of the converted number.

_fcvt *(Win 9X, Win NT)*
This routine converts a floating-point number to a string.

```
char* _fcvt(double value, int count, int* dec, int* sign);
```

_fcvt returns a pointer to a string of digits.

It contains the following parameters:

- *value*—The number to be converted.
- *count*—The maximum number of digits to be converted.
- *dec*—The implied decimal point position.
- *sign*—The sign of the converted number.

free *(ANSI, Win 9X, Win NT)*
This routine frees allocated memory.

```
void free(void* block);
```

free contains the following parameter:

- *block*—The address of the previously allocated memory block to be freed.

_fullpath *(Win 9X, Win NT)*
_wfullpath *(Win NT)*
These routines create an absolute (full) pathname for the specified relative pathname.

```
char* _fullpath(char* abs, const char* rel, size_t max);
wchar_t* _wfullpath(wchar_t* abs, const wchar_t* rel,
    size_t max);
```

They return a pointer to a buffer containing the absolute pathname, or **NULL** if an error occurred.

The **_fullpath** and **_wfullpath** routines contain the following parameters:

- *abs*—The buffer into which the absolute pathname is to be placed.
- *rel*—The relative pathname.
- *max*—The maximum length of the absolute pathname.

_gcvt *(Win 9X, Win NT)*

This routine converts a floating-point value to a string.

```
char* _gcvt(double value, int digits, char* buffer);
```

_gcvt returns a pointer to the buffer containing the string of digits.

It contains the following parameters:

- *value*—The value to be converted to a string.
- *digits*—The maximum number of digits to be processed.
- *buffer*—The buffer that is to receive the string.

getenv *(ANSI, Win 9X, Win NT)*
_wgetenv *(Win 9X, Win NT)*

These routines retrieve a string from the process environment.

```
char* getenv(const char* varname);
wchar_t* _wgetenv(const wchar_t* varname);
```

They return a pointer to the environment string that contains *varname*, or **NULL** if *varname* is not found.

The **getenv** and **_wgetenv** routines contain the following parameter:

- *varname*—The environment variable for which to search.

_itoa, _i64toa, _ui64toa, _itow, _i64tow, And _ui64tow *(Win 9X, Win NT)*

These routines convert an integer to a string.

```
char* _itoa(int value, char* string, int radix);
char* _i64toa(__int64 value, char* string, int radix);
char* _ui64toa(unsigned _int64 value, char* string,
  int radix);
```

```
wchar_t* _itow(int value, wchar_t* string, int radix);
wchar_t* _i64tow(__int64 value, wchar_t* string, int radix);
wchar_t* _ui64tow(unsigned __int64 value, wchar_t* string,
   int radix);
```

They return a pointer to the result string.

The **_itoa**, **_i64toa**, **_ui64toa**, **_itow**, **_i64tow**, and **_ui64tow** routines contain the following parameters:

- *value*—The value to be converted.

- *string*—The buffer that receives the string result.

- *radix*—The base of the value (2 through 36).

ldiv (ANSI, Win 9X, Win NT)
This routine divides two long values.

```
ldiv_t ldiv(long int numerator, long int denominator);
```

ldiv returns a structure of type **ldiv_t**, which contains the quotient and the remainder.

It contains the following parameters:

- *numerator*—The numerator.

- *denominator*—The denominator.

_lrotl And _lrotr (Win 9X, Win NT)
These routines rotate the bits of a long value left (**_lrotl**) or right (**_lrotr**).

```
unsigned long _lrotl(unsigned long value, int shift);
unsigned long _lrotr(unsigned long value, int shift);
```

They return the rotated value.

The **_lrotl** and **_lrotr** routines contain the following parameters:

- *value*—The value to be rotated.

- *shift*—The number of bits to be rotated.

_ltoa And _ltow (Win 9X, Win NT)
Converts a long integer to a string.

```
char* _ltoa(long value, char* string, int radix);
wchar_t* _ltow(long value, wchar_t* string, int radix);
```

They return a pointer to the result string.

The **_ltoa** and **_ltow** routines contain the following parameters:

- *value*—The number to be converted.
- *string*—The buffer to hold the result.
- *radix*—The base of *value*.

_makepath And _wmakepath (Win 9X, Win NT)
These routines create a pathname from components.

```
void _makepath(char* path, const char* drive,
  const char* dir, const char* fname, const char* ext);
void _wmakepath(wchar_t* path, const wchar_t* drive,
  const wchar_t* dir, const wchar_t* fname,
  const wchar_t* ext);
```

The **_makepath** and **_wmakepath** routines contain the following parameters:

- *path*—The buffer to hold the result.
- *drive*—The drive letter.
- *dir*—The directory.
- *fname*—The file name.
- *ext*—The file extension.

malloc (ANSI, Win 9X, Win NT)
This routine allocates a memory block.

```
void* malloc(size_t size);
```

It contains the following parameter:

- *size*—The number of bytes to allocate.

__max (Win 9X, Win NT)
This routine returns the larger of two values of any numeric type.

```
type __max(type a, type b);
```

It contains the following parameters:

- *type*—Any numeric type.
- *a*—The first value.
- *b*—The second value.

mblen *(ANSI, Win 9X, Win NT)*
This routine determines the validity of a multibyte character and returns its length.

```
int mblen(const char* mbstr, size_t count);
```

mblen returns one of the following:

- The length in bytes of the multibyte character if the operation was successful.

- If *mbstr* is **NULL** or points to a wide-character null character, the value 0.

- If *mbstr* is not a valid multibyte character within its first *count* characters, the value –1.

It contains the following parameters:

- *mbstr*—The multibyte character string to be checked.

- *count*—The maximum number of bytes to be checked.

mbstowcs *(ANSI, Win 9X, Win NT)*
This routine converts a string of multibyte characters to a string of wide characters.

```
size_t mbstowcs(wchar_t* wcstr, const char* mbstr,
  size_t count);
```

mbstowcs returns the number of converted multibyte characters, or –1 if an error occurred.

It contains the following parameters:

- *wcstr*—The buffer to receive the wide-character string.

- *mbstr*—The multibyte string.

- *count*—The number of multibyte characters to convert.

mbtowc *(ANSI, Win 9X, Win NT)*
This routine converts a multibyte character to a wide character.

```
int mbtowc(wchar_t* wchar, const char* mbchar, size_t count);
```

mbtowc returns the length in bytes of the multibyte character, or –1 if an error occurred.

It contains the following parameters:

- **wchar**—The buffer to receive the wide character.
- **mbchar**—The sequence of bytes containing the multibyte character.
- **count**—The number of bytes to process.

_ _min *(Win 9X, Win NT)*
This routine returns the smaller of two values.

```
type __min(type a, type b);
```

It contains the following parameters:

- **type**—Any numeric type.
- **a**—The first value.
- **b**—The second value.

_onexit *(Win 9X, Win NT)*
This routine specifies a routine to be called at program termination.

```
_onexit_t _onexit(_onexit_t f);
```

_onexit returns a pointer to the function if successful; otherwise, it returns **NULL**.

It contains the following parameter:

- **f**—A pointer to the function to be called at termination.

_putenv *(Win 9X, Win NT)*
_wputenv *(Win NT)*
These routines create, modify, or remove an environment variable.

```
int _putenv(const char* envstr);
int _wputenv(const wchar_t* envstr);
```

They return the value 0 if successful, or –1 if an error occurred.

The **_putenv** and **_wputenv** routines contain the following parameter:

- **envstr**—An environment string definition.

qsort *(ANSI, Win 9X, Win NT)*
This routine sorts an array using the quicksort algorithm.

```
void qsort(void* base, size_t num, size_t width,
    int (__cdecl* y) (const void* x1, const void* x2));
```

It contains the following parameters:

- *base*—The base of the array to be searched.
- *num*—The number of elements in the array.
- *width*—The width of each array element.
- *y*—A function that compares two elements, *x1* and *x2*.
- *x1*—The pointer to an array element for comparison.
- *x2*—The pointer to an array element for comparison.

rand *(ANSI, Win 9X, Win NT)*
This routine generates a pseudorandom number.

```
int rand(void);
```

rand returns the pseudorandom number in the range 0 to **RAND_MAX**.

realloc *(ANSI, Win 9X, Win NT)*
This routine reallocates a memory block.

```
void* realloc(void* block, size_t size);
```

realloc returns a **void** pointer to the reallocated block, or **NULL** if an error occurred.

It contains the following parameters:

- *block*—A pointer to the previously allocated memory block.
- *size*—The new size of the block, in bytes.

_rotl *And* _rotr *(ANSI, Win 9X, Win NT)*
These routines rotate the bits of an **int** value left (**_rotl**) or right (**_rotr**).

```
unsigned int _rotl(unsigned int value, int shift);
unsigned int _rotr(unsigned int value, int shift);
```

They return the rotated value.

The **_rotl** and **_rotr** routines contain the following parameters:

- *value*—The value to be rotated.
- *shift*—The number of bits to be rotated.

_searchenv *(Win 9X, Win NT)*
_wsearchenv *(Win NT)*

These routines search for a file using path information from the process environment.

```
void _searchenv(const char* file, const char* var,
  char* path);
void _wsearchenv(const wchar_t* file, const wchar_t* var,
  wchar_t* path);
```

The **_searchenv** and **_wsearchenv** routines contain the following parameters:

- *file*—The name of the file for which to search.

- *var*—The environment variable that contains the list of paths.

- *path*—The buffer that is to receive the path.

_splitpath *And* _wsplitpath *(Win 9X, Win NT)*

These routines split a pathname into components.

```
void _splitpath(const char* path, char* drive, char* dir,
  char* fname, char* ext);
void _wsplitpath(const wchar_t* path, wchar_t* drive,
  wchar_t* dir, wchar_t* fname, wchar_t* ext);
```

The **_splitpath** and **_wsplitpath** routines contain the following parameters:

- *path*—The absolute (full) path.

- *drive*—The optional drive letter, followed by a colon (:).

- *dir*—The optional directory path, including a trailing slash. The path may include forward slashes (/), backward slashes (\), or both.

- *fname*—The base file name, without an extension.

- *ext*—The optional file name extension, including a leading period (.).

srand *(ANSI, Win 9X, Win NT)*

This routine sets a starting point (seed) for the random-number generator.

```
void srand(unsigned int seed);
```

It contains the following parameter:

- **seed**—The seed for random-number generation.

stroul And wcstoul *(ANSI, Win 9X, Win NT)*
These routines convert a string to an unsigned long value.

```
unsigned long stroul(const char* nptr, char** endptr,
  int base);
unsigned long wcstoul(const wchar_t* nptr, wchar_t** endptr,
  int base);
```

They return the converted value if the operation succeeds, the value 0 if no conversion can be performed, or the value **ULONG_MAX** if overflow occurred.

The **stroul** and **wcstoul** routines contain the following parameters:

- **nptr**—The string to be converted.

- **endptr**—A pointer to a character that stops the scan, or **NULL**.

- **base**—The number base.

strtol And wcstol *(ANSI, Win 9X, Win NT)*
These routines convert a string to a long value.

```
long strtol(const char* nptr, char** endptr, int base);
long wcstol(const wchar_t* nptr, wchar_t** endptr, int base);
```

They return the long value represented in **nptr** if the operation was successful, the value 0 if no conversion can be performed, or the value **LONG_MAX** or **LONG_MIN** if overflow occurred.

The **strtol** and **wcstol** routines contain the following parameters:

- **nptr**—The string to be converted.

- **endptr**—A pointer to a character that stops the scan, or **NULL**.

- **base**—The number base.

_swab *(Win 9X, Win NT)*
This routine swaps the adjacent bytes of a buffer.

```
void _swab(char* src, char* dest, int n);
```

6. General-Purpose Library Components

It contains the following parameters:

- *src*—The source buffer.
- *dest*—The destination buffer.
- *n*—The number of bytes to be swapped and copied.

_ultoa And _ultow *(Win 9X, Win NT)*

These routines convert an unsigned long integer to a string.

```
char* _ultoa(unsigned long value, char* string, int radix);
wchar_t* _ultow(unsigned long value, wchar_t* string,
  int radix);
```

They return a pointer to the string containing the result.

The **_ultoa** and **_ultow** routines contain the following parameters:

- *value*—The number to be converted.
- *string*—The buffer to receive the result string.
- *radix*—The number base of *value*.

va_arg, va_end, And va_start *(ANSI, Win 9X, Win NT, Unix)*

These routines provide access to a list of arguments.

```
type va_arg(va_list arg_ptr, type);
void va_end(va_list arg_ptr);
void va_start(va_list arg_ptr); // Unix
void va_start(va_list arg_ptr, prev); // ANSI
```

The **va_arg** routine returns the current argument. Neither the **va_start** nor the **va_end** routine returns a value.

The **va_arg**, **va_end**, and **va_start** routines contain the following parameters:

- *type*—The type of the argument to be retrieved.
- *arg_ptr*—The pointer to the list of arguments.
- *prev*—The parameter preceding the first optional argument (ANSI form only).

wcstombs *(ANSI, Win 9X, Win NT)*

This routine converts a string of wide characters to a string of multibyte characters.

```
size_t wcstombs(char* mbstr, const wchar_t* wcstr, size_t count);
```

wcstombs returns the number of bytes written to the output string.

It contains the following parameters:

- *mbstr*—The buffer to receive the multibyte character string.
- *wcstr*—The wide-character string.
- *count*—The maximum number of bytes to be stored in the multibyte character string.

wctomb (ANSI, Win 9X, Win NT)
This routine converts a wide character to a multibyte character.

```
int wctomb(char* mbchar, wchar_t wchar);
```

wctomb returns the number of bytes in the wide character if the operation was successful, or the value –1 if conversion was not possible.

It contains the following parameters:

- *mbchar*—The address of a buffer that receives the multibyte character.
- *wchar*—The wide character.

_wtoi, _wtoi64, And _wtol (Win 9X, Win NT)
These routines convert a wide-character string to an integer.

```
int _wtoi(const wchar_t* string);
__int64 _wtoi64(const wchar_t* string);
long _wtol(const wchar_t* string);
```

They return the converted value if the operation was successful, or 0 if the input cannot be converted. The return value is undefined if overflow occurred.

The **_wtoi**, **_wtoi64**, and **_wtol** routines contain the following parameter:

- *string*—The string to be converted.

6. General-Purpose Library Components

Buffers, Characters, And Strings

In Brief

Manipulating Buffers, Characters, And Strings

This chapter presents five header files that provide routines that manipulate buffers, characters, and strings:

- **cctype** and **ctype.h**
- **ciso646** and **iso646.h**
- **cstring** and **string.h**
- **cwchar** and **wchar.h**
- **cwctype** and **wctype.h**

The **cctype/ctype.h** header provides routines that let you test and alter characters. The **ciso646/iso646.h** header defines macros that provide readable alternatives to several C++ operators. The **cstring/string.h** header provides routines that let you manipulate text stored as an array of characters. The **cwchar/wchar.h** header provides routines that let you manipulate text stored as an array of wide characters. The **cwctype/wctype.h** header provides routines that let you test and alter wide characters.

Immediate Solutions

cctype And ctype.h

The template class **ctype** provides routines that let you test and alter characters. The **cctype** header provides a convenient way to include the **ctype.h** header file and define the contents of that file within the **std** namespace. You must reference the names introduced by **cctype** by qualifying them using the namespace (**std**) and the scope resolution operator. Alternatively, you can incorporate the members of the **std** namespace into the current namespace by including the following line after the **#include** directives:

```
using namespace std;
```

Routines

isalnum And iswalnum (ANSI, Win 9x, Win NT)
These routines return true (a non-zero value) if a specified character, *c*, is alphanumeric; otherwise, they return 0.

```
int isalnum(int c);
int iswalnum(wint_t c);
```

isalpha And iswalpha (ANSI, Win 9x, Win NT)
These routines return true (a non-zero value) if a specified character, *c*, is alphabetic; otherwise, they return 0.

```
int isalpha(int c)
int iswalpha(wint_t c)
```

__isascii (Win 9x, Win NT)
iswascii (ANSI, Win 9x, Win NT)
These routines return true (a non-zero value) if a specified integer value, *c*, represents an ASCII character; otherwise, they return 0.

```
int __isascii(int c)
int iswascii(wint_t c)
```

7. Buffers, Characters, And Strings

155

iscntrl And *iswcntrl* (ANSI, Win 9x, Win NT)

These routines return true (a non-zero value) if a specified character, *c*, is a control character (**0x00-0x1F** or **0x7F**); otherwise, they return 0.

```
int iscntrl(int c)
int iswcntrl(wint_t c)
```

__iscsyn And *__iscsymf* (Win 9x, Win NT)

These routines return true (a non-zero value) if a specified character, *c*, is a letter, underscore, or digit (**__iscsyn**), or a letter or underscore (**__iscsymf**); otherwise, they return 0.

```
int __iscsyn (int c)
int __iscsymf (int c)
```

isdigit And *iswdigit* (ANSI, Win 9x, Win NT)

These routines return true (a non-zero value) if a specified character, *c*, represents a decimal digit; otherwise, they return 0.

```
int isdigit(int c)
int iswdigit(wint_t c)
```

isgraph And *iswgraph* (ANSI, Win 9x, Win NT)

These routines return true (a non-zero value) if a specified character, *c*, is a printable character other than a space; otherwise, they return 0.

```
int isgraph(int c)
int iswgraph(wint_t c)
```

islower And *iswlower* (ANSI, Win 9x, Win NT)

These routines return true (a non-zero value) if a specified character, *c*, is lowercase; otherwise, they return 0.

```
int islower(int c)
int iswlower(wint_t c)
```

isprint And *iswprint* (ANSI, Win 9x, Win NT)

These routines return true (a non-zero value) if a specified character, *c*, is printable; otherwise, they return 0.

```
int isprint(int c)
int iswprint(wint_t c)
```

ispunct And *iswpunct* (ANSI, Win 9x, Win NT)

These routines return true (a non-zero value) if a specified character, *c*, is a printable character but is not a space or an alphanumeric character; otherwise, they return 0.

```
int ispunct(int c)
int iswpunct(wint_t c)
```

isspace And *iswspace* (ANSI, Win 9x, Win NT)

These routines return true (a non-zero value) if a specified character, *c*, is a space; otherwise, they return 0.

```
int isspace(int c)
int iswspace(wint_t c)
```

isupper And *iswupper* (ANSI, Win 9x, Win NT)

These routines return true (a non-zero value) if a specified character, *c*, is uppercase; otherwise, they return 0.

```
int isupper(int c)
int iswupper(wint_t c)
```

iswctype (ANSI, Win 9x, Win NT)

This routine returns true (a non-zero value) if the specified character has the specified property.

```
int iswctype(wint_t c, wctype_t desc)
```

iswctype returns a non-zero value if the specified character, *c*, has the property *desc*; otherwise, it returns 0.

It contains the following parameters:

- *c*—The character to be tested.
- *desc*—The property for which to test.

isxdigit And *iswxdigit* (ANSI, Win 9x, Win NT)

These routines return true (a non-zero value) if a specified character, *c*, represents a hexadecimal digit; otherwise, they return 0.

```
int isxdigit(int c)
int iswxdigit(wint_t c)
```

7. Buffers, Characters, And Strings

157

isleadbyte *(ANSI, Win 9x, Win NT)*

This routine returns true (a non-zero value) if the argument, **c**, holds the first byte of a multibyte character; otherwise, it returns 0.

```
int isleadbyte(int c)
```

ciso646 And iso646.h

The **iso646.h** header file defines macros that provide readable alternatives to several C++ operators, as shown in Table 7.1. The **ciso646** header provides a convenient way to include the **iso646.h** header file and define the contents of that file within the **std** namespace. You must reference the names introduced by **ciso646** by qualifying them using the namespace (**std**) and the scope resolution operator. Alternatively, you can incorporate the members of the **std** namespace into the current namespace by including the following line after the **#include** directives:

```
using namespace std;
```

Table 7.1   Macros defined by iso646.h.

Macro	C++ Alternative
and	&&
and_eq	&=
bitand	&
bitor	|
compl	~
not	!
not_eq	!=
or	||
or_eq	|=
xor	^
xor_eq	^=

cstring And string.h

The **string.h** header file defines macros that let you manipulate strings, which are sequences of characters terminated by a null character. The **cstring** header provides a convenient way to include the **string.h** header file and define the contents of that file within the **std** namespace. You must reference the names introduced by **cstring** by qualifying them using the namespace (**std**) and the scope resolution operator. Alternatively, you can incorporate the members of the **std** namespace into the current namespace by including the following line after the **#include** directives:

```
using namespace std;
```

Routines

_memccpy (Win 9x, Win NT)
This routine copies characters from a buffer, stopping when a specified number of characters have been copied or a specified character has been copied.

```
void* _memccpy(void* dest, const void* src, int c,
  unsigned int count);
```

If the character **c** was copied, **_memccpy** returns a pointer to the byte in **dest** that immediately follows the character; otherwise, it returns **NULL**.

It contains the following parameters:

* **dest**—A pointer to a destination buffer.
* **src**—A pointer to the source buffer.
* **c**—The last character to copy.
* **count**—The maximum number of bytes to be copied.

memchr (ANSI, Win 9x, Win NT)
This routine finds a specified character in a buffer.

```
void* memchr(const void* buf, int c, size_t count);
```

memchr returns a pointer to the first location of **c** in **buf**, or **NULL** if **c** does not occur in **buf**.

7. Buffers, Characters, And Strings

It contains the following parameters:

- **buf**—A pointer to the buffer to be searched.
- **c**—The character for which to search.
- **count**—The maximum number of bytes to search.

memcmp *(ANSI, Win 9x, Win NT)*
This routine compares the contents of two buffers.

```
int memcmp(const void* buf1, const void* buf2, size_t count);
```

If the buffers have identical contents, it returns the value 0. If the contents of the first buffer collate before those of the second buffer, it returns a negative value; if the contents of the first buffer collate after those of the second buffer, it returns a positive value.

It contains the following parameters:

- **buf1**—A pointer to the first buffer.
- **buf2**—A pointer to the second buffer.
- **count**—The number of characters to be compared.

memcpy *(ANSI, Win 9x, Win NT)*
This routine copies characters from a source buffer to a destination buffer.

```
void* memcpy(void* dest, const void* src, size_t count);
```

memcpy returns the value of the destination buffer.

It contains the following parameters:

- **dest**—The destination buffer.
- **src**—The source buffer.
- **count**—The number of characters to be copied.

_memicmp *(Win 9x, Win NT)*
This routine compares the contents of two buffers, without regard to case.

```
int _memicmp(const void* buf1, const void* buf2, unsigned int
    count);
```

If the buffers have identical contents, it returns the value 0. If the contents of the first buffer collate before those of the second buffer, it returns a negative value; if the contents of the first buffer collate after those of the second buffer, it returns a positive value.

It contains the following parameters:

- ***buf1***—A pointer to the first buffer.
- ***buf2***—A pointer to the second buffer.
- ***count***—The number of characters to be compared.

memmove *(ANSI, Win 9x, Win NT)*
This routine moves the contents of one buffer to another, ensuring that overlapping regions are handled properly.

```
void* memmove(void* dest, const void* src, size_t count);
```

memmove returns the value of ***dest***.

It contains the following parameters:

- ***dest***—The destination buffer.
- ***src***—The source buffer.
- ***count***—The number of bytes to be copied.

memset *(ANSI, Win 9x, Win NT)*
This routine sets a buffer to a specified character.

```
void* memset(void* dest, int c, size_t count);
```

memset returns the value of the destination buffer.

It contains the following parameters:

- ***dest***—The destination buffer.
- ***c***—The character to be set as the buffer's contents.
- ***count***—The number of characters.

strcat *And* wscat *(ANSI, Win 9x, Win NT)*
These routines append one string to another.

```
char* strcat(char* dest, const char* src);
wchar_t* wscat(wchar_t* dest, const wchar_t* src);
```

They return the destination string ***dest***.

The **strcat** and **wscat** routines contain the following parameters:

- *dest*—The null-terminated destination string.
- *src*—The null-terminated source string.

strchr And wcschr (ANSI, Win 9x, Win NT)
These routines find a character in a string.

```
char* strchr(const char * str, int c);
wchar_t* wcschr(const wchar_t * str, int c);
```

They return a pointer to the first occurrence of *c* in *str*, or **NULL** if no such occurrence exists.

The **strchr** and **wcschr** routines contain the following parameters:

- *str*—The null-terminated string to be searched.
- *c*—The character for which to search.

strcmp And wcscmp (ANSI, Win 9x, Win NT)
These routines compare two strings.

```
int strcmp(const char* str1, const char* str2);
int wcscmp(const wchar_t* str1, const wchar_t* str2);
```

If the strings have the same contents, they return the value 0. If the first string collates before the second, they return a negative value; otherwise, they return a positive value.

The **strcmp** and **wcscmp** routines contain the following parameters:

- *str1*—The first null-terminated string.
- *str2*—The second null-terminated string.

strcoll And wcscoll
For a detailed look at these routines, see Chapter 13, which describes routines that support locales.

strcpy And wcscpy (ANSI, Win 9x, Win NT)
These routines copy a string.

```
char* strcpy(char* dest, const char* src);
char* wcscpy(wchar_t* dest, const wchar_t* src);
```

They return the destination string *dest*.

The **strcpy** and **wcscpy** routines contain the following parameters:

- *dest*—The null-terminated destination string.
- *src*—The null-terminated source string.

strcspn *And* wcscspn *(ANSI, Win 9x, Win NT)*

These routines return an index to the first character in a string that does not belong to a specified set of characters.

```
size_t strcspn(const char* str, const char* set);
size_t wcscspn(const wchar_t* str, const wchar_t* set);
```

They return an integer that specifies the length of the initial segment of *str* that consists entirely of characters not in *set*.

The **strcspn** and **wcscspn** routines contain the following parameters:

- *str*—The null-terminated string to be searched.
- *set*—A null-terminated string that specifies the character set.

_strdup *And* _wcsdup *(ANSI, Win 9x, Win NT)*

These routines duplicate a string.

```
char* _strdup(const char* str);
wchar_t* _strdup(const wchar_t* str);
```

They return a pointer to the copied string if the operation succeeds; otherwise, they return **NULL**.

The **_strdup** and **_wcsdup** routines contain the following parameter:

- *str*—The null-terminated string to be copied.

strerror *(ANSI, Win 9x, Win NT)*
_strerror *(Win 9x, Win NT)*

These routines return a system error message (**strerror**) or print a user-supplied error message (**_strerror**).

```
char* strerror(int err);
char* _strerror(const char* str);
```

strerror contains the following parameters:

- *err*—The error number. Errors are specified using the value of **errno** corresponding to the error.

_sterror contains the following parameter:

- *str*—The null-terminated error message.

_stricmp *And* _wcsicmp *(Win 9x, Win NT)*
These routines compare two strings, without regard to case.

```
int _stricmp(const char* str1, const char* str2);
int _wcsicmp(const wchar_t* str1, const wchar_t* str2);
```

If the strings have the same contents, they return the value 0. If the first string collates before the second, they return a negative value; otherwise, they return a positive value.

The **_stricmp** and **_wcsicmp** routines contain the following parameters:

- *str1*—The first null-terminated string.
- *str2*—The second null-terminated string.

strlen *And* wcslen *(ANSI, Win 9x, Win NT)*
These routines return the number of characters contained in a string, not including the terminating **NULL** value.

```
size_t strlen(const char* str);
size_t wcslen(const wchar_t* str);
```

The **strlen** and **wcslen** routines contain the following parameter:

- *str*—The null-terminated string.

_strlwr *And* _wcslwr *(Win 9x, Win NT)*
These routines convert a string to lowercase.

```
char* _strlwr(char* str);
wchar_t* _wcslwr(wchar_t* str);
```

They return a pointer to the converted string.

The **_strlwr** and **_wcslwr** routines contain the following parameter:

- *str*—The null-terminated string to be converted.

strncat *And* wcsncat *(ANSI, Win 9x, Win NT)*
These routines append one string to another.

```
char* strncat(char* dest, const char* src, size_t count);
wchar_t* wcsncat(wchar_t* dest, const wchar_t* src,
  size_t count);
```

They return a pointer to the destination string.

The **strncat** and **wcsncat** routines contain the following parameters:

- *dest*—The null-terminated destination string.
- *src*—The null-terminated source string.
- *count*—The maximum number of characters to be appended.

strncmp And wcsncmp (ANSI, Win 9x, Win NT)
These routines compare two strings.

```
int strncmp(const char* str1, const char* str2, size_t count);
int wcsncmp(const wchar_t* str1, const wchar_t* str2,
  size_t count);
```

If the strings have the same contents, these routines return the value 0. If the first string collates before the second, these routines return a negative value; otherwise, they return a positive value.

The **strncmp** and **wcsncmp** routines contain the following parameters:

- *str1*—The first null-terminated string.
- *str2*—The second null-terminated string.
- *count*—The maximum number of characters to be compared.

strncpy And wcsncpy (ANSI, Win 9x, Win NT)
These routines copy characters of one string to another.

```
char* strncpy(char* dest, const char* src, size_t count);
wchar_t* wcsncpy(wchar_t* dest, const wchar_t* src,
  size_t count);
```

They return the destination string.

The **strncpy** and **wcsncpy** routines contain the following parameters:

- *dest*—The null-terminated destination string.
- *src*—The null-terminated source string.
- *count*—The maximum number of characters to be copied.

_strnicmp And _wcsnicmp (Win 9x, Win NT)
These routines compare two strings, without regard to case.

```
int _strnicmp(const char* str1, const char* str2, size_t count);
int _wcsnicmp(const wchar_t* str1, const wchar_t* str2,
  size_t count);
```

7. Buffers, Characters, And Strings

If the strings have the same contents, these routines return the value 0. If the first string collates before the second, these routines return a negative value; otherwise, they return a positive value.

The **_strnicmp** and **_wcsnicmp** routines contain the following parameters:

- **str1**—The first null-terminated string.
- **str2**—The second null-terminated string.
- **count**—The maximum number of characters to be compared.

_strnset And _wcsnset (ANSI, Win 9x, Win NT)
These routines set the contents of a string to a specified character.

```
char* _strnset(char* str, int c, size_t count);
wchar_t* _wcsnset(wchar_t* str, int c, size_t count);
```

They return a pointer to the resulting string.

The **_strnset** and **_wcsnset** routines contain the following parameters:

- **str**—The string to be altered.
- **c**—The character to be set as the contents of the string.
- **count**—The number of characters to be set.

strpbrk And wcspbrk (ANSI, Win 9x, Win NT)
These routines scan a string for a character in a specified set.

```
char* strpbrk(const char* str, const char* set);
wchar_t* wcspbrk(const wchar_t* str, const wchar_t* set);
```

They return a pointer to the first occurrence within **str** of a character in **set**, or **NULL** if no such occurrence exists.

The **strpbrk** and **wcspbrk** routines contain the following parameters:

- **str**—The null-terminated string to be searched.
- **set**—A null-terminated string that specifies the characters to be searched for.

strrchr and wcsrchr (ANSI, Win 9x, Win NT)
These routines scan a string for the last occurrence of a specified character.

```
char* strrchr(const char* str, int c);
wchar_t* wcsrchr(const wchar_t* str, int c);
```

They return a pointer to the last occurrence of *c* in *str*, or **NULL** if no such occurrence exists.

The **strrchr** and **wesrchr** routines contain the following parameters:

- *str*—The null-terminated string to be scanned.
- *c*—The character for which to scan.

_strrev And _wcsrev *(Win 9x, Win NT)*
These routines reverse the characters of a string.

```
char* _strrev(char* str);
wchar_t* _wcsrev(wchar_t* str);
```

They return a pointer to the resulting string.

The **_strrev** and **_wcsrev** routines contain the following parameter:

- *str*—The null-terminated string to be reversed.

_strset And _wcsset *(Win 9x, Win NT)*
These routines set each character of a string to a specified character.

```
char* _strset(char* str, int c);
wchar_t* _wcsset(wchar_t* str, int c);
```

They return a pointer to the resulting string.

The **_strset** and **_wcsset** routines contain the following parameters:

- *str*—The null-terminated string.
- *c*—The character to be set as the contents of the string.

strspn And wcsspn *(Win 9x, Win NT)*
These routines find the first occurrence of a specified substring.

```
size_t strspn(const char *string, const char *strCharSet);
size_t wcsspn(const wchar_t *string, const wchar_t *strCharSet);
```

These routines return an integer value that specifies the length of the first substring in *string* that consists entirely of characters in *strCharSet*. If *string* begins with a character not in *strCharSet*, they return 0.

The **strspn** and **wcsspn** routines contain the following parameters:

- *string*—The null-terminated string to be searched.

- **strCharSet**—The character set that defines a substring.

strstr *And* wcsstr *(ANSI, Win 9x, Win NT)*
These routines scan a substring that matches a specified string.

```
char* strstr(const char* str, const char* sub);
wchar_t* wcsstr(const wchar_t* str, const wchar_t* sub);
```

They return a pointer to the first occurrence in **str** of the substring **set**, or **NULL** if no such occurrence exists.

The **strstr** and **wcsstr** routines contain the following parameters:

- **str**—The null-terminated string to be scanned.
- **sub**—A null-terminated string that specifies the substring for which to scan.

strtok *And* wcstok *(ANSI, Win 9x, Win NT)*
These routines return the next token in a string.

```
char* strtok(char* str, const char* delim);
wchar_t* wcstok (wchar_t* str, const wchar_t* delim);
```

They return a pointer to the next token found in **str**, or **NULL** if no more tokens are found.

The **strtok** and **wcstok** routines contain the following parameters:

- **str**—The null-terminated string to be searched.
- **delim**—A null-terminated string that specifies the set of delimiter characters.

_strupr *And* wcsupr *(Win 9x, Win NT)*
These routines convert a string to uppercase.

```
char* _strupr(char* str);
wchar_t* _wcsupr(wchar_t* str);
```

They return a pointer to the converted string.

The **_strupr** and **wcsupr** routines contain the following parameter:

- **str**—The null-terminated string to be converted.

strxfrm And *wcsxfrm* (ANSI, Win 9x, Win NT)

These routines transform a string in a locale-specific manner to accommodate diverse collating sequences.

```
size_t strxfrm (char* dest, const char* src, size_t count);
size_t wcsxfrm (wchar_t* dest, const wchar_t* src,
  size_t count);
```

They return the length of the transformed string, not counting the terminating **NULL** character. The transformed string can be used as an argument of **strcmp**.

The **strxfrm** and **wcsxfrm** routines contain the following parameter:

- *dest*—The null-terminated destination string.

- *src*—The null-terminated source string.

- *count*—The maximum number of characters to be transformed.

cwchar And wchar.h

The **wchar.h** header file defines macros that let you manipulate wide strings and perform input/output operations on wide streams. The **cwchar** header provides a convenient way to include the **wchar.h** header file and define the contents of that file within the **std** namespace. You must reference the names introduced by **cwchar** by qualifying them using the namespace (**std**) and the scope resolution operator. Alternatively, you can incorporate the members of the **std** namespace into the current namespace by including the following line after the **#include** directives:

```
using namespace std;
```

Many of the routines found in **wchar.h** are also found in **string.h**. Table 7.2 identifies these routines, described in the previous section.

Variables And Constants

Table 7.3 shows the major variables defined by the **wchar.h** header file.

Types

Table 7.4 shows the major types defined by the **wchar.h** header file.

*Table 7.2   **wchar.h** routines also found in **string.h**.*

Routine	Function
wcsxfrm	Transform a string in a locale-specific manner.
wcscat	Append one string to another.
wcschr	Search a string for the first occurrence of a character.
wcscmp	Compare two strings.
wcscoll	Compare two strings using locale-specific information.
wcscpy	Copy a string.
wcscspn	Search a string for characters in a specific set.
wcslen	Return the length of a string.
wcsncat	Append characters to a string.
wcsncmp	Compare characters of two strings.
wcsncpy	Copy characters from one string to another.
wcspbrk	Scan a string for characters in a specified set.
wcsrchr	Scan a string for the last occurrence of a specified character.
wcsspn	Scan a string for the first character not within a specified set.
wcsstr	Scan a string for a substring that matches a specified string.
wcstok	Find the next token in a string.

*Table 7.3   Variables defined by **wchar.h**.*

Variable	Description
WCHAR_MAX	The maximum value for the type **wchar_t**.
WCHAR_MIN	The minimum value for the type **wchar_t**.

*Table 7.4   Types defined by **wchar.h**.*

Type	Description
wctype_t	An integer type that can represent all characters of any national character set.
wint_t	An integer type that can hold any wide character.

Routines

In addition to routines for manipulating wide characters, the **wchar.h** header defines several routines for performing wide-character input/output. These routines, which are also defined in the **stdio.h** header, are summarized in Table 7.5. See the **stdio.h** header in Chapter 6 for a description of these routines.

*Table 7.5   Wide-character input/output routines defined within **stdio.h.***

Routine	Function
fgetwc	Read a wide character from a stream.
fgetws	Read a string of wide characters from a stream.
fputwc	Write a wide character to a stream.
fputws	Write a string of wide characters to a stream.
fwprintf	Write a formatted string of wide characters to a stream.
fwscanf	Read formatted data from a wide-character stream.
getwc	Read a wide character from a stream.
getwchar	Read a wide character from **stdin**.
putwc	Write a wide character to a stream.
putwchar	Write a wide character to **stdout**.
swprintf	Write a formatted string of wide characters to a buffer.
swscanf	Read formatted data from a wide-character buffer.
ungetwc	Push a wide character back onto an input stream.
vfwprintf	Write a formatted string of wide characters to a stream by using a pointer to a list of arguments.
vswprintf	Write a formatted string of wide characters to a buffer by using a pointer to a list of arguments.
wprintf	Write a formatted string of wide characters to **stdout**.
wscanf	Read formatted data from **stdin**.

btowc *(ANSI, Win 9x, Win NT)*

This routine converts a character to a wide character.

```
wint_t btowc(int c);
```

btowc returns the value **WEOF** if *c* is **EOF**; otherwise, it returns a wide character equivalent to *c*.

It contains the following parameter:

• *c*—The character to be converted.

fwide *(ANSI, Win 9x, Win NT)*

This routine sets a stream to wide-character or byte mode, or determines whether a stream is a wide-character stream or a byte stream.

```
int fwide(FILE *stream, int mode);
```

fwide returns a positive value if the stream is a wide-character stream; a negative value if the stream is a byte stream; or the value 0 if the orientation of the stream has not been set.

It contains the following parameters:

- *stream*—The stream to be set or tested.

- *mode*—A flag that specifies whether the orientation of the stream should be set. A positive value causes the routine to set the stream's orientation to wide character. A negative value causes the routine to set the stream's orientation to byte. A 0 value specifies that the routine should not attempt to set the orientation of the stream.

mbrlen (ANSI, Win 9x, Win NT)
This routine determines the number of bytes in the initial multibyte character of a string.

```
size_t mbrlen(const char *s, size_t n, mbstate_t *ps);
```

mbrlen returns one of the following:

- **(size_t)-2** if the multibyte character is incomplete.

- **(size_t)-1** if an encoding error exists. In this case, the **errno** global variable is set to the value **EILSEQ**.

- The value 0 if the multibyte character is a null character.

- The number of bytes in the multibyte character.

It contains the following parameters:

- *s*—The string that contains the multibyte character.

- *n*—The maximum number of bytes of the multibyte character.

- *ps*—A pointer to an object that represents the conversion state, or **NULL**, which specifies that an object internal to the routine will be used.

mbrtowc (ANSI, Win 9x, Win NT)
This routine determines the number of bytes in a multibyte string that completes the next multibyte character.

```
size_t mbrtowc(wchar_t *pwc, const char *s, size_t n, mbstate_t
    *ps);
```

mbrtowc returns one of the following:

- **(size_t)-2** if the multibyte character is incomplete.

- **(size_t)-1** if an encoding error exists. In this case, the **errno** global variable is set to the value **EILSEQ**.
- The value 0 if the next completed character is a null character.
- The number of bytes needed to complete the multibyte character.

It contains the following parameters:

- *pwc*—A pointer to the initial byte of the multibyte character.
- *s*—A string that contains the remaining bytes of the multibyte character.
- *n*—The maximum number of remaining bytes of the multibyte character.
- *ps*—A pointer to an object that represents the conversion state, or **NULL**, which specifies that an object internal to the routine will be used.

mbsinit *(ANSI, Win 9x, Win NT)*
This routine determines the status of the conversion of a multibyte character.

```
int mbsinit(const mbstate_t *ps);
```

mbsinit returns a non-zero value if *ps* refers to an initial conversion state or is **NULL**; otherwise, it returns 0.

It contains the following parameter:

- *ps*—A pointer to an object that represents the conversion state, or **NULL**, which specifies that an object internal to the routine will be used.

mbsrtowcs *(ANSI, Win 9x, Win NT)*
This routine converts a multibyte string to a sequence of wide characters.

```
size_t mbsrtowcs(wchar_t *dst, const char **src, size_t len,
    mbstate_t *ps);
```

mbsrtowcs returns one of the following:

- **(size_t)-1** if an encoding error exists. In this case, the **errno** global variable is set to the value **EILSEQ**.
- The number of multibyte characters converted, not including the terminating null character is returned.

7. Buffers, Characters, And Strings

It contains the following parameters:

- **dst**—A buffer that receives the converted wide characters.
- **src**—An array of pointers to the characters of the multibyte string.
- **len**—The length of the multibyte string.
- **ps**—A pointer to an object that represents the conversion state, or **NULL**, which specifies that an object internal to the routine will be used.

wcrtomb (ANSI, Win 9x, Win NT)

This routine determines the number of bytes needed to represent a wide character as a multibyte character and performs the conversion.

```
size_t wcrtomb(char *s, wchar_t wc, mbstate_t *ps);
```

wcrtomb returns one of the following:

- **(size_t)-1** if the wide character is invalid. In this case, the **errno** global variable is set to the value **EILSEQ**.
- The number of multibyte characters needed to represent the wide character, not including the terminating null character.

It contains the following parameters:

- **s**—The buffer that receives the multibyte character sequence.
- **wc**—The wide character to be converted.
- **ps**—A pointer to an object that represents the conversion state, or **NULL**, which specifies that an object internal to the routine will be used.

wcsrtombs (ANSI, Win 9x, Win NT)

This routine converts a wide-character string to a sequence of multibyte characters.

```
size_t wcsrtombs(char *dst, const wchar_t **src, size_t len,
    mbstate_t *ps);
```

wcsrtombs returns one of the following:

- **(size_t)-1** if the wide-character string contains an invalid character. In this case, the **errno** global variable is set to the value **EILSEQ**.
- The number of multibyte characters needed to represent the contents of the wide-character string, not including the terminating null character.

It contains the following parameters:

- **dst**—The buffer that receives the resulting sequence of multibyte characters.

- **src**—The wide-character string to be converted.

- **len**—The maximum length of the wide-character string.

- **ps**—A pointer to an object that represents the conversion state, or **NULL**, which specifies that an object internal to the routine will be used.

wcstod (ANSI, Win 9x, Win NT)

This routine converts a string to a double-precision floating-point value.

```
double wcstod(const wchar_t *nptr, wchar_t **endptr);
```

wcstod returns the value of the valid floating-point number contained in the string. The routine returns the value **HUGE_VAL** or **–HUGE_VAL** if an overflow occurs, or the value 0 if an underflow occurs; in either case, the routine sets the global variable **errno** to indicate that an error occurred.

It contains the following parameters:

- **nptr**—The string to be converted.

- **endptr**—A pointer to a character that stops the scan, or **NULL** if the entire string is to be scanned.

wcstoul (ANSI, Win 9x, Win NT)

This routine converts a string to an unsigned long-integer value.

```
unsigned long wcstoul(const wchar_t *nptr, wchar_t **endptr, int
    base);
```

wcstoul returns the value of the valid integer number contained in the string. The routine returns the value **ULONG_MAX** if an overflow occurs, or the value 0 if no conversion can be performed; in either case, the routine sets the global variable **errno** to indicate that an error occurred.

It contains the following parameters:

- **nptr**—The string to be converted.

- **endptr**—A pointer to a character that stops the scan, or **NULL** if the entire string is to be scanned.

- **base**—The base in which the number is represented in the string.

wctob *(ANSI, Win 9x, Win NT)*
This routine determines whether a wide character can be represented as a one-byte multibyte character.

```
int wctob(wint_t c);
```

wctob returns the multibyte representation of *c* if *c* can be represented as a one-byte multibyte character; otherwise, it returns the value **WEOF**.

It contains the following parameter:

- *c*—The wide character to be tested.

wmemchr *(ANSI, Win 9x, Win NT)*
This routine searches an array of wide characters for the first occurrence of a specified wide character.

```
const wchar_t *wmemchr(const wchar_t *s, wchar_t c, size_t n);
wchar_t *wmemchr(wchar_t *s, wchar_t c, size_t n);
```

wmemchr returns a pointer to the matching array element, or **NULL** if no such element exists.

It contains the following parameters:

- *s*—The wide-character array to be searched.
- *c*—The wide character for which to search.
- *n*—The number of wide-character elements to be tested.

wmemcmp *(ANSI, Win 9x, Win NT)*
This routine compares two wide-character arrays.

```
int wmemcmp(const wchar_t *s1, const wchar_t *s2, size_t n);
```

wmemcmp returns the value 0 if the two arrays have the same contents; a positive number if the first different element of *s1* is greater than the corresponding element of *s2*; or a negative number if the first different element of *s1* is less than the corresponding element of *s2*.

It contains the following parameters

- *s1*—The first wide-character string.
- *s2*—The second wide-character string.
- *n*—The number of wide characters to be compared.

wmemcpy *(ANSI, Win 9x, Win NT)*
This routine copies the elements of a wide-character array.

```
wchar_t *wmemcpy(wchar_t *dest, const wchar_t *src, size_t n);
```

wmemcpy returns the value of ***dest***.

It contains the following parameters:

- ***dest***—The buffer that receives the copied characters.
- ***src***—The wide-character array to be copied.
- ***n***—The number of characters to be copied.

wmemmove *(ANSI, Win 9x, Win NT)*
This routine moves the contents of one wide-character buffer to another, which may overlap the first.

```
wchar_t *wmemmove(wchar_t *dest, const wchar_t *src, size_t n);
```

wmemmove returns the value of ***dest***.

It contains the following parameters:

- ***dest***—The buffer that receives the characters.
- ***src***—The wide-character array to be moved.
- ***n***—The number of characters to be moved.

wmemset *(ANSI, Win 9x, Win NT)*
This routine sets the contents of a wide-character buffer to a specified character.

```
wchar_t *wmemset(wchar_t *dest, wchar_t c, size_t n);
```

wmemset returns the value of ***dest***.

It contains the following parameters:

- ***dest***—The buffer that is to be set.
- ***c***—The character to be set as the contents of the buffer.
- ***n***—The number of characters to be inserted into the buffer.

7. Buffers, Characters, And Strings

cwctype And wctype.h

The **wctype.h** header file defines macros that determine a classification rule for wide-character codes. The **cwctype** header provides a convenient way to include the **wctype.h** header file and define the contents of that file within the **std** namespace. You must reference the names introduced by **cwctype** by qualifying them using the namespace (**std**) and the scope resolution operator. Alternatively, you can incorporate the members of the **std** namespace into the current namespace by including the following line after the **#include** directives:

```
using namespace std;
```

Types

wftrans_t
An integer type that represents locale-specific character mappings.

Routines

wctype (Win 9x, Win NT)
This routine determines a classification rule for wide-character codes.

```
wctype_t wctype(const char* property);
```

If the current locale does not define a classification rule whose name matches the property string *property*, the function returns the 0 value; otherwise, it returns a non-zero value that you can use as the second argument of a call to **towctrans**.

It contains the following parameter:

• *property*—The property string.

NOTE: The **wctype.h** header file uses **wctype** to define several macros that classify wide characters by type. Table 7.6 summarizes these macros.

---

*Table 7.6   Routines based on **wctype**.*

Routine	Meaning
iswalnum(c)	iswctype(c, wctype("alnum"))
iswalpha(c)	iswctype(c, wctype("alpha"))
iswcntrl(c)	iswctype(c, wctype("cntrl"))
iswdigit(c)	iswctype(c, wctype("digit"))
iswgraph(c)	iswctype(c, wctype("graph"))
iswlower(c)	iswctype(c, wctype("lower"))
iswprint(c)	iswctype(c, wctype("print"))
iswpunct(c)	iswctype(c, wctype("punct"))
iswspace(c)	iswctype(c, wctype("space"))
iswupper(c)	iswctype(c, wctype("upper"))
iswxdigit(c)	iswctype(c, wctype("xdigit"))

Bits And Numerics

In Brief

Working With Bit And Numeric Values

This chapter describes two template classes (**bitset** and **complex**) and three header files (**float.h**, **limits.h**, and **math.h**) that define variables, constants, and routines useful for working with bit and numeric values.

The **bitset** template class represents a sequence of bits. Its methods let you manipulate, compare, and convert the values of the constituent bits.

The **float.h** header defines a set of constants that describe the properties of the floating-point types **float**, **double**, and **long double**.

The **limits.h** header defines a set of constants that describe the properties of the integer types **char**, **unsigned char**, **short int**, **int**, **unsigned int**, **long**, and **unsigned long**.

The **math.h** header defines a set of routines that implement common mathematical functions, including trigonometric, logarithmic, and exponential functions.

The **complex** template class represents a complex number as a pair of numeric values of a specified type. Its methods let you manipulate, compare, and convert complex values.

Immediate Solutions

---

bitset

The template class **bitset** represents an object that stores a sequence of bits; the template parameter N specifies the maximum number of bits. A bit is considered set if its value is 1, or reset if its value is 0. Flipping a bit changes its value from 1 to 0 or from 0 to 1. When converting between an object of class **bitset<N>** and an object of some integral type, bit position j corresponds to the bit value $1 << j$. The integral value corresponding to two or more bits is the sum of the bit values.

Variables And Constants

bitset_size
```
static const size_t bitset_size = N;
```

The constant **bitset_size** holds the maximum number of bits in the bit sequence.

Types

typedef element_type
```
typedef bool element_type;
```

The **typedef element_type** is an alias for the type **bool**, which is the type of the elements of the sequence.

Routines

bitset (Win 9x, Win NT)
This routine constructs a bitset.

```
bitset();
bitset(unsigned long val);
```

It contains the following parameter:

• *val*—The size of the bitset to be constructed.

any *(Win 9x, Win NT)*
This routine determines if any bits are set.

```
bool any() const;
```

any returns a non-zero value if any bit is set; otherwise, it returns the value 0.

at *(Win 9x, Win NT)*
This routine retrieves the value of the specified bit.

```
bool at(size_t pos) const;
reference at(size_t pos);
```

at returns the value of the specified bit. The routine throws an exception object of the class **out_of_range** if an error occurs. The routine returns an object of type ***reference*** if the element can be modified; otherwise, it returns a **bool**.

It contains the following parameter:

• ***pos***—The index of the bit whose value is to be returned.

count *(Win 9x, Win NT)*
This routine retrieves the number of bits in the bit sequence.

```
size_t count() const;
```

count returns the number of bits in the bit sequence.

flip *(Win 9x, Win NT)*
This routine flips the value of all bits or the specified bit of a bit sequence.

```
bitset<N>& flip();
bitset<N>& flip(size_t pos);
```

flip returns the modified bit set.

It contains the following parameter:

• ***pos***—The index of the bit to be flipped.

none *(Win 9x, Win NT)*
This routine determines if none of the bits is set.

```
bool none() const;
```

none returns a non-zero value if none of the bits is set; otherwise, it returns the value 0.

operator== And operator!= (Win 9x, Win NT)

These routines compare two bit sequences.

```
bool operator==(const bitset<N>& rhs) const;
bool operator!=(const bitset<N>& rhs) const;
```

operator== returns a non-zero value if the two bitsets have the same value and **operator!=** returns a non-zero value if the two bitsets have different values; otherwise, they return the value 0.

They contain the following parameter:

* *rhs*—The bitsct to be compared with the current bitset.

operator<< , operator >>, operator<<=, And operator>>= (Win 9x, Win NT)

These routines shift a bit sequence left (**operator<<, operator<<=**) or right (**operator>>, operator>>=**).

```
bitset<N> operator<<(size_t pos) const;
bitset<N> operator>>(size_t pos) const;
bitset<N>& operator<<=(const bitset<N>& pos);
bitset<N>& operator>>=(const bitset<N>& pos);
```

They return the modified bitset, in which each bit position is shifted *pos* positions to the left (**operator<<, operator<<=**) or right (**operator>>, operator>>=**) of its place in the original bitset. Vacated positions are reset.

The **operator<<, operator>>, operator<<=**, and **operator>>=** routines contain the following parameter:

* *pos*—The number of bits by which to shift.

operator~ (Win 9x, Win NT)

This routine flips each bit of a bit sequence.

```
bitset<N> operator~();
```

operator~ returns the modified bitset, in which each bit has the opposite of its value in the original bitset.

operator&= *(Win 9x, Win NT)*
This routine logically ANDs one bit sequence with another.

```
bitset<N>& operator&=(const bitset<N>& rhs);
```

operator&= returns the modified bitset, in which each element has been replaced by the logical AND of its original value and the value of the corresponding bit in *rhs*.

It contains the following parameter:

• *rhs*—The bitset to be logically ANDed with the current bitset.

operatorl= *(Win 9x, Win NT)*
This routine logically ORs one bit sequence with another.

```
bitset<N>& operator|=(const bitset<N>& rhs);
```

operatorl= returns the modified bitset, in which each element has been replaced by the inclusive logical OR of its original value and the value of the corresponding bit in *rhs*.

It contains the following parameter:

• *rhs*—The bitset to be logically ORed with the current bitset.

operator^= *(Win 9x, Win NT)*
This routine exclusively ORs one bit sequence with another.

```
bitset<N>& operator^=(const bitset<N>& rhs);
```

operator^= returns the modified bitset, in which each element has been replaced by the exclusive logical OR of its original value and the value of the corresponding bit in *rhs*.

It contains the following parameter:

• *rhs*—The bitset to be exclusively ORed with the current bitset.

operator[ ] *(Win 9x, Win NT)*
This routine returns the specified element of a bit sequence.

```
bool operator[](size_t pos) const;
reference operator[](size_t pos);
```

operator[] returns the value of the specified element, or an undefined value if the specified position is not valid. The routine returns an object of type *reference* if the element can be modified; otherwise, it returns a **bool**.

It contains the following parameter:

• *pos*—The index of the element to be returned.

reset *(Win 9x, Win NT)*
This routine resets the values of all elements or the specified element of a bit sequence.

```
bitset<N>& reset();
bitset<N>& reset(size_t pos);
```

reset returns the modified bitset, in which each element, or the specified element, has been reset.

It contains the following parameter:

• *pos*—The index of the element to be reset.

set *(Win 9x, Win NT)*
This routine sets the values of all elements or the specified element of a bit sequence.

```
bitset<N>& set();
bitset<N>& set(size_t pos, bool val = true);
```

set returns the modified bitset, in which each element, or the specified element, has been set.

It contains the following parameters:

• *pos*—The index of the element to be set.

• *val*—The value to which the elements are to be set.

size *(Win 9x, Win NT)*
This routine retrieves the maximum number of elements in the bit sequence.

```
size_t size() const;
```

size returns the maximum number of elements in the bitset.

test *(Win 9x, Win NT)*
This routine retrieves the value of the specified element of a bitset.

8. Bits And Numerics

```
bool test(size_t pos) const;
```

test returns a non-zero value if the specified element is set; otherwise, it returns the value 0.

It contains the following parameter:

• **pos**—The index of the element to be tested.

to_string *(Win 9x, Win NT)*
This routine retrieves the value of a bit sequence, represented as a string.

```
string to_string() const;
```

to_string returns a string that corresponds to the bitset. Characters in the string are **'1'** if the corresponding element is set and **'0'** if the corresponding element is reset.

to_ulong *(Win 9x, Win NT)*
This routine retrieves the value of a bit sequence, represented as an **unsigned long**.

```
unsigned long to_ulong() const;
```

to_ulong returns an **unsigned long** value that represents the value of the bitset. The routine throws **overflow_error** if overflow error occurs.

cfloat And float.h

The **float.h** header provides routines that describe the representation of floating-point values. The **cfloat** header provides a convenient way to include the **float.h** header file and define the contents of that file within the **std** namespace. You must reference the names introduced by **cfloat** by qualifying them using the namespace (**std**) and the scope resolution operator. Alternatively, you can incorporate the members of the **std** namespace into the current namespace by including the following line after the **#include** directives:

```
using namespace std;
```

Variables And Constants

Table 8.1 summarizes the constants defined in the **float.h** header file.

Table 8.1   Constants defined in float.h.

Constant	Description
DBL_DIG	The number of decimal digits, q, such that any **double** number with q decimal digits can be rounded into a radix b floating-point number with p digits and back without change to the q decimal digits.
DBL_EPSILON	The difference between 1 and the least value greater than 1 that is representable as a **double**.
DBL_MANT_DIG	The number of digits in the mantissa of a **double**, represented in radix **FLT_RADIX**.
DBL_MAX	The maximum representable finite **double** value.
DBL_MAX_10_EXP	The maximum integer, n, such that 10^n is a representable finite **double**.
DBL_MAX_EXP	The maximum integer, n, such that **FLT_RADIX** raised to the power $n-1$ is a representable finite **double**.
DBL_MIN	The minimum normalized positive **double** value.
DBL_MIN_10_EXP	The smallest negative integer, n, such that 10^n is in the range of normalized **double** values.
DBL_MIN_DIG	The smallest negative integer, n, such that **FLT_RADIX** raised to the power $n-1$ is a normalized **double** number.
FLT_DIG	The number of decimal digits, q, such that any **float** number with q decimal digits can be rounded into a radix b floating-point number with p digits and back without change to the q decimal digits.
FLT_EPSILON	The difference between 1 and the least value greater than 1 that is representable as a **float**.
FLT_MANT_DIG	The number of digits in the mantissa of a **float**, represented in radix **FLT_RADIX**.
FLT_MAX	The maximum representable finite **float** value.
FLT_MAX_10_EXP	The maximum integer, n, such that 10^n is a representable finite **float**.
FLT_MAX_EXP	The maximum integer, n, such that **FLT_RADIX** raised to the power $n-1$ is a representable finite **float**.
FLT_MIN	The minimum normalized positive **float** value.
FLT_MIN_10_EXP	The smallest negative integer, n, such that 10^n is in the range of normalized **float** values.
FLT_MIN_DIG	The smallest negative integer, n, such that **FLT_RADIX** raised to the power $n-1$ is a normalized **float** number.

(continued)

Table 8.1   Constants defined in float.h (continued).

Constant	Description
FLT_RADIX	The radix in which the exponent of a floating-point number is represented.
FLT_ROUNDS	Indicates the rounding mode for floating-point addition: • -1 — Indeterminate • 0 — Toward zero • 1 — To nearest • 2 — Toward positive infinity • 3 — Toward negative infinity
LDBL_DIG	The number of decimal digits, q, such that any **long double** number with q decimal digits can be rounded into a radix b floating-point number with p digits and back without change to the q decimal digits.
LDBL_EPSILON	The difference between 1 and the least value greater than 1 that is representable as a **long double**.
LDBL_MANT_DIG	The number of digits in the mantissa of a **long double**, represented in radix **FLT_RADIX**.
LDBL_MAX	The maximum representable finite **long double** value.
LDBL_MAX_10_EXP	The maximum integer, n, such that 10^n is a representable finite **long double**.
LDBL_MAX_EXP	The maximum integer, n, such that **FLT_RADIX** raised to the power $n-1$ is a representable finite **long double**.
LDBL_MIN	The minimum normalized positive **long double** value.
LDBL_MIN_10_EXP	The smallest negative integer, n, such that 10^n is in the range of normalized **long double** values.
LDBL_MIN_DIG	The smallest negative integer, n, such that **FLT_RADIX** raised to the power $n-1$ is a normalized **long double** number.

climits And limits.h

The **limits.h** header describes the representation of integer values. The **climits** header provides a convenient way to include the **limits.h** header file and define the contents of that file within the **std** namespace. You must reference the names introduced by **climits** by qualifying them using the namespace (**std**) and the scope resolution operator. Alternatively, you can incorporate the members of the **std** namespace into the current namespace by including the following line after the **#include** directives:

```
using namespace std;
```

Variables And Constants

Table 8.2 summarizes the constants defined in the **limits.h** header file.

*Table 8.2   Constants defined in **limits.h**.*

Constant	Description
CHAR_BIT	The number of bits used to represent the smallest object that is not a bit-field.
CHAR_MAX	The maximum **char** value.
CHAR_MIN	The minimum **char** value.
INT_MAX	The maximum **int** value.
INT_MIN	The minimum **int** value.
LONG_MAX	The maximum **long int** value.
LONG_MIN	The minimum **long int** value.
MB_LEN_MAX	The maximum number of bytes in a multibyte character (for any supported locale).
SCHAR_MAX	The maximum value of a **signed char**.
SCHAR_MIN	The minimum value of a **signed char**.
SHRT_MAX	The maximum value of a **short int**.
SHRT_MIN	The minimum value of a **short int**.
UCHAR_MAX	The maximum value of an **unsigned char**.
UINT_MAX	The maximum value of an **unsigned int**.
ULONG_MAX	The maximum value of an **unsigned long**.
USHRT_MAX	The maximum value of an **unsigned short int**.

cmath And math.h

The **math.h** header provides routines that let you perform common mathematical functions in your programs. The **cmath** header provides a convenient way to include the **math.h** header file and define the contents of that file within the **std** namespace. You must reference the names introduced by **cmath** by qualifying them using the namespace (**std**) and the scope resolution operator. Alternatively, you can incorporate the members of the **std** namespace into the current namespace by including the following line after the **#include** directives:

```
using namespace std;
```

Routines

acos *(ANSI, Win 9x, Win NT)*
This routine computes the principal value of the arc cosine.

```
double acos(double x);
```

acos returns the principal arc cosine of *x*, measured in radians, which falls within the range [0, π].

It contains the following parameter:

- *x*—The cosine, which must be in the range [–1, +1].

asin *(ANSI, Win 9x, Win NT)*
This routine computes the principal value of the arc sine.

```
double asin(double x);
```

asin returns the principal arc sine of *x*, measured in radians, which falls within the range [–π/2, +π/2].

It contains the following parameter:

- *x*—The sine, which must be in the range [–1, +1].

atan *(ANSI, Win 9x, Win NT)*
This routine computes the principal value of the arc tangent.

```
double atan(double x);
```

atan returns the principal arc tangent of *x*, measured in radians, which falls within the range [–π/2, +π/2].

It contains the following parameter:

- *x*—The tangent.

atan2 *(ANSI, Win 9x, Win NT)*
This routine computes the principal value of the arc tangent, using the signs of its arguments to determine the quadrant of the return value.

```
double atan2(double y, double x);
```

It returns the principal value of the arc tangent of *y/x*; at least one argument must be non-zero.

It contains the following parameters:

- *x*—The denominator of the tangent.
- *y*—The numerator of the tangent.

ceil *(ANSI, Win 9x, Win NT)*

This routine computes the ceiling of a specified value—the smallest integral value not less than the specified value.

```
double ceil(double x);
```

ceil returns the smallest integral value not less than *x*.

It contains the following parameter:

- *x*—The value whose ceiling is to be returned.

cos *(ANSI, Win 9x, Win NT)*

This routine computes the cosine.

```
double cos (double x);
```

cos returns the cosine of *x*.

It contains the following parameter:

- *x*—The angle, measured in radians.

cosh *(ANSI, Win 9x, Win NT)*

This routine computes the hyperbolic cosine.

```
double cosh(double x);
```

cosh returns the hyperbolic cosine of *x*.

It contains the following parameter:

- *x*—The angle, measured in radians.

exp *(ANSI, Win 9x, Win NT)*

This routine computes the exponential function.

```
double exp(double x);
```

exp returns the exponential value.

It contains the following parameter:

- *x*—The power to which the base *e* will be raised.

fabs (ANSI, Win 9x, Win NT)

This routine computes the absolute value.

```
double fabs(double x);
```

fabs returns the absolute value of x.

It contains the following parameter:

- x—The number whose absolute value is to be returned.

floor (ANSI, Win 9x, Win NT)

This routine computes the floor of a specified value—the largest integral value not greater than the specified value.

```
double floor(double x);
```

floor returns the floor of x.

It contains the following parameter:

- x—The value whose floor is to be returned.

fmod (ANSI, Win 9x, Win NT)

This routine computes the floating-point modulus—the remainder of an integral division.

```
double fmod(double x, double y);
```

fmod returns the floating-point remainder of the division x/y. The result can be represented as $x - i * y$ for some integer i, such that if y is non-zero, the result has the same sign as x and an absolute value less than the absolute value of y. If y is 0, the routine may return 0 or a domain error may occur.

fmod contains the following parameters:

- x—The numerator.
- y—The denominator.

frexp (ANSI, Win 9x, Win NT)

This routine breaks a floating-point number into a normalized fraction and an integral power of 2.

```
double frexp(double value, int* exp);
```

frexp returns the normalized fraction—the value x such that **value** is equal to $x*2^{exp}$.

It includes the following parameters

- *value*—The value to be broken.

- *exp*—A pointer to the **int** that receives the integral power of 2 used to represent *value*.

idexp *(ANSI, Win 9x, Win NT)*

This routine multiplies a floating-point number by an integral power of 2.

```
double idexp(double x, double exp);
```

idexp returns the value $x*2^{exp}$.

It contains the following parameters:

- *x*—The number to be multiplied.

- *exp*—The exponent of the power of 2.

log *(ANSI, Win 9x, Win NT)*

This routine computes the natural logarithm.

```
double log(double x);
```

log returns the natural logarithm of x.

It contains the following parameter:

- *x*—The number whose natural logarithm is to be returned.

log10 *(ANSI, Win 9x, Win NT)*

This routine computes the base-10 logarithm.

```
double log10(double x);
```

log10 returns the base-10 logarithm of *x*.

It contains the following parameter:

- *x*—The number whose base-10 logarithm is to be returned.

modf *(ANSI, Win 9x, Win NT)*

This routine breaks a floating-point number into fractional and integral parts having the same sign.

```
double modf(double value, double* iptr);
```

modf returns the signed fractional part of *value*.

It contains the following parameters:

- *value*—The value to be broken.
- *iptr*—A pointer to the **double** that receives the signed integral part of *value*.

pow *(ANSI, Win 9x, Win NT)*
This routine computes x raised to the power y.

```
double pow(double x, double y);
```

pow returns the value x^y.

It contains the following parameters:

- x—The base.
- y—The exponent, which must be integral if x is negative.

sin *(ANSI, Win 9x, Win NT)*
This routine computes the sine.

```
double sin(double x);
```

sin returns the sine of x.

It contains the following parameter:

- x—The angle, measured in radians.

sinh *(ANSI, Win 9x, Win NT)*
This routine computes the hyperbolic sine.

```
double sinh(double x);
```

sinh returns the hyperbolic sine.

It contains the following parameter:

- x—The angle, measured in radians.

sqrt *(ANSI, Win 9x, Win NT)*
This routine computes the square root.

```
double sqrt(double x);
```

sqrt returns the square root of x.

It contains the following parameter:

* *x*—The nonnegative number whose square root is to be returned.

tan *(ANSI, Win 9x, Win NT)*
This routine computes the tangent.

```
double tan(double x);
```

tan returns the tangent of *x*.

It contains the following parameter:

* *x*—The angle, measured in radians.

tanh *(ANSI, Win 9x, Win NT)*
This routine computes the hyperbolic tangent.

```
double tanh(double x);
```

tanh returns the hyperbolic tangent.

It contains the following parameter:

* *x*—The angle, measured in radians.

complex

The template class **complex** describes an object that represents a complex number. The template parameter *T* specifies the type of two stored objects that represent the real and imaginary parts of a complex number. The class has a public default constructor, destructor, copy constructor, and assignment operator; it also defines the conventional arithmetic operators. An instance of **complex** can be assigned integer or floating-point values and can be cast to integer or floating-point types.

Routines

complex *(ANSI, Win 9x, Win NT)*
This routine constructs a complex object.

```
complex(const T& re = 0, const T& im = 0);
complex(const complex& x);
```

8. Bits And Numerics

It contains the following parameters:

- *re*—The real part of the complex number.
- *im*—The imaginary part of the complex number.
- *x*—A complex number.

const *(ANSI, Win 9x, Win NT)*
This routine returns the imaginary part of a complex number.

```
T imag() const;
```

const returns the imaginary part of the complex number.

operator= *(ANSI, Win 9x, Win NT)*
This routine assigns a value to a complex object.

```
complex& operator=(const complex& rhs);
complex& operator=(const T& rhs);
```

operator= returns the complex value that was assigned.

It contains the following parameter:

- *rhs*—The complex value to be assigned. If *rhs* has type *T*, the imaginary part of the complex value is set to 0.

operator+= *(ANSI, Win 9x, Win NT)*
This routine increments a complex number.

```
complex& operator+=(const complex& rhs);
complex& operator+=(const T& rhs);
```

operator+= returns the incremented complex value.

It contains the following parameter:

- *rhs*—The increment. If *rhs* has type *T*, the imaginary part of the increment is taken to be 0.

operator−= *(ANSI, Win 9x, Win NT)*
This routine decrements a complex number.

```
complex& operator-=(const complex& rhs);
complex& operator-=(const T& rhs);
```

operator−= returns the decremented complex value.

It contains the following parameter:

- ***rhs***—The decrement. If ***rhs*** has type ***T***, the imaginary part of the decrement is taken to be 0.

operator*= (ANSI, Win 9x, Win NT)
This routine multiplies a complex number.

```
complex& operator*=(const complex& rhs);
complex& operator*=(const T& rhs);
```

operator*= returns the multiplied value.

It contains the following parameter:

- ***rhs***—The multiplier. If ***rhs*** has type ***T***, the imaginary part of the multiplier is taken to be 0.

operator/= (ANSI, Win 9x, Win NT)
This routine divides a complex number.

```
complex& operator/=(const complex& rhs);
complex& operator/=(const T& rhs);
```

operator/= returns the divided complex value.

It contains the following parameter:

- ***rhs***—The divisor. If ***rhs*** has type ***T***, the imaginary part of the divisor is taken to be 0.

operator+ (ANSI, Win 9x, Win NT)
This routine adds two complex numbers.

```
friend complex<T>
  operator+(const complex<T>& lhs, const T& rhs);
friend complex<T>
  operator+(const T& lhs, const complex<T>& rhs);
```

operator+ returns the sum of the complex numbers.

It contains the following parameters:

- ***lhs***—One term of the sum.
- ***rhs***—The other term of the sum.

operator– (ANSI, Win 9x, Win NT)
This routine subtracts two complex numbers.

8. Bits And Numerics

```
friend complex<T>
  operator-(const complex<T>& lhs, const T& rhs);
friend complex<T>
  operator-(const T& lhs, const complex<T>& rhs);
```

operator– returns the difference of the complex numbers.

It contains the following parameters:

- *lhs*—One term of the difference (the subtrahend).
- *rhs*—The other term of the difference (the minuend).

operator* (ANSI, Win 9x, Win NT)
This routine multiplies two complex numbers.

```
friend complex<T>
  operator*(const complex<T>& lhs, const T& rhs);
friend complex<T>
  operator*(const T& lhs, const complex<T>& rhs);
```

operator* returns the product of the complex numbers.

It contains the following parameters:

- *lhs*—One factor of the product.
- *rhs*—The other factor of the product.

operator/ (ANSI, Win 9x, Win NT)
This routine divides two complex numbers.

```
friend complex<T>
  operator/(const complex<T>& lhs, const T& rhs);
friend complex<T>
  operator/(const T& lhs, const complex<T>& rhs);
```

operator/ returns the quotient of the complex numbers.

It contains the following parameters:

- *lhs*—The numerator (the dividend).
- *rhs*—The denominator (the divisor).

operator== And operator!= (ANSI, Win 9x, Win NT)
These routines compare two complex numbers.

```
friend bool
  operator==(const complex<T>& lhs, const T& rhs);
```

```
friend bool
   operator==(const T& lhs, const complex<T>& rhs);
friend bool
   operator!=(const complex<T>& lhs, const T& rhs);
friend bool
   operator!=(const T& lhs, const complex<T>& rhs);
```

They return a non-zero value if the two complex numbers are equal (**operator ==**) or not equal (**operator!=**); otherwise, they return the value 0.

The **operator==** and **operator!=** routines contain the following parameters:

- *lhs*—The first complex number.

- *rhs*—The other complex number.

real *(ANSI, Win 9x, Win NT)*
This routine returns the real part of a complex number.

```
T real() const;
```

Input And Output, Files, And Directories

In Brief

Advanced Input/Output Facilities

In addition to the stream-oriented input/output routines summarized in Chapter 6, Visual C++ provides low-level input/output routines, console input/output routines, and port input/output routines. Visual C++ also provides routines for file handling and directory control.

Low-level input/output lets you manipulate files at the operating-system level. Low-level input/output is performed without buffering.

The predefined input/output devices **stdin**, **stdout**, and **stderr** are collectively termed the *console. Console input/output* lets you read and write to the console.

Port input/output lets you read and write data to input/output ports. Such ports are typically associated with input/output devices, rather than with disk files.

The Visual C++ routines for file handling and directory control let you create and delete files, construct and parse paths, and perform other useful functions.

Immediate Solutions

Low-Level Input/Output

The low-level input/output functions access the operating system directly, neither buffering nor formatting data. Three predefined streams provide access to standard input/output devices, as shown in Table 9.1. The low-level input/output routines set the **errno** global variable when an error occurs. When you use the low-level input/output routines, you do not need to include a header file unless your program requires a constant that is defined in **stdio.h**, such as the end-of-file indicator (**EOF**). The **io.h** header file defines prototypes for the low-level input/output functions.

Routines

_close *(Win 9x, Win NT)*
This routine closes a file.

```
int _close(int handle);
```

_close returns the value 0 if the file was successfully closed; otherwise, it returns the value –1.

It contains the following parameter:

• *handle*—The handle of the open file.

_commit *(Win 9x, Win NT)*
This routine flushes a file to disk.

```
int _commit(int handle);
```

Table 9.1   Predefined streams.

Stream	Handle
stdin	0
stdout	1
stderr	2

_commit returns the value 0 if the file was successfully flushed; otherwise, it returns the value –1.

It contains the following parameter:

• *handle*—The handle of the file to be flushed.

_creat And _wcreat (Win 9x, Win NT)
These routines create a file.

```
int _creat(const char* filename, int pmode);
int _wcreat(const wchar_t* filename, int pmode);
```

They return a handle to the created file if the file was successfully created; otherwise, they return the value –1.

The **_creat** and **_wcreat** routines use the following parameters:

• *filename*—The name of the file to be created.

• *pmode*—The permission setting, which can be any of the following values defined in **sys\stat.h**:

  • **_S_IREAD**, which specifies that reading is permitted.

  • **_S_IWRITE**, which specifies that writing is permitted.

  • **_S_IREAD | _S_IWRITE**, which specifies that reading and writing are permitted.

_dup (Win 9x, Win NT)
This routine creates a second handle for an open file. It is typically used to associate a predefined file handle with a different file.

```
int _dup(int handle);
```

_dup returns the new file handle if the operation was successful; otherwise, it returns the value –1.

It contains the following parameter:

• *handle*—The handle of the open file.

_dup2 (Win 9x, Win NT)
This routine reassigns a file handle.

```
int _dup2(int handle1, int handle2);
```

_dup2 returns the value 0 if the operation was successful; otherwise, it returns the value –1.

It contains the following parameters:

- **handle1**—The handle of the open file.
- **handle2**—Any handle value.

_eof (Win 9x, Win NT)
This routine tests for the end-of-file condition.

```
int _eof(int handle);
```

_eof returns the value 1 if the file is at the end of the file, the value 0 if the file is not at the end of the file, or the value –1 if an error occurred.

It contains the following parameter:

- **handle**—The handle of the open file.

_lseek And _lseeki64 (Win 9x, Win NT)
These routines reposition the file pointer to a given location.

```
long _lseek(int handle, long offset, int origin);
__int64 _lseeki64(int handle, __int64 offset, nt origin);
```

They return the offset, in bytes, of the new file pointer position if the operation was successful; otherwise, they return the value –1L.

The **_lseek** and **_lseek64** routines use the following parameters:

- **handle**—The handle of the open file.
- **offset**—The number of bytes relative to origin.
- **origin**—One of the following constants:
  - **SEEK_SET**, which specifies the beginning of the file.
  - **SEEK_CUR**, which specifies the current file pointer position.
  - **SEEK_END**, which specifies the end of the file.

_open And _wopen (Win 9x, Win NT)
These routines open a file.

```
int _open(const char* filename, int oflag, [, int pmode]);
int _wopen(const wchar_t* filename, int oflag, [, int pmode]);
```

They return the handle of the open file if the operation was successful; otherwise, they return the value –1.

The **_open** and **_wopen** routines contain the following parameters:

- *filename*—The name of the file to be opened.
- *oflag*—An integer expression formed from constants defined in the **fcntrl.h** header:
  - **_O_APPEND**, which moves the file pointer to the end of file before each write operation.
  - **_O_BINARY**, which opens the file in binary mode.
  - **_O_CREAT**, which creates a new file and opens it for writing.
  - **_O_CREAT I O_SHORT_LIVED**, which creates a temporary file.
  - **_O_CREAT I O_TEMPORARY**, which creates a temporary file that is automatically deleted when closed.
  - **_O_CREAT I O_EXCL**, which returns an error value if the file exists.
  - **_O_RANDOM**, which specifies random access.
  - **_O_RDONLY**, which opens the file for read-only access.
  - **_O_RDWR**, which opens the file for read and write access.
  - **_O_SEQUENTIAL**, which specifies sequential access.
  - **_O_TEXT**, which opens the file in text mode, providing for translation of certain special characters (see the section describing the **fdopen** and **wfdopen** routines in Chapter 6).
  - **_O_TRUNC**, which truncates the file to zero length.
  - **_O_WRONLY**, which opens the file for write-only access.

NOTE: *You must specify either **_O_RDONLY**, **_O_RDWR**, or **_O_WRONLY**.*

- *pmode*—The permission setting, which can be any of the following values defined in **sys\stat.h**:
  - **_S_IREAD**, which specifies that reading is permitted.
  - **_S_IWRITE**, which specifies that writing is permitted.
  - **_S_IREAD I _S_IWRITE**, which specifies that reading and writing are permitted.

_read *(Win 9x, Win NT)*
This routine reads data from a file.

```
int _read(nit handle, void* buffer, unsigned int count);
```

_read returns the number of bytes read, the value 0 if end-of-file condition occurred, or the value –1 if an error occurred.

It contains the following parameters:

- *handle*—The handle of the open file.
- *buffer*—The buffer that receives the bytes read.
- *count*—The number of bytes to be read.

_sopen *And* _wsopen *(Win 9x, Win NT)*
These routines open a file for file sharing.

```
int _sopen(const char* filename, int oflag, int shflag
  [, int pmode]);
int _wsopen(const wchar_t* filename, int oflag, int shflag
  [, int pmode]);
```

They return the file handle of the open file if the operation was successful; otherwise, they return the value –1.

The **_sopen** and **_wsopen** routines contain the following parameters:

- *filename*—The name of the file to be opened.
- *oflag*—An integer expression formed from constants defined in the **fcntrl.h** header:
  - **_O_APPEND**, which moves the file pointer to the end of file before each write operation.
  - **_O_BINARY**, which opens the file in binary mode.
  - **_O_CREAT**, which creates a new file and opens it for writing.
  - **_O_CREAT | O_SHORT_LIVED**, which creates a temporary file.
  - **_O_CREAT | O_TEMPORARY**, which creates a temporary file that is automatically deleted when closed.
  - **_O_CREAT | O_EXCL**, which returns an error value if the file exists.
  - **_O_RANDOM**, which specifies random access.
  - **_O_RDONLY**, which opens the file for read-only access.
  - **_O_RDWR**, which opens the file for read and write access.
  - **_O_SEQUENTIAL**, which specifies sequential access.

9. Input And Output, Files, And Directories

- **_O_TEXT**, which opens the file in text mode, providing for translation of certain special characters (see the section describing the **fdopen** and **wfdopen** routines in Chapter 6).

- **_O_TRUNC**, which truncates the file to zero length.

- **_O_WRONLY**, which opens the file for write-only access.

NOTE: *You must specify either **_O_RDONLY**, **_O_RDWR**, or **_O_WRONLY**.*

- *shflag*—The file-sharing mode, specified by one of the following constants defined in **share.h**:

  - **_SH_DENYRW**, which denies read and write access to the file.

  - **_SH_DENYWR**, which denies write access to the file.

  - **_SH_DENYRD**, which denies read access to the file.

  - **_SH_DENYNO**, which permits read and write access to the file.

- *pmode*—The permission setting, required only when you specify **_O_CREAT**. The permission can be any of the following values defined in **sys\stat.h**:

  - **_S_IREAD**, which specifies that reading is permitted.

  - **_S_IWRITE**, which specifies that writing is permitted.

  - **_S_IREAD | _S_IWRITE**, which specifies that reading and writing are permitted.

_tell And _telli64 *(Win 9x, Win NT)*
These routines retrieve the current file pointer position.

```
long _tell(intd handle);
__int64 _telli64(int handle);
```

They return the position of the file pointer if the operation was successful; otherwise, they return the value –1.

The routines use the following parameter:

- *handle*—The handle of the open file.

_umask *(Win 9x, Win NT)*
This routine sets the file permission mask.

```
int _umask(int pmode);
```

_unmask returns the previous value of the file permission mask.

It contains the following parameter:

- *pmode*—The desired permission mode, which can be any of the following values defined in **sys\stat.h**:
  - **_S_IWRITE**, which specifies that writing is permitted.
  - **_S_IREAD**, which specifies that reading is permitted.
  - **_S_IREAD | _S_IWRITE**, which specifies that reading and writing are permitted.

_write *(Win 9x, Win NT)*
This routine writes data to a file.

```
int _write(int handle, const void* buffer, unsigned int count);
```

_write returns the number of bytes written if the operation was successful; otherwise, it returns the value –1.

It contains the following parameters:

- *handle*—The handle of the open file.
- *buffer*—The buffer that contains the bytes to be written.
- *count*—The number of bytes to be written.

Console And Port Input/Output

The **conio.h** header file contains routines that read and write on the console or an input/output port. You do not need to open the console or an input/output port before using it, nor do you need to close it. Under Windows 9x and Windows NT, console input and output cannot be redirected.

Routines

_cgets *(Win 9x, Win NT)*
This routine reads a string from the console.

```
char* _cgets(char* buffer);
```

_cgets returns a pointer to the string, stored beginning at *buffer[2]*. The routine ceases reading characters when it encounters a carriage return/linefeed combination or when it has read the specified number of bytes.

The routine contains the following parameter:

- **buffer**—The buffer that receives the bytes read. The element **buffer[0]** must contain the maximum number of bytes to be read. On completion, the element **buffer[1]** contains the actual number of bytes read.

_cprintf *(Win 9x, Win NT)*

This routine writes formatted data to the console.

```
int _cprintf(const char* format [, argument] ...);
```

_cprintf returns the number of characters written.

It contains the following parameters:

- **format**—The format control string containing text, which appears in the output verbatim, and specifications that determine the form in which arguments are printed. Each specification has the form:

```
%[flags][width][.precision][{h|I|I64|L}]type
```

Table 9.2 summarizes the flags and Table 9.3 summarizes the types. For further information on format specifiers, consult the Visual C++ documentation.

- **argument**—The arguments whose values are to be printed.

_cputs *(Win 9x, Win NT)*

This routine writes a string to the console.

```
int _cputs(const char* string);
```

Table 9.2   *printf* flags.

Flag	Meaning
–	Left align
+	Prefix with sign
0	Zero pad
blank	Pad with spaces
#	With the **o**, **x**, or **X** format, prefix the output with 0, 0x, or 0X With the **e**, **E**, or **f** format, force a decimal point With the **g** or **G** format, force a decimal point and do not truncate trailing zeroes

Table 9.3   printf types.

Character	Type	Format
c	**int**	Single-byte character
	wint_t	Wide character
C	**int**	Single-byte character
	wint_t	Wide character
d	**int**	Signed decimal integer
i	**int**	Signed decimal integer
o	**int**	Unsigned octal integer
u	**int**	Unsigned decimal integer
x	**int**	Unsigned hexadecimal integer
X	**int**	Unsigned hexadecimal integer
e	**double**	Signed value in exponential format
E	**double**	Signed value in exponential format
f	**double**	Signed value in decimal format
g	**double**	Signed value in exponential or decimal format
G	**double**	Signed value in exponential or decimal format
n	Pointer to integer	Stores the number of characters written to the stream buffer in the associated integer argument
p	Pointer to **void**	Address in segment/offset format
s	String	A single-byte character string
S	String	A wide-character string

_cputs returns the value 0 if the operation was successful; otherwise, it returns a non-zero value.

It contains the following parameter:

• *string*—The string to be written.

_cscanf *(Win 9x, Win NT)*
This routine reads formatted data from the console.

```
int _cscanf(const char* format [, argument] ...);
```

_cscanf returns the number of fields converted and assigned, or **EOF** to indicate an error or end-of-file condition.

It contains the following parameters:

- *format*—A format control string specifying the format of the input (see the description of **_cprintf** earlier in this chapter). The string can contain whitespace characters, non-whitespace characters other than the percent sign (%), and format specifications. Each specification has the form:

```
%[*][width][.precision][{h|I|I64|L}]type
```

For further information on format specifiers, consult the Visual C++ documentation.

- *argument*—The arguments that are to receive the data read.

_getch *(Win 9x, Win NT)*
This routine reads a character from the console.

```
int _getch(void);
```

_getch returns the character read.

_getche *(Win 9x, Win NT)*
This routine reads a character from the console and echoes it.

```
int _getche(void);
```

_getche returns the character read.

_inp *(Win 9x, Win NT)*
This routine reads a byte from the specified input/output port.

```
int _inp(unsigned short port);
```

_inp returns the byte read.

It contains the following parameter:

- *port*—The port number, which must be in the range 0 through 65,535.

_inpd *(Win 9x, Win NT)*
This routine reads a double word from the specified input/output port.

```
unsigned long _inpd(unsigned short port);
```

_inpd returns the double word read.

It contains the following parameter:

- *port*—The port number, which must be in the range 0 through 65,535.

_inpw *(Win 9x, Win NT)*
This routine reads a 2-byte word from the specified input/output port.

```
unsigned short _inpw(unsigned short port);
```

_inpw returns the word read.

It contains the following parameter:

- *port*—The port number, which must be in the range 0 through 65,535.

_kbhit *(Win 9x, Win NT)*
This routine checks for a keystroke at the console. You typically use this before attempting to read from the console.

```
int _kbhit(void);
```

_kbhit returns a non-zero value if a key has been pressed; otherwise, it returns the value 0.

_outp *(Win 9x, Win NT)*
This routine writes a byte to the specified input/output port.

```
int _outp(unsigned short port, int data);
```

_outp returns the data output.

It contains the following parameters:

- *port*—The port number, which must be in the range 0 through 65,535.
- *data*—The byte to be written.

_outpd *(Win 9x, Win NT)*
This routine writes a double word to the specified input/output port.

```
int _outpd(unsigned short port, unsigned long data);
```

9. Input And Output, Files, And Directories

_outpd returns the data output.

It contains the following parameters:

- **port**—The port number, which must be in the range 0 through 65,535.

- **data**—The double word to be written.

_outpw *(Win 9x, Win NT)*
This routine writes a word to the specified input/output port.

```
int _outp(unsigned short port, unsigned short data);
```

_outpw returns the data output.

It contains the following parameters:

- **port**—The port number, which must be in the range 0 through 65,535.

- **data**—The word to be written.

_putch *(Win 9x, Win NT)*
This routine writes a character to the console.

```
int _putch(int c);
```

_putch returns the character, **c**, if the operation was successful; otherwise, it returns the value **EOF**.

It contains the following parameter:

- **c**—The character to be written.

_ungetch *(Win 9x, Win NT)*
This routine replaces a character into the console buffer, so it becomes the next character read.

```
int _ungetch(int c);
```

_ungetch returns the character, **c**, if the operation was successful; otherwise, it returns the value **EOF**.

It contains the following parameter:

- **c**—The character to be pushed back.

File Handling

The header file **io.h** provides low-level routines that create, delete, and manipulate files and set and check file access permissions. Some of these routines, like other low-level input/output routines, operate on files designated by a file handle. The runtime library imposes a limit on the number of available file handles. If you link your program with the single-thread, static library (LIBC.LIB), your program can access no more than 64 file handles; if you link your program with a multithread library (LIBCMT.LIB or MSVCRT.LIB and MSVCRT.DLL), your program can access no more than 256 file handles.

Routines

_access And _waccess *(Win 9x, Win NT)*
These routines check the file permission setting.

```
int _access(const char* path, int mode);
int _waccess(const wchar_t* path, int mode);
```

They return the value 0 if the file can be accessed in the specified manner; otherwise, they return the value –1.

The **_access** and **_waccess** routines contain the following parameters:

• *path*—The file or directory path.

• *mode*—The permission to be checked, which must be one of the following values:

  • 0, which checks for existence of the file.

  • 2, which checks for write permission.

  • 4, which checks for read permission.

  • 6, which checks for read and write permission.

_chmod *(Win 9x, Win NT)*
_wchmod *(Win NT)*
These routines change the file permission setting.

```
int _chmod(const char* filename, int pmode);
int _wchmod(const wchar_t* filename, int pmode);
```

They return the value 0 if the operation was successful; otherwise, they return the value –1.

The **_chmod** and **_wchmod** routines contain the following parameters:

- *filename*—The name of the existing file.
- *pmode*—The types of access permitted, specified by the following constants defined in the **sys/stat.h** header file:
  - **_S_IWRITE**, which specifies that writing is permitted.
  - **_S_IREAD**, which specifies that reading is permitted.
  - **_S_IREAD | _S_IWRITE**, which specifies that reading and writing are permitted.

_chsize *(Win 9x, Win NT)*
This routine changes the size of a file.

```
int _chsize(int handle, long size);
```

_chsize returns the value 0 if the operation was successful; otherwise, it returns the value –1.

It contains the following parameters:

- *handle*—The handle of the open file.
- *size*—The new length of the file, in bytes.

_filelength *(Win 9x, Win NT)*
This routine returns the length of a file.

```
long _filelength(int handle);
__int64 _filelength(int handle);
```

_filelength returns the length, in bytes, of the file, or it returns the value –1L, indicating that an error occurred.

It contains the following parameter:

- *handle*—The handle of the open file.

_fstat *And* _fstati64 *(Win 9x, Win NT)*
These routines return file status information.

```
int _fstat(int handle, struct _stat* buffer);
__int64 _fstati64(int handle, struct _stat* buffer);
```

They return the value 0 if the operation was successful; otherwise, they return the value –1.

The **_fstat** and **_fstati64** routines contain the following parameters:

- *handle*—The handle of the open file.
- *buffer*—A pointer to the buffer in which results are placed. The **_stat** structure, which defines the format of the buffer, has the following fields:
  - **st_atime**, which is the time of the last file access.
  - **st_ctime**, which is the time of file creation.
  - **st_dev**, which is the value handle if the file is a device file; otherwise, it is the value 0.
  - **st_mode**, which is a bit mask for file mode information. The **S_IFCHR** bit indicates that the handle refers to a device. The **S_IFREG** bit indicates that the handle refers to an ordinary file.
  - **st_mtime**, which is the time of the last file modification.
  - **st_nlink**, which is the value 1 on a non-NTFS file system.
  - **st_rdev**, which is the value handle if the file is a device file; otherwise, it is the value 0.
  - **st_size**, which is the size of the file, in bytes.

The **_fstat** and **_fstati64** routines are defined in the **sys/stat.h** header file, rather than the **io.h** header file.

_fullpath *(Win 9x, Win NT)*
_wfullpath *(Win NT)*
These routines expand a relative path to the equivalent absolute (full) path. They use the current drive and directory to determine the absolute path.

```
char* _fullpath(char* abs, const char* rel, size_t max);
wchar_t* _wfullpath(wchar_t* abs, const wchar_t* rel,
  size_t max);
```

They return a pointer to the buffer containing the absolute path if the operation was successful; otherwise, they return the value **NULL**.

The **_fullpath** and **_wfullpath** routines contain the following parameters:

9. Input And Output, Files, And Directories

- **abs**—A pointer to the buffer that receives the absolute pathname.

- **rel**—The relative pathname.

- **max**—The maximum length of the full pathname, measured in bytes for **_fullpath** and in wide characters for **_wfullpath**.

_get_osfhandle *(Win 9x, Win NT)*

This routine returns the operating system file handle associated with an existing user file handle.

```
long __get_osfhandle(int filehandle);
```

_get_osfhandle returns a file handle associated with the user file handle.

It contains the following parameter:

- **filehandle**—The user file handle.

_isatty *(Win 9x, Win NT)*

This routine checks for a character-oriented device.

```
int _isatty(int handle);
```

_isatty returns a non-zero value if **handle** is associated with a character device (a terminal, console, printer, or serial port); otherwise, it returns the value 0.

It contains the following parameter:

- **handle**—The handle of the open file.

_locking *(Win 9x, Win NT)*

This routine locks areas of a file.

```
int _locking(int handle, int mode, long nbytes);
```

_locking returns the value 0 if the operation was successful; otherwise, it returns the value –1.

It contains the following parameters:

- **handle**—The handle of the open file.

- **mode**—The locking mode, which must be one of the following constants defined in the **locking.h** header file:

- **_LK_LOCK** or **_LK_RLCK**, which attempts 10 times to lock the specified bytes.

- **_LK_NBLCK** or **_LK_NBRLCK**, which locks the specified bytes

- **_LK_UNLCK**, which unlocks previously locked bytes

- *nbytes*—The number of bytes to be locked, beginning at the current file pointer position

_makepath *And* _wmakepath *(Win 9x, Win NT)*

These routines merge path components into a single path.

```
void _makepath(char* path, const char* drive,
  const char* dir, const char* fname, const char* ext);
void _wmakepath(wchar_t* path, const wchar_t* drive,
  const wchar_t* dir, const wchar_t* fname,
  const wchar_t* ext);
```

The **_makepath** and **_wmakepath** routines contain the following parameters:

- *path*—The full path.

- *drive*—The drive letter.

- *dir*—The directory path.

- *fname*—The file name.

- *ext*—The file extension.

_mktemp *And* _wmktemp *(Win 9x, Win NT)*

These routines create a unique file name.

```
char* _mktemp(char* template);
wchar_t* _wmktemp(wchar_t* template);
```

They return a pointer to the modified template if the operation was successful; otherwise, they return the value **NULL**.

The **_mktemp** and **_wmktemp** routines contain the following parameter:

- *template*—The file name pattern, which has the form *baseXNNNNN*. The routine leaves *base* intact, replaces the *X* with an alphabetic character, and replaces *NNNNN* with a five-digit unique value. The routine can make a maximum of 27 unique file names for any combination of base and template values.

_open_osfhandle *(Win 9x, Win NT)*

This routine associates a runtime file handle with an existing operating system file handle.

```
int _open_osfhandle(long osfhandle, int flags);
```

_open_osfhandle returns the runtime file handle if the operation was successful; otherwise, it returns the value –1.

It contains the following parameters:

- *osfhandle*—The operating system file handle.

- *flags*—The types of operations allowed, specified by using the following constants defined in the **fcntl.h** header file:

  - **_O_APPEND**, which repositions the file pointer to the end of the file before every write operation.

  - **_O_RDONLY**, which opens the file for reading only.

  - **_O_TEXT**, which opens the file in text (translated) mode.

remove *(ANSI, Win 9x, Win NT),*
_wremove *(Win NT)*

These routines delete a file.

```
int remove(const char* path);
int _wremove(const wchar_t* path);
```

They return the value 0 if the operation was successful; otherwise, they return the value –1.

The **remove** and **_wremove** routines contain the following parameter:

- *path*—The path of the file to be removed.

rename *(ANSI, Win 9x, Win NT),*
_wrename *(Win NT)*

These routines rename a file.

```
int rename(const char* oldname, const char* newname);
int _wrename(const wchar_t* oldname, const wchar_t* newname);
```

They return the value 0 if the operation was successful; otherwise, they return the value –1.

The **rename** and **_wrename** routines contain the following parameters:

- *oldname*—A pointer to the old file name.
- *newname*—A pointer to the new file name.

_setmode *(Win 9x, Win NT)*
This routine sets the file translation mode.

```
int _setmode(int handle, int mode);
```

_setmode returns the previous translation mode if the operation was successful; otherwise, it returns the value –1.

It contains the following parameters:

- *handle*—The handle of the open file.
- *mode*—The file translation mode, which must be **_O_TEXT** or **_O_BINARY**.

_splitpath *And* _wsplitpath *(Win 9x, Win NT)*
These routines parse a path into components.

```
void _splitpath(const char* path, char* drive, char* dir,
  char* fname, char* ext);
void _wsplitpath(const wchar_t* path, wchar_t* drive,
  wchar_t* dir, wchar_t* fname, wchar_t* ext);
```

The **_splitpath** and **_wsplitpath** routines contain the following parameters:

- *path*—The path to be parsed.
- *drive*—The buffer that is to receive the drive letter, which includes a trailing colon (:).
- *dir*—The buffer that is to receive the directory path, which may contain forward slashes (/), backward slashes (\), or both.
- *fname*—The buffer that is to receive the file name.
- *ext*—The buffer that is to receive the file extension, which includes a leading period (.).

_stat *And* _stati64 *(Win 9x, Win NT)*
_wstat *And* _wstati64 *(Win NT)*
These routines retrieve file status information on a file.

9. Input And Output, Files, And Directories

```
int _stat(const char* path, struct _stat buffer);
__int64 _stati64(const char* path, struct _stat buffer);
int _wstat(const wchar_t* path, struct _stat buffer);
__int64 _wstati64(const wchar_t* path, struct _stat buffer);
```

They return the value 0 if the operation was successful; otherwise, they return the value –1.

The **_stat**, **_stati64**, **_wstat**, and **_wstati64** routines contain the following parameters:

- **path**—The path of the existing file.
- **buffer**—A pointer to the **_stat** structure that stores the result. The structure contains the following fields:
  - **st_gid**, which is the identifier of the group that owns the file (Unix) or 0 (9x, NT).
  - **st_atime**, which is the time of the last access of the file.
  - **st_ctime**, which is the time of creation of the file.
  - **st_dev**, which is the drive number of the disk containing the file.
  - **st_ino**, which is the i-node number (Unix).
  - **st_mode**, which is a bit mask that describes the file type. The **_S_IFDIR** bit indicates that the file is a directory. The **_S_IFREG** bit indicates that the file is an ordinary file or device.
  - **st_mtime**, which is the time of the last modification of the file.
  - **st_nlink**, which is always 1 on non-NTFS systems.
  - **st_rdev**, which is the drive number of the disk containing the file (same as **st_dev**).
  - **st_size**, which is a 64-bit integer that holds the size of the file in bytes.
  - **st_uid**, which is the identifier of the user that owns the file (Unix) or 0 (9x, NT).

These routines and their associated constants are defined in the header files **sys/types.h** and **sys/stat.h**.

_umask *(Win 9x, Win NT)*
This routine sets the default permission mask for new files.

```
int _umask(int pmode);
```

_umask returns the previous value of *pmode*.

It contains the following parameter:

* *pmode*—The default permission setting, which can be any of the following values defined in **sys\stat.h**:

    * **_S_IWRITE**, which specifies that writing is permitted.

    * **_S_IREAD**, which specifies that reading is permitted.

    * **_S_IREAD | _S_IWRITE**, which specifies that reading and writing are permitted.

_unlink *(Win 9x, Win NT)*
_wunlink *(Win NT)*
These routines delete a file.

```
int _unlink(const char* filename);
int _wunlink(const wchar_t* filename);
```

They return the value 0 if the operation was successful; otherwise, they return the value –1.

The **_unlink** and **_wunlink** routines contain the following parameter:

* *filename*—The name of the file to be deleted.

Directory Control

The directory control routines access, modify, and obtain information about directory structures and paths. They work with drives, paths, and files. Because various operating systems use different conventions for naming drives and paths, special care is needed in writing portable programs that use directory control routines.

Routines

_chdir *(Win 9x, Win NT)*
_wchdir *(Win NT)*
These routines change the current working directory.

```
int _chdir(const char* dir);
int _wchdir(const wchar_t* dir);
```

They return the value 0 if the operation was successful; otherwise, they return the value –1.

The **_chdir** and **_wchdir** routines contain the following parameter:

- **dir**—The directory that is to become the current directory.

_chdrive *(Win 9x, Win NT)*

This routine changes the current drive.

```
int _chdrive(int drive);
```

_chdrive returns the value 0 if the operation was successful; otherwise, it returns the value –1.

It contains the following parameter:

- **drive**—The number of the drive that is to become the current drive (0=A, 1=B, and so on).

_getcwd *(Win 9x, Win NT)*
_wgetcwd *(Win NT)*

These routines return the current working directory for the default drive.

```
char* _getcwd(char* buffer, int max);
wchar_t* _wgetcwd(wchar_t* buffer, int max);
```

They return a pointer to **buffer** if the operation was successful; otherwise, they return the value **NULL**.

The **_getcwd** and **_wgetcwd** routines contain the following parameters:

- **buffer**—The buffer that receives the current working directory.
- **max**—The maximum length of the path in characters (**_getcwd**) or wide characters (**_wgetcwd**).

_getdcwd *(Win 9x, Win NT)*
_wgetdcwd *(Win NT)*

These routines retrieve the current working directory for the specified drive.

```
char* _getdcwd(int drive, char* buffer, int max);
wchar_t* _wgetdcwd(int drive, wchar_t* buffer, int max);
```

They return a pointer to *buffer* if the operation was successful; otherwise, they return the value **NULL**.

The **_getdcwd** and **_wgetdcwd** routines contain the following parameters:

- *drive*—The number of the drive for which the current working directory is to be returned (0=A, 1=B, and so on).
- *buffer*—The buffer that receives the current working directory.
- *max*—The maximum length of the path in characters (**_getdcwd**) or wide characters (**_wgetdcwd**).

_getdrive *(Win 9x, Win NT)*
This routine retrieves the current (default) drive.

```
int _getdrive(void);
```

It returns the number of the current drive (0=A, 1=B, and so on).

_mkdir *(Win 9x, Win NT)*
_wmkdir *(Win NT)*
These routines make a new directory.

```
int _mkdir(const char* dir);
int _wmkdir(const wchar_t* dir);
```

They return the value 0 if the operation was successful; otherwise, they return the value –1.

The **_mkdir** and **_wmkdir** routines contain the following parameter:

- *dir*—The name of the directory to be created.

_rmdir *(Win 9x, Win NT)*
_wrmdir *(Win NT)*
These routines remove a directory.

```
int _rmdir(const char* dir);
int _wrmdir(const wchar_t* dir);
```

They return the value 0 if the operation was successful; otherwise, they return the value –1.

The **_rmdir** and **_wrmdir** routines contain the following parameter:

- *dir*—The name of the directory to be deleted.

9. Input And Output, Files, And Directories

_searchenv And _wsearchenv *(Win 9x, Win NT)*

These routines search paths within an environment variable for a given file.

```
void _searchenv(const char *filename, const char *varname,
  char *pathname );
void _wsearchenv(const wchar_t *filename, const wchar_t *varname,
  wchar_t *pathname );
```

The **_searchenv** and **_wsearchenv** routines contain the following parameters:

- *filename*—The name of the file for which to search.
- *varname*—The environment variable to be searched.
- *pathname*—The buffer that receives the path name. The routine stores an empty string in the buffer if the file was not found.

Errors, Jumps, And Signals

In Brief

Error Handling

Visual C++ provides several facilities and mechanisms that are useful for handling unusual program conditions. The **errno.h** header file defines a set of integral constants used to identify various program error conditions. The **setjmp.h** header defines routines that let programs execute nonlocal jumps. This facility may be useful in recovering from exceptional or error conditions. The **signal.h** header file defines routines that let programs asynchronously handle signals, which are specific conditions that may occur during program execution.

Debugging

The **assert.h** header file provides the **assert** routine, which can be very useful during program debugging. The **assert** routine takes a **true/false** argument, which it tests. If the evaluation of the **true/false** argument yields **true**, the routine takes no action. If the evaluation of the **true/false** argument yields **false**, the **assert** routine prints a message on the console (**stderr**) device.

Immediate Solutions

cerrno And errno.h

The **errno.h** header file defines macros that identify program error conditions. The **cerrno** header provides a convenient way to include the **errno.h** header file and define the contents of that file within the **std** namespace. You must reference the names introduced by **cerrno** by qualifying them using the namespace (**std**) and the scope resolution operator. Alternatively, you can incorporate the members of the **std** namespace into the current namespace by including the following line after the **#include** directives:

```
using namespace std;
```

Table 10.1 summarizes the macros defined by the **errno.h** file and indicates which of these macros are defined by the ANSI standard, and therefore portable, and which are not.

Table 10.1   Initial capitalization.

Constant	ANSI	Description
E2BIG	No	Argument list is too long.
EACCES	No	Permission to access the file or directory was denied.
EAGAIN	No	No more processes are available.
EBADF	No	The specified file handle does not refer to an open file or specified a read-only file to which the program attempted to write.
ECHILD	No	No spawned processes exist.
EDEADLOCK	No	Resource deadlock would occur.
EDOM	Yes	Argument to math function not within function's domain.
EEXIST	No	The program attempted to create a file that already exists.
EINVAL	No	Invalid argument value.
EMFILE	No	Too many open files.
ENOENT	No	No such file or directory.
ENOEXEC	No	The program attempted to execute a file that is not executable or that has an invalid executable-file format.
ENOMEM	No	Insufficient memory is available.

(continued)

Table 10.1   Initial capitalization (continued).

Constant	ANSI	Description
ENOSPC	No	No space left on device.
ERANGE	Yes	The result of an operation is too large and cannot be represented.
EXDEV	No	The program attempted to move a file to a different device (using the **rename** function).

csetjmp And setjmp.h

The **setjmp.h** header file provides routines that let your program perform nonlocal jumps. The **csetjmp** header provides a convenient way to include the **setjmp.h** header file and define the contents of that file within the **std** namespace. You must reference the names introduced by **csetjmp** by qualifying them using the namespace (**std**) and the scope resolution operator. Alternatively, you can incorporate the members of the **std** namespace into the current namespace by including the following line after the **#include** directives:

```
using namespace std;
```

Type

The **setjmp.h** header file defines the type **jmp_buf**, which is an array that holds information needed to restore the calling environment when a program executes a nonlocal jump.

Routines

longjmp *(ANSI, Win 9x, Win NT)*

This routine restores the environment saved by the **setjmp** routine.

```
void longjmp(jmp_buf env, int val);
```

After the **longjmp** routine has completed, the program behaves as though a call of the **setjmp** routine had returned the value *val*.

The **longjmp** routine contains the following parameters:

- *env*—The array created by the **setjmp** routine, containing the information describing the calling environment.

- *val*—The value returned as though by the **setjmp** routine.

setjmp *(ANSI, Win 9x, Win NT)*

This routine, which may be a macro or an identifier declared with external linkage, saves the calling environment.

```
int setjmp(jmp_buf env);
```

When directly invoked, the **setjmp** routine returns the value 0; when the return is from a call to the **longjmp** routine, the **setjmp** routine returns a non-zero value.

The **setjmp** routine contains the following parameter:

- *env*—The array that receives the information describing the calling environment.

A call of the **setjmp** routine may occur only in the following contexts:

- As an expression statement

- As the conditional expression of a selection or iteration statement

- As an operand of a relational or equality operator, where the other operand is an integral constant and the resulting expression is the conditional expression of a selection or iteration statement

- As the operand of the unary operator (!), where the resulting expression is the conditional expression of a selection or iteration statement

osignal And signal.h

The **signal.h** header file provides routines that let your program raise and handle signals, which are conditions that may occur during program execution. The **csignal** header provides a convenient way to include the **signal.h** header file and define the contents of that file within the **std** namespace. You must reference the names introduced by **csignal** by qualifying them using the namespace (**std**) and the scope resolution operator. Alternatively, you can incorporate the members of the **std** namespace into the current namespace by including the following line after the **#include** directives:

```
using namespace std;
```

Variables And Constants

Table 10.2 summarizes the constants defined in the **signal.h** header file. These constants correspond to signals, actions to be taken when a signal is received, or the result of handling a signal.

Type

The **signal.h** header file defines the type **sig_atomic_t**, which represents an integral type that can be accessed atomically, despite the possibility of asynchronous interrupts.

Routines

raise (ANSI, Win 9x, Win NT)

This routine sends the specified signal to the executing program.

```
int raise(int sig);
```

The **raise** routine returns the value 0 if the operation was successful; otherwise, it returns a non-zero value.

The **raise** routine contains the following parameter:

- **sig**—Specifies the signal to be sent (see the constants described in Table 10.2).

signal (ANSI, Win 9x, Win NT)

This routine specifies the action taken in response to a specified signal.

```
void (*signal(int sig, void (*func) (int))) (int);
```

Table 10.2   Constants defined in signal.h.

Constant	Type	Description
SIGABRT	Signal	Abnormal termination.
SIG_DFL	Action	Perform the default action.
SIG_ERR	Result	Error occurred during signal handling.
SIGFPE	Signal	Arithmetic error.
SIG_IGN	Action	Perform no action: ignore the signal.
SIGILL	Signal	Invalid function image or illegal instruction.
SIGINT	Signal	Attention signal.
SIGSEGV	Signal	Invalid access to storage.
SIGTERM	Signal	Termination request.

The **signal** routine contains the following parameters:

- *sig*—The signal for which the action is to be specified.
- *func*—A pointer to the function that will be executed when the specified signal is received, or one of the following values:
  - **SIG_DFL**, which specifies that the signal should be handled in a default manner
  - **SIG_IGN**, which specifies that the signal should be ignored

cassert And assert.h

The **assert.h** header file provides a macro that puts diagnostics into programs. The **cassert** header provides a convenient way to include the **assert.h** header file and define the contents of that file within the **std** namespace. You must reference names introduced by **cassert** by qualifying them using the namespace (**std**) and the scope resolution operator. Alternatively, you can incorporate the members of the **std** namespace into the current namespace by including the following line after the **#include** directives:

```
using namespace std;
```

assert (ANSI, Win 9x, Win NT)
This routine, which is implemented as a macro, puts a diagnostic into a program.

```
void assert(int expression);
```

The **assert** macro contains the following parameter:

- *expression*—The expression to be tested.

The **assert** macro tests the value of its argument and takes no action if the argument evaluates to **true**; otherwise, it displays a message on the console (**stdout**) device. The message identifies the source file, the source file line number, and the text of the argument. The **assert** macro then calls the **abort** routine.

System Calls

In Brief

Handling Processes

The **process.h** header file defines constants and routines that facilitate working with processes and threads. The routines defined in the **process.h** header file let your programs create and execute processes and threads, and control their execution.

Handling Time Values

The **time.h** header file defines constants, types, and routines that facilitate working with time values, including calendar times, local times, and daylight-saving times. The routines let your program obtain the current system time, compute the difference between two times, and convert times to and from a variety of formats.

Immediate Solutions

process.h

The **process.h** header defines constants and routines that are useful for working with processes. Unlike most other Visual C++ header files, the **process.h** header file has no associated header file that automatically defines the contents of **process.h** within the **std** namespace.

Several additional routines useful for working with processes are defined by other header files.

Related solutions:	Found on page:
_pclose	126
perror, _wperror	126
_popen, _wpopen	127
abort	139
getenv, _wgetenv	142
_putenv, _wputenv	146
_onexit	146
longjmp	232
setjmp	233
raise	234
signal	234

Constants

Table 11.1 summarizes the constants defined by the **process.h** header file, identifying the routine that uses each.

Routines

_beginthread And _beginthreadex (Win 9x, Win NT)
These routines create a thread.

Table 11.1   Constants defined in process.h.

Constant	Routine	Meaning
_P_DETACH	**spawn**	Spawns a background process; the calling process continues to run.
_P_NOWAIT	**spawn**	Spawns a process; the calling process continues to run.
_P_NOWAITO	**spawn**	Same as **_P_NOWAIT**.
_P_OVERLAY	**spawn**	Overlays the calling process with new process.
_P_WAIT	**spawn**	Suspends the calling thread until execution of new process is complete.
_WAIT_CHILD	**cwait**	Calling process waits until new process terminates.
_WAIT_GRANDCHILD	**cwait**	Calling process waits until new process, and all processes created by the new process, terminate.

```
unsigned long _beginthread(void(__cdecl *start_address)(void *),
    unsigned stack_size, void *arglist);
unsigned long _beginthreadex(void *security, unsigned stack_size,
    unsigned (__stdcall *start_address)(void *), void *arglist,
    unsigned initflag, unsigned *thrdaddr);
```

They return a handle to the created thread if the operation was successful; otherwise, **_beginthread** returns the value –1 and **_beginthreadex** returns the value 0.

The **_beginthread** and **_beginthreadex** routines contain the following parameters:

- *start_address*—The start address of the routine to be executed as the new thread.

- *stack_size*—The stack size for the new thread.

- *arglist*—The argument list to be passed to the new thread.

- *security*—The Windows NT security descriptor for the new thread (must be 0 for Win 9x).

- *initflag*—The initial state of the new thread. The possible values are:

  - 0—The thread should run immediately.

  - **CREATE_SUSPEND**—The thread is to be left in a suspended state.

- *thrdaddr*—The variable that receives the identifier of the new thread.

_cexit And _c_exit *(Win 9x, Win NT)*
These routines perform exit termination procedures.

```
void _cexit(void);
void _c_exit(void);
```

The **_cexit** routine performs a complete termination that includes executing registered **atexit** and **_onexit** functions, flushing all input/output buffers, closing all open streams, and returning. The **_c_exit** routine performs an abbreviated termination, by closing all open streams and returning.

_cwait *(Win 9x, Win NT)*
This routine waits until a specified process terminates.

```
int _cwait(int *termstat, int handle, int action);
```

The **_cwait** routine returns the handle of the specified process if the operation was successful; otherwise, it returns the value –1.

The **_cwait** routine contains the following parameters:

- *termstat*—The variable that receives the result code of the terminated process.
- *handle*—The handle of the process or thread.
- *action*—The routine ignores this parameter, which must be **NULL**.

_endthread And _endthreadex *(Win 9x, Win NT)*
These routines terminate a Windows NT or Windows 95 thread

```
void _endthread(void);
void _endthreadex(unsigned val);
```

The **_endthreadex** routine contains the following parameter:

- *val*—The thread exit code

The **_endthread** routine automatically closes the thread handle. The **_endthreadex** routine, however, does not; you should use the Win32 **CloseHandle** API to close the thread handle of a thread terminated via **_endthreadex**.

_execl And _wexecl *(Win 9x, Win NT)*
These routines execute a new process with an argument list.

11. System Calls

```
int _execl(const char *cmdname, const char *arg0,
  ... const char *argn, NULL);
int _wexecl(const wchar_t *cmdname, const wchar_t *arg0,
  ... const wchar_t *argn, NULL);
```

If the operation is successful, these routines do not return; otherwise, they return the value −1.

The **_execl** and **_wexecl** routines contain the following parameters:

- *cmdname*—The path of the file to be executed

- *arg0, ... , argn*—The argument list to be passed to the new process.

_execle And _wexecle (Win 9x, Win NT)
These routines execute a new process with an argument list and environment.

```
int _execle(const char *cmdname, const char *arg0,
  ... const char *argn, NULL, const char *const *envp);
int _wexecle(const wchar_t *cmdname, const wchar_t *arg0,
  ... const wchar_t *argn, NULL, const char *const *envp);
```

If the operation is successful, these routines do not return; otherwise, they return the value −1.

The **_execle** and **_wexecle** routines contain the following parameters:

- *cmdname*—The path of the file to be executed.

- *arg0, ... , argn*—The argument list to be passed to the new process.

- *envp*—The array of pointers to environment strings.

_execlp And _wexeclp (Win 9x, Win NT)
These routines execute a new process using the **PATH** variable and an argument list.

```
int _execlp(const char *cmdname, const char *arg0,
  ... const char *argn, NULL);
int _wexeclp(const wchar_t *cmdname, const wchar_t *arg0,
  ... const wchar_t *argn, NULL);
```

If the operation is successful, these routines do not return; otherwise, they return the value −1.

The **_execlp** and **_wexeclp** routines contain the following parameters:

- *cmdname*—The path of the file to be executed.
- *arg0*, ... , *argn*—The argument list to be passed to the new process.

_execlpe And _wexeclpe *(Win 9x, Win NT)*

These routines execute a new process using the **PATH** variable, a specified environment, and an argument list.

```
int _execlpe(const char *cmdname, const char *arg0,
  ... const char *argn, NULL, const char *const *envp);
int _wexeclpe(const wchar_t *cmdname, const wchar_t *arg0,
  ... const wchar_t *argn, NULL, const wchar_t *const *envp);
```

If the operation is successful, these routines do not return; otherwise, they return the value –1.

The **_execlpe** and **_wexeclpe** routines contain the following parameters:

- *cmdname*—The path of the file to be executed.
- *arg0*, ... , *argn*—The argument list to be passed to the new process.
- *envp*—The array of pointers to environment strings.

_execv And _wexecv *(Win 9x, Win NT)*

These routines execute a new process with a specified argument array.

```
int _execv(const char *cmdname,
  const char *const *argv);
int _wexecv(const wchar_t *cmdname,
  const wchar_t *const *argv);
```

If the operation is successful, these routines do not return; otherwise, they return the value –1.

The **_execv** and **_wexecv** routines contain the following parameters:

- *cmdname*—The path of the file to be executed.
- *argv*—The array holding pointers to the argument values.

_execve And _wexecve *(Win 9x, Win NT)*

These routines execute a new process with an argument array and a specified environment.

```
int _execve(const char *cmdname,
  const char *const *argv, const char *const *envp);
int _wexecve(const wchar_t *cmdname,
  const wchar_t *const *argv, const wchar_t *const *envp);
```

If the operation is successful, these routines do not return; otherwise, they return the value –1.

The **_execve** and **_wexecve** routines contain the following parameters:

- *cmdname*—The path of the file to be executed.

- *argv*—The array holding pointers to the argument values.

- *envp*—The array of pointers to environment strings.

_execvp And _wexecvp *(Win 9x, Win NT)*

These routines execute a new process using the **PATH** variable and an argument array.

```
int _execvp(const char *cmdname,
  const char *const *argv);
int _wexecvp(const wchar_t *cmdname,
  const wchar_t *const *argv);
```

If the operation is successful, these routines do not return; otherwise, they return the value –1.

The **_execvp** and **_wexecvp** routines contain the following parameters:

- *cmdname*—The path of the file to be executed.

- *argv*—The array holding pointers to the argument values.

_execvpe And _wexecvpe *(Win 9x, Win NT)*

These routines execute a new process using the **PATH** variable, a specified environment, and an argument array.

```
int _execvpe(const char *cmdname,
  const char *const *argv, const char *const *envp);
int _wexecvpe(const wchar_t *cmdname,
  const wchar_t *const *argv, const wchar_t *const *envp);
```

If the operation is successful, these routines do not return; otherwise, they return the value –1.

The **_execvpe** and **_wexecvpe** routines contain the following parameters:

- *cmdname*—The path of the file to be executed.
- *argv*—The array holding pointers to the argument values.
- *envp*—The array of pointers to environment strings.

exit And _exit (Win 9x, Win NT)
These routines perform exit termination procedures.

```
void exit(void);
void _exit(void);
```

The **exit** routine performs a complete termination that includes executing registered **atexit** and **_onexit** functions, flushing all input/output buffers, closing all open streams, and terminating. The **_exit** routine performs an abbreviated termination, by closing all open streams and terminating.

_getpid (Win 9x, Win NT)
This routine returns the process ID number of the current process.

```
int _getpid(void);
```

_spawnl And _wspawnl (Win 9x, Win NT)
These routines create and execute a new process with a specified argument list.

```
int _spawnl(int mode, const char *cmdname,
  const char *arg0, const char *arg1,
  ... const char *argn, NULL);
int _wspawnl(int mode, const wchar_t *cmdname,
  const wchar_t *arg0, const wchar_t *arg1,
  ... const wchar_t *argn, NULL);
```

The return value from a synchronous spawn (**_P_WAIT** specified for *mode*) is the exit status of the new process. The return value from an asynchronous spawn (**_P_NOWAIT** or **_P_NOWAITO** specified for *mode*) is the process handle. A return value of –1 indicates an error.

The **_spawnl** and **_wspawnl** routines contain the following parameters:

- *mode*—The execution mode of the calling process (see Table 11.1).

- *cmdname*—The path of the file to be executed.

- *arg0*, ... , *argn*—The list of pointers to arguments.

_spawnle And _wspawnle (Win 9x, Win NT)

These routines create and execute a new process with a specified argument list and environment.

```
int _spawnle(int mode, const char *cmdname,
  const char *arg0, const char *arg1,
  ... const char *argn, NULL,
  const char *const *envp);
int _wspawnle(int mode, const wchar_t *cmdname,
  const wchar_t *arg0, const wchar_t *arg1,
  ... const wchar_t *argn, NULL,
  const wchar_t *const *envp);
```

The return value from a synchronous spawn (**_P_WAIT** specified for *mode*) is the exit status of the new process. The return value from an asynchronous spawn (**_P_NOWAIT** or **_P_NOWAITO** specified for *mode*) is the process handle. A return value of –1 indicates an error.

The **_spawnle** and **_wspawnle** routines contain the following parameters:

- *mode*—The execution mode of the calling process (see Table 11.1).

- *cmdname*—The path of the file to be executed.

- *arg0*, ... , *argn*—The list of pointers to arguments.

- *envp*—The array of pointers to environment strings.

_spawnlp And _wspawnlp (Win 9x, Win NT)

These routines create and execute a new process using the **PATH** variable and a specified argument list.

```
int _spawnlp(int mode, const char *cmdname,
  const char *arg0, const char *arg1,
  ... const char *argn, NULL);
int _wspawnlp(int mode, const wchar_t *cmdname,
  const wchar_t *arg0, const wchar_t *arg1,
  ... const wchar_t *argn, NULL);
```

The return value from a synchronous spawn (**_P_WAIT** specified for *mode*) is the exit status of the new process. The return value from an asynchronous spawn (**_P_NOWAIT** or **_P_NOWAITO** specified for *mode*) is the process handle. A return value of −1 indicates an error.

The **_spawnlp** and **_wspawnlp** routines contain the following parameters:

- *mode*—The execution mode of the calling process (see Table 11.1).

- *cmdname*—The path of the file to be executed.

- *arg0, ... , argn*—The list of pointers to arguments.

_spawnlpe And _wspawnlpe (Win 9x, Win NT)

These routines create and execute a new process using the **PATH** variable, a specified environment, and an argument list.

```
int _spawnlpe(int mode, const char *cmdname,
  const char *arg0, const char *arg1,
  ... const char *argn, NULL,
  const char *const *envp);
int _wspawnlpe(int mode, const wchar_t *cmdname,
  const wchar_t *arg0, const wchar_t *arg1,
  ... const wchar_t *argn, NULL,
  const wchar_t *const *envp);
```

The return value from a synchronous spawn (**_P_WAIT** specified for *mode*) is the exit status of the new process. The return value from an asynchronous spawn (**_P_NOWAIT** or **_P_NOWAITO** specified for *mode*) is the process handle. A return value of −1 indicates an error.

The **_spawnlpe** and **_wspawnlpe** routines contain the following parameters:

- *mode*—The execution mode of the calling process (see Table 11.1).

- *cmdname*—The path of the file to be executed.

- *arg0, ... , argn*—The list of pointers to arguments.

- *envp*—The array of pointers to environment strings.

_spawnv And _wspawnv (Win 9x, Win NT)

These routines create and execute a new process with a specified argument array.

```
int _spawnv(int mode, const char *cmdname,
  const char *const *argv);
int _wspawnv(int mode, const wchar_t *cmdname,
  const wchar_t *const *argv);
```

The return value from a synchronous spawn (**_P_WAIT** specified for **mode**) is the exit status of the new process. The return value from an asynchronous spawn (**_P_NOWAIT** or **_P_NOWAITO** specified for **mode**) is the process handle. A return value of –1 indicates an error.

The **_spawnv** and **_wspawnv** routines contain the following parameters:

- **mode**—The execution mode of the calling process (see Table 11.1).

- **cmdname**—The path of the file to be executed.

- **argv**—The array of pointers to arguments.

_spawnve And _wspawnve *(Win 9x, Win NT)*

These routines create and execute a new process with a specified environment and an argument array.

```
int _spawnve(int mode, const char *cmdname,
  const char *const *argv,
  const char *const *envp);
int _wspawnve( int mode, const wchar_t *cmdname,
  const wchar_t *const *argv,
  const wchar_t *const *envp);
```

The return value from a synchronous spawn (**_P_WAIT** specified for **mode**) is the exit status of the new process. The return value from an asynchronous spawn (**_P_NOWAIT** or **_P_NOWAITO** specified for **mode**) is the process handle. A return value of –1 indicates an error.

The **_spawnve** and **_wspawnve** routines contain the following parameters:

- **mode**—The execution mode of the calling process (see Table 11.1).

- **cmdname**—The path of the file to be executed.

- **argv**—The array of pointers to arguments.

- **envp**—The array of pointers to environment strings.

_spawnvp And _wspawnvp (Win 9x, Win NT)

These routines create and execute a new process using the **PATH** variable and a specified argument array.

```
int _spawnvp(int mode, const char *cmdname,
  const char *const *argv);
int _wspawnvp(int mode, const wchar_t *cmdname,
  const wchar_t *const *argv);
```

The return value from a synchronous spawn (**_P_WAIT** specified for *mode*) is the exit status of the new process. The return value from an asynchronous spawn (**_P_NOWAIT** or **_P_NOWAITO** specified for *mode*) is the process handle. A return value of –1 indicates an error.

The **_spawnvp** and **_wspawnvp** routines contain the following parameters:

- *mode*—The execution mode of the calling process (see Table 11.1).
- *cmdname*—The path of the file to be executed.
- *argv*—The array holding pointers to the argument values.

_spawnvpe And _wspawnvpe (Win 9x, Win NT)

These routines create and execute a new process using the **PATH** variable, a specified environment, and an argument array.

```
int _spawnvpe(int mode, const char *cmdname,
  const char *const *argv, const char *const *envp);
int _wspawnvpe(int mode, const wchar_t *cmdname,
  const wchar_t *const *argv, const wchar_t *const *envp);
```

The return value from a synchronous spawn (**_P_WAIT** specified for *mode*) is the exit status of the new process. The return value from an asynchronous spawn (**_P_NOWAIT** or **_P_NOWAITO** specified for *mode*) is the process handle. A return value of –1 indicates an error.

The **_spawnvpe** and **_wspawnvpe** routines contain the following parameters:

- *mode*—The execution mode of the calling process (see Table 11.1).
- *cmdname*—The path of the file to be executed.
- *argv*—The array holding pointers to the argument values.
- *envp*—The array of pointers to environment strings.

11. System Calls

system And *_wsystem* (Win 9x, Win NT)

These routines execute a specified operating system command.

```
int system(const char *command);
int _wsystem(const wchar_t *command);
```

If the command string is not **NULL**, these routines return the value returned by the command interpreter, if the operation was successful; otherwise, they return the value –1. If the command string is **NULL** and the routine finds the command interpreter, these routines return a non-zero value; otherwise, they return the value 0.

The **system** and **_wsystem** routines contain the following parameter:

- *command*—The string that contains the command to be executed.

ctime And ctime.h

The **ctime.h** header file defines macros that facilitate working with time. The **ctime** header provides a convenient way to include the **ctime.h** header file and define the contents of that file within the **std** namespace. You must reference the names introduced by **ctime** by qualifying them using the namespace (**std**) and the scope resolution operator. Alternatively, you can incorporate the members of the **std** namespace into the current namespace by including the following line after the **#include** directives:

```
using namespace std;
```

The **ctime.h** header file works with three sorts of time:

- Calendar time that represents a date and time using the Gregorian calendar
- Local time, which is the calendar time for a specific time zone
- Daylight-saving time, which is an adjusted local time

Variables And Constants

In addition to the constant **NULL**, which is also defined in **stdlib.h**, the **ctime.h** header file defines one constant: **CLOCKS_PER_SEC**.

This constant holds the number of clock ticks per second; it is used to interpret the value returned by the **clock** routine.

Types

clock_t
An arithmetic type that can hold a time value.

time_t
An arithmetic type that can hold a time value.

struct tm
A structure that holds the components of a calendar time. Table 11.2 summarizes the components of the **tm** structure.

Routines

asctime (ANSI, Win 9x, Win NT)
_wasctime (Win 9x, Win NT)
These routines convert time from type **struct tm** to a string.

```
char *asctime(const struct tm *timeptr);
wchar_t *_wasctime(const struct tm *timeptr);
```

They return a pointer to the string result.

The **asctime** and **_wasctime** routines contain the following parameter:

- *timeptr*—A pointer to the **tm** structure to be converted.

*Table 11.2   Components of the **tm** structure.*

Component	Description
int tm_sec;	The number of seconds after the minute—[0, 59]
int tm_min;	The number of minutes after the hour—[0, 59]
int tm_hour;	The number of hours since midnight—[0, 23]
int tm_mday;	The day of the month—[1, 31]
int tm_mon;	The number of months since January—[0, 11]
int tm_year;	The number of years since 1900
int tm_wday;	The number of days since Sunday—[0, 6]
int tm_yday;	The number of days since January 1—[0, 365]
int tm_isdest;	Daylight-saving-time flag*

* The **tm_isdest** flag is positive if daylight-saving time is in effect in the local time zone, zero if daylight-saving time is not in effect in the local time zone, or negative if the status of daylight-saving time is unknown.

clock *(ANSI, Win 9x, Win NT)*
This routine returns the elapsed CPU time for the current process.

```
clock_t clock(void);
```

ctime *(ANSI, Win 9x, Win NT)*
_wctime *(, Win 9x, Win NT)*
These routines convert a time from type **time_t** to a string.

```
char *ctime(const time_t *timer);
wchar_t *_wctime(const time_t *timer);
```

They return a pointer to the string result, or **NULL** if the result falls outside the range of times that can be represented.

The **ctime** and **_wctime** routines contain the following parameter:

• *timer*—A pointer to the stored time.

difftime *(ANSI, Win 9x, Win NT)*
This routine computes the difference between two times.

```
double difftime(time_t timer1, time_t timer0);
```

difftime returns the difference between the times, in seconds.

It contains the following parameters:

• *timer0*—The beginning time.
• *timer1*—The ending time.

_ftime *(Win 9x, Win NT)*
This routine stores the current system time in a variable of type **struct _timeb**.

```
void _ftime(struct _timeb *timeptr);
```

The **_ftime** routine contains the following parameter:

• *timeptr*—A pointer to the **_timeb** structure that receives the result.

The **_ftime** routine and the associate **_timeb** structure are defined in the **sys\timeb.h** header file, rather than the **time.h** header file. The **_timeb** structure contains the following components:

• **dstflag**—A non-zero value if daylight-saving time is currently in effect for the local time zone.

- **millitm**—The fraction of a second (in milliseconds).
- **time**—The time in seconds since midnight (00:00:00), January 1, 1970, universal coordinated time (UTC).
- **timezone**—The difference (in minutes) between UTC and local time.

_futime *(ANSI, Win 9x, Win NT)*

This routine sets the modification time on an open file.

```
int _futime(int handle, struct _utimbuf *filetime);
```

It returns the value 0 if the operation was successful; otherwise, it returns the value –1.

The **_futime** routine contains the following parameters:

- *handle*—The handle of the open file.
- *filetime*—The **_utimbuf** structure that contains the time to be set.

The **_futime** routine and the associate **_utimbuf** structure are defined in the **sys\utime.h** header file, rather than the **time.h** header file. The **_utimbuf** structure contains the following components:

- **actime**—A **time_t** variable that holds the time of file access.
- **modtime**—A **time_t** variable that holds the time of file modification.

gmtime *(ANSI, Win 9x, Win NT)*

This routine converts time from type **time_t** to **struct tm**.

```
struct tm *gmtime(const time_t *timer);
```

The **gmtime** routine returns a pointer to a **tm** structure that receives the value of the *timer* argument in UTC (universal coordinated time).

It contains the following parameter:

- *timer*—The time to be converted.

localtime *(ANSI, Win 9x, Win NT)*

This routine converts time from type **time_t** to **struct tm** with local correction.

```
struct tm *localtime(const time_t *timer);
```

The **localtime** routine returns a pointer to a **tm** structure that receives the local time result.

It contains the following parameter:

• *timer*—The time to be converted.

mktime *(ANSI, Win 9x, Win NT)*
This routine converts a time to a calendar value.

```
time_t mktime(struct tm *timeptr);
```

The **mktime** routine returns the calendar time.

It contains the following parameter:

• *timeptr*—The time to be converted.

_strdate *And* _wstrdate *(Win 9x, Win NT)*
These routines return the current system date as a string.

```
char *_strdate(char *datestr);
wchar_t *_wstrdate(wchar_t *datestr);
```

They return a pointer to the string result.

The **_strdate** and **_wstrdate** routines contain the following parameter:

• *datestr*—A pointer to the buffer that receives the result.

strftime *(ANSI, Win 9x, Win NT)*
wcsftime *(Win 9x, Win NT)*
These routines format a date-and-time string for international use.

```
size_t strftime(char *strDest, size_t maxsize,
  const char *format, const struct tm *timeptr);
size_t wcsftime(wchar_t *strDest, size_t maxsize,
  const wchar_t *format, const struct tm *timeptr);
```

They return the number of characters placed in the *strDest* buffer, if the operation was successful; otherwise, they return **NULL**.

The **strftime** and **wcsftime** routines contain the following parameters:

• *strDest*—A pointer to the destination buffer.

• *maxsize*—The number of characters (or wide characters) that can be placed in the destination buffer.

- *format*—The format control string.
- *timeptr*—A pointer to the time to be converted.

_strtime And _wstrtime *(Win 9x, Win NT)*
These routines return the current system time as a string.

```
char *_strtime(char *timestr);
wchar_t *_wstrtime(wchar_t *timestr);
```

The **_strtime** and **_wstrime** routines contain the following parameter:

- *timestr*—A pointer to the buffer that receives the result.

time *(ANSI, Win 9x, Win NT)*
This routine returns the current system time as a value of type **time_t**.

```
time_t time(time_t *timer);
```

The **time** routine contains the following parameter:

- *timer*—A pointer to the buffer that receives the result.

_tzset *(Win 9x, Win NT)*
This routine sets external time variables from the environment time variable **TZ**.

```
void _tzset(void);
```

The **_tzset** routine sets the values of three global variables: **_daylight**, **_timezone**, and **_tzname**. The **_ftime** and **localtime** functions use these variables to make corrections from universal coordinated time (UTC) to local time, and the **time** function uses them to compute UTC from system time.

You set the **TZ** environment variable using the following syntax:

```
set TZ=tzn[+ | -]hh[:mm[:ss] ][dzn]
```

The values used to set the **TZ** environment variable are:

- *tzn*—The three-letter time-zone name, such as **PST**.
- *hh*—The difference in hours between UTC and local time.
- *mm*—The minutes.
- *ss*—The seconds.
- *dzn*—The three-letter daylight-savings time zone, such as **PDT**.

If the **TZ** value is not set, **_tzset** uses the time-zone information specified by the operating system. Under Windows NT and Windows 9x, the Control Panel's Date/Time application lets the user set the time zone. If **_tzset** cannot obtain this information, it uses **PST8PDT**, which signifies the U.S. Pacific time zone.

_utime And _wutime (Win 9x, Win NT)

These routines set the file modification time.

```
int _utime(unsigned char *filename, struct _utimbuf *times);
int _wutime(wchar_t *filename, struct _utimbuf *times);
```

They return the value 0 if the operation was successful; otherwise, they return the value -1.

These **_utime** and **_wutime** routines contain the following parameters:

- *filename*—The name of the file whose modification time is to be set.

- *times*—The time to be set.

The **_utime** and **_wutime** routines and the **_utimbuf** structure are defined in the header file **sys/utime.h**, rather than **time.h**. The **_utimbuf** structure contains the following components:

- **actime**—A **time_t** variable that holds the time of file access.

- **modtime**—A **time_t** variable that holds the time of file modification.

Chapter 12

Collections

In Brief

Working With Collection Classes

This chapter presents three header files that help you work with collections: the **string** header file, the **valarray** header file, and the **search** header file.

The **string** header file defines a template collection class that facilitates working with text strings. You can use this class to work with strings that consist of characters or wide characters.

The **valarray** header file defines a collection class that resembles a vector. The collection class includes routines that let you perform a variety of operations, particularly numeric operations, on the elements of the collection class.

The **search.h** header file defines several routines that facilitate searching and sorting. These same routines are also defined in the **stdlib.h** header file, so programs that include **stdlib.h** do not need to also include **search.h**.

Immediate Solutions

string

The **string** header defines a template collection class that facilitates working with text strings. In particular, it defines the template class **basic_string**, which it uses to define the classes **string** (which represents a sequence of characters) and **wstring** (which represents a sequence of wide characters). Most programs do not use the **basic_string** template class itself, but instead use the **string** or **wstring** classes that it defines.

The **basic_string** template class uses three parameters:

- **class E**—Specifies the type of the elements of the collection. The **string** class uses elements of type **char**, whereas the **wstring** class uses elements of type **wchar_t**.

- **class T**—Describes traits of the elements. This class must have the same interface as the **char_traits** template class.

- **class A**—Describes a protected object that allocates and frees storage for the collection. This class must have the same interface as the **allocator** template class.

Routines

operator+ (ANSI, Win 9x, Win NT)
This routine appends a **basic_string** (or constant of the type underlying the **basic_string**) to a **basic_string** (or constant of the type underlying the **basic_string**) and returns the result.

```
template<class E, class T, class A>
    basic_string<E, T, A> operator+(
        const basic_string<E, T, A>& lhs,
        const basic_string<E, T, A>& rhs);
template<class E, class T, class A>
    basic_string<E, T, A> operator+(
        const basic_string<E, T, A>& lhs,
        const E *rhs);
```

```
template<class E, class T, class A>
    basic_string<E, T, A> operator+(
        const basic_string<E, T, A>& lhs, E rhs);
template<class E, class T, class A>
    basic_string<E, T, A> operator+(
        const E *lhs,
        const basic_string<E, T, A>& rhs);
template<class E, class T, class A>
    basic_string<E, T, A> operator+(
        E lhs,
        const basic_string<E, T, A>& rhs);
```

operator+ contains the following parameters:

- *lhs*—The left **basic_string** object.

- *rhs*—The right **basic_string** object.

operator== (ANSI, Win 9x, Win NT)

This routine compares a **basic_string** (or constant of the type underlying the **basic_string**) with a **basic_string** (or constant of the type underlying the **basic_string**), returning **true** if their contents are the same and **false** otherwise.

```
template<class E, class T, class A>
    bool operator==(
        const basic_string<E, T, A>& lhs,
        const basic_string<E, T, A>& rhs);
template<class E, class T, class A>
    bool operator==(
        const basic_string<E, T, A>& lhs,
        const E *rhs);
template<class E, class T, class A>
    bool operator==(
        const E *lhs,
        const basic_string<E, T, A>& rhs);
```

operator== contains the following parameters:

- *lhs*—The left **basic_string** object.

- *rhs*—The right **basic_string** object.

operator!= (ANSI, Win 9x, Win NT)

This routine compares a **basic_string** (or constant of the type underlying the **basic_string**) to a **basic_string** (or constant of the type underlying the **basic_string**), returning **true** if their contents are different and **false** otherwise.

```
template<class E, class T, class A>
    bool operator!=(
        const basic_string<E, T, A>& lhs,
        const basic_string<E, T, A>& rhs);
template<class E, class T, class A>
    bool operator!=(
        const basic_string<E, T, A>& lhs,
        const E *rhs);
template<class E, class T, class A>
    bool operator!=(
        const E *lhs,
        const basic_string<E, T, A>& rhs);
```

operator!= contains the following parameters:

- *lhs*—The left **basic_string** object.
- *rhs*—The right **basic_string** object.

operator< (ANSI, Win 9x, Win NT)
This routine compares a **basic_string** (or constant of the type underlying the **basic_string**) to a **basic_string** (or constant of the type underlying the **basic_string**), returning **true** if the left object collates lower than the right object and **false** otherwise.

```
template<class E, class T, class A>
    bool operator<(
        const basic_string<E, T, A>& lhs,
        const basic_string<E, T, A>& rhs);
template<class E, class T, class A>
    bool operator<(
        const basic_string<F, T, A>& lhs,
        const E *rhs);
template<class E, class T, class A>
    bool operator<(
        const E *lhs,
        const basic_string<E, T, A>& rhs);
```

operator< contains the following parameters:

- *lhs*—The left **basic_string** object or constant.
- *rhs*—The right **basic_string** object or constant.

operator> (ANSI, Win 9x, Win NT)
This routine compares a **basic_string** (or constant of the type underlying the **basic_string**) to a **basic_string** (or constant of the type underlying the **basic_string**), returning **true** if the left object collates higher than the right object and **false** otherwise.

```
template<class E, class T, class A>
    bool operator>(
        const basic_string<E, T, A>& lhs,
        const basic_string<E, T, A>& rhs);
template<class E, class T, class A>
    bool operator>(
        const basic_string<E, T, A>& lhs,
        const E *rhs);
template<class E, class T, class A>
    bool operator>(
        const E *lhs,
        const basic_string<E, T, A>& rhs);
```

operator> contains the following parameters:

- *lhs*—The left **basic_string** object or constant.
- *rhs*—The right **basic_string** object or constant.

operator<= (ANSI, Win 9x, Win NT)

This routine compares a **basic_string** (or constant of the type underlying the **basic_string**) to a **basic_string** (or constant of the type underlying the **basic_string**), returning **true** if the left object collates lower than or the same as the right object and **false** otherwise.

```
template<class E, class T, class A>
    bool operator<=(
        const basic_string<E, T, A>& lhs,
        const basic_string<E, T, A>& rhs);
template<class E, class T, class A>
    bool operator<=(
        const basic_string<E, T, A>& lhs,
        const E *rhs);
template<class E, class T, class A>
    bool operator<=(
        const E *lhs,
        const basic_string<E, T, A>& rhs);
```

operator<= contains the following parameters:

- *lhs*—The left **basic_string** object or constant.
- *rhs*—The right **basic_string** object or constant.

operator>= (ANSI, Win 9x, Win NT)

The **operator>=** routine compares a **basic_string** (or constant of the type underlying the **basic_string**) to a **basic_string** (or constant of the type underlying the **basic_string**), returning **true** if the left object collates higher than or the same as the right object and **false** otherwise.

```
template<class E, class T, class A>
    bool operator>=(
        const basic_string<E, T, A>& lhs,
        const basic_string<E, T, A>& rhs);
template<class E, class T, class A>
    bool operator>=(
        const basic_string<E, T, A>& lhs,
        const E *rhs); template<class E, class T, class A>
    bool operator>=(
        const E *lhs,
        const basic_string<E, T, A>& rhs);
```

operator>= contains the following parameters:

- *lhs*—The left **basic_string** object or constant.

- *rhs*—The right **basic_string** object or constant.

swap *(ANSI, Win 9x, Win NT)*
This routine exchanges the contents of the **basic_string** objects provided as arguments.

```
template<class E, class T, class A>
    void swap(
        const basic_string<E, T, A>& lhs,
        const basic_string<E, T, A>& rhs);
```

swap contains the following parameters:

- *lhs*—The left **basic_string** object or constant.

- *rhs*—The right **basic_string** object or constant.

operator<< *(ANSI, Win 9x, Win NT)*
This routine inserts a **basic_string** object into an output stream and returns the resulting stream.

```
template<class E, class T, class A>
    basic_ostream<E>& operator<<(
        basic_ostream <E>& os,
        const basic_string<E, T, A>& str);
```

operator<< contains the following parameters:

- *os*—The output stream.
- *str*—The string to be inserted.

operator>> (ANSI, Win 9x, Win NT)

This routine extracts a sequence of elements from an input stream, placing them in the specified **basic_string** object and returning the modified input stream.

```
template<class E, class T, class A>
    basic_istream<E>& operator>>(
        basic_istream <E>& is,
        basic_string<E, T, A>& str);
```

operator>> contains the following parameters:

- *is*—The input stream.
- *str*—The **basic_string** that is to receive the sequence of elements.

The extraction process stops:

- When the end of file is reached.
- When the routine has extracted **is.width()** elements, if that value is non-zero.
- When the routine has extracted **is.max_size()** elements.
- When the routine has extracted an element *c* for which **use_facet< ctype<E> >(getloc()). is(ctype<E>::space,** *c* **)** is true, in which case the element *c* is put back on the input stream.

getline (ANSI, Win 9x, Win NT)

This routine extracts a sequence of elements from an input stream, placing them in the specified **basic_string** object and returning the modified input stream.

```
template<class E, class T, class A>
    basic_istream<E, T>& getline(
        basic_istream <E, T>& is,
        basic_string<E, T, A>& str);
template<class E, class T, class A>
    basic_istream<E, T>& getline(
        basic_istream <E, T>& is,
        basic_string<E, T, A>& str,
        E delim);     };
```

getline contains the following parameters:

- *is*—The input stream.
- *str*—The **basic_string** that is to receive the sequence of elements.
- *delim*—A character that stops the extraction process.

The extraction process stops:

- When the end of file is reached.
- When the routine has extracted an element that compares equal to *delim*. The *delim* character is neither put back onto the input stream nor appended to the controlled sequence.
- When the routine has extracted **is.max_size( )** elements, in which case the function calls **setstate(ios_base::failbit)**.

valarray

The **valarray** header file defines a template class **valarray** that provides a variable-length sequence of objects of type **T** that behaves something like a vector. The template class provides many useful ways to reference and manipulate the elements of the sequence.

Routines

operator* (ANSI, Win 9x, Win NT)
This routine multiplies the corresponding elements of two **valarray** objects (or a **valarray** object and a constant) and returns the result.

```
template<class T>
    valarray<T> operator*(const valarray<T>& lhs,
        const valarray<T>& rhs);
template<class T>
    valarray<T> operator*(const valarray<T> lhs,
        const T& rhs);
template<class T>
    valarray<T> operator*(const T& lhs,
        const valarray<T>& rhs);
```

The routine contains the following parameters:

- *lhs*—The left **valarray** object or constant.
- *rhs*—The right **valarray** object or constant.

operator/ *(ANSI, Win 9x, Win NT)*

This routine divides the corresponding elements of two **valarray** objects (or a **valarray** object and a constant) and returns the result.

```
template<class T>
    valarray<T> operator/(const valarray<T>& lhs,
        const valarray<T>& rhs);
template<class T>
    valarray<T> operator/(const valarray<T> lhs,
        const T& rhs);
template<class T>
    valarray<T> operator/(const T& lhs,
        const valarray<T>& rhs);
```

operator/ contains the following parameters:

- *lhs*—The left (dividend) **valarray** object or constant.

- *rhs*—The right (divisor) **valarray** object or constant.

operator% *(ANSI, Win 9x, Win NT)*

This routine computes the modulus of corresponding elements of two **valarray** objects (or a **valarray** object and a constant) and returns the result.

```
template<class T>
    valarray<T> operator%(const valarray<T>& lhs,
        const valarray<T>& rhs);
template<class T>
    valarray<T> operator%(const valarray<T> lhs,
        const T& rhs);
template<class T>
    valarray<T> operator%(const T& lhs,
        const valarray<T>& rhs);
```

operator% contains the following parameters:

- *lhs*—The left (dividend) **valarray** object or constant.

- *rhs*—The right (divisor) **valarray** object or constant.

operator+ *(ANSI, Win 9x, Win NT)*

This routine adds the corresponding elements of two **valarray** objects (or a **valarray** object and a constant) and returns the result.

```
template<class T>
    valarray<T> operator+(const valarray<T>& lhs,
        const valarray<T>& rhs);
```

12. Collections

```
template<class T>
    valarray<T> operator+(const valarray<T> lhs,
        const T& rhs);
template<class T>
    valarray<T> operator+(const T& lhs,
        const valarray<T>& rhs);
```

operator+ contains the following parameters:

- **lhs**—The left **valarray** object or constant.

- **rhs**—The right **valarray** object or constant.

operator- (ANSI, Win 9x, Win NT)
This routine subtracts the corresponding elements of two **valarray** objects (or a **valarray** object and a constant) and returns the result.

```
template<class T>
    valarray<T> operator-(const valarray<T>& lhs,
        const valarray<T>& rhs);
template<class T>
    valarray<T> operator-(const valarray<T> lhs,
        const T& rhs);
template<class T>
    valarray<T> operator-(const T& lhs,
        const valarray<T>& rhs);
```

operator- contains the following parameters:

- **lhs**—The left (subtrahend) **valarray** object or constant.

- **rhs**—The right (minuend) **valarray** object or constant.

operator^ (ANSI, Win 9x, Win NT)
This routine exclusively ORs the bits of the corresponding elements of two **valarray** objects (or a **valarray** object and a constant) and returns the result.

```
template<class T>
    valarray<T> operator^(const valarray<T>& lhs,
        const valarray<T>& rhs);
template<class T>
    valarray<T> operator^(const valarray<T> lhs,
        const T& rhs);
template<class T>
    valarray<T> operator^(const T& lhs,
        const valarray<T>& rhs);
```

operator^ contains the following parameters:

- *lhs*—The left **valarray** object or constant.

- *rhs*—The right **valarray** object or constant.

operator& (ANSI, Win 9x, Win NT)

This routine ANDs the bits of the corresponding elements of two **valarray** objects (or a **valarray** object and a constant) and returns the result.

```
template<class T>
    valarray<T> operator&(const valarray<T>& lhs,
        const valarray<T>& rhs);
template<class T>
    valarray<T> operator&(const valarray<T> lhs,
        const T& rhs);
template<class T>
    valarray<T> operator&(const T& lhs,
        const valarray<T>& rhs);
```

operator& contains the following parameters:

- *lhs*—The left **valarray** object or constant.

- *rhs*—The right **valarray** object or constant.

operator| (ANSI, Win 9x, Win NT)

This routine inclusively ORs the bits of the corresponding elements of two **valarray** objects (or a **valarray** object and a constant) and returns the result.

```
template<class T>
    valarray<T> operator|(const valarray<T>& lhs,
        const valarray<T>& rhs);
template<class T>
    valarray<T> operator|(const valarray<T> lhs,
        const T& rhs);
template<class T>
    valarray<T> operator|(const T& lhs,
        const valarray<T>& rhs);
```

operator| contains the following parameters:

- *lhs*—The left **valarray** object or constant.

- *rhs*—The right **valarray** object or constant.

operator<< (ANSI, Win 9x, Win NT)

This routine shifts the bits of each element of a **valarray** object to the left by the number of positions given by the value of the corresponding element of a second **valarray** object (or a constant).

```
template<class T>
    valarray<T> operator<<(const valarray<T>& lhs,
        const valarray<T>& rhs);
template<class T>
    valarray<T> operator<<(const valarray<T> lhs,
        const T& rhs);
template<class T>
    valarray<T> operator<<(const T& lhs,
        const valarray<T>& rhs);
```

operator<< contains the following parameters:

- *lhs*—The left **valarray** object, which contains the values to be shifted.

- *rhs*—The right **valarray** object or constant, which contains the number of positions by which to shift.

operator>> (ANSI, Win 9x, Win NT)

This routine shifts the bits of each element of a **valarray** object to the right by the number of positions given by the value of the corresponding element of a second **valarray** object (or a constant).

```
template<class T>
    valarray<T> operator>>(const valarray<T>& lhs,
        const valarray<T>& rhs);
template<class T>
    valarray<T> operator>>(const valarray<T> lhs,
        const T& rhs);
template<class T>
    valarray<T> operator>>(const T& lhs,
        const valarray<T>& rhs);
```

operator>> contains the following parameters:

- *lhs*—The left **valarray** object, which contains the values to be shifted.

- *rhs*—The right **valarray** object or constant, which contains the number of positions by which to shift.

12. Collections

operator&& *(ANSI, Win 9x, Win NT)*

This routine logically ANDs the elements of two **valarray** objects (or a **valarray** object and a constant).

```
template<class T>
    valarray<bool> operator&&(const valarray<T>& lhs,
        const valarray<T>& rhs);
template<class T>
    valarray<bool> operator&&(const valarray<T> lhs,
        const T& rhs);
template<class T>
    valarray<bool> operator&&(const T& lhs,
        const valarray<T>& rhs);
```

operator&& contains the following parameters:

- *lhs*—The left **valarray** object or constant.
- *rhs*—The right **valarray** object or constant.

operator|| *(ANSI, Win 9x, Win NT)*

This routine logically ORs the elements of two **valarray** objects (or a **valarray** object and a constant).

```
template<class T>
    valarray<bool> operator||(const valarray<T>& lhs,
        const valarray<T>& rhs);
template<class T>
    valarray<bool> operator||(const valarray<T> lhs,
        const T& rhs);
template<class T>
    valarray<bool> operator||(const T& lhs,
        const valarray<T>& rhs);
```

operator|| contains the following parameters:

- *lhs*—The left **valarray** object or constant.
- *rhs*—The right **valarray** object or constant.

operator== *(ANSI, Win 9x, Win NT)*

This routine uses the equality operator to compare the corresponding elements of two **valarray** objects (or a **valarray** object and a constant) and returns a **valarray** object whose elements indicate the result of the comparison.

```
template<class T>
    valarray<bool> operator==(const valarray<T>& lhs,
        const valarray<T>& rhs);
template<class T>
    valarray<bool> operator==(const valarray<T> lhs,
        const T& rhs);
template<class T>
    valarray<bool> operator==(const T& lhs,
        const valarray<T>& rhs);
```

The routine contains the following parameters:

- *lhs*—The left **valarray** object or constant.

- *rhs*—The right **valarray** object or constant.

operator!= *(ANSI, Win 9x, Win NT)*

This routine uses the inequality operator to compare the corresponding elements of two **valarray** objects (or a **valarray** object and a constant) and returns a **valarray** object whose elements indicate the result of the comparison.

```
template<class T>
    valarray<bool> operator!=(const valarray<T>& lhs,
        const valarray<T>& rhs);
template<class T>
    valarray<bool> operator!=(const valarray<T> lhs,
        const T& rhs);
template<class T>
    valarray<bool> operator!=(const T& lhs,
        const valarray<T>& rhs);
```

operator!= contains the following parameters:

- *lhs*—The left **valarray** object or constant.

- *rhs*—The right **valarray** object or constant.

operator< *(ANSI, Win 9x, Win NT)*

This routine uses the less than operator to compare the corresponding elements of two **valarray** objects (or a **valarray** object and a constant) and returns a **valarray** object whose elements indicate the result of the comparison.

```
template<class T>
    valarray<bool> operator<(const valarray<T>& lhs,
        const valarray<T>& rhs);
```

12. Collections

```
template<class T>
    valarray<bool> operator<(const valarray<T> lhs,
        const T& rhs);
template<class T>
    valarray<bool> operator<(const T& lhs,
        const valarray<T>& rhs);
```

operator< contains the following parameters:

- *lhs*—The left **valarray** object or constant.
- *rhs*—The right **valarray** object or constant.

operator<= (ANSI, Win 9x, Win NT)

This routine uses the less than or equal to operator to compare the corresponding elements of two **valarray** objects (or a **valarray** object and a constant) and returns a **valarray** object whose elements indicate the result of the comparison.

```
template<class T>
    valarray<bool> operator<=(const valarray<T>& lhs,
        const valarray<T>& rhs);
template<class T>
    valarray<bool> operator<=(const valarray<T> lhs,
        const T& rhs);
template<class T>
    valarray<bool> operator<=(const T& lhs,
        const valarray<T>& rhs);
```

operator<= contains the following parameters:

- *lhs*—The left **valarray** object or constant.
- *rhs*—The right **valarray** object or constant.

operator>= (ANSI, Win 9x, Win NT)

This routine uses the greater than or equal to operator to compare the corresponding elements of two **valarray** objects (or a **valarray** object and a constant) and returns a **valarray** object whose elements indicate the result of the comparison.

```
template<class T>
    valarray<bool> operator>=(const valarray<T>& lhs,
        const valarray<T>& rhs);
template<class T>
    valarray<bool> operator>=(const valarray<T> lhs,
        const T& rhs);
```

```
template<class T>
    valarray<bool> operator>=(const T& lhs,
      const valarray<T>& rhs);
```

The routine contains the following parameters:

- *lhs*—The left **valarray** object or constant.

- *rhs*—The right **valarray** object or constant.

operator> *(ANSI, Win 9x, Win NT)*

This routine uses the greater than operator to compare the corresponding elements of two **valarray** objects (or a **valarray** object and a constant) and returns a **valarray** object whose elements indicate the result of the comparison.

```
template<class T>
    valarray<bool> operator>(const valarray<T>& lhs,
      const valarray<T>& rhs);
template<class T>
    valarray<bool> operator>(const valarray<T> lhs,
      const T& rhs);
template<class T>
    valarray<bool> operator>(const T& lhs,
      const valarray<T>& rhs);
```

operator> contains the following parameters:

- *lhs*—The left **valarray** object or constant.

- *rhs*—The right **valarray** object or constant.

max *(ANSI, Win 9x, Win NT)*

This routine returns the largest element within a **valarray**.

```
template<class T>
    T max(const valarray<T>& x);
```

max contains the following parameter:

- *x*—The **valarray** object.

min *(ANSI, Win 9x, Win NT)*

This routine returns the largest element within a **valarray**.

```
template<class T>
    T min(const valarray<T>& x);
```

min contains the following parameter:

* *x*—The **valarray** object.

abs *(ANSI, Win 9x, Win NT)*
This routine returns the largest element within a **valarray**.

```
template<class T>
    T abs(const valarray<T>& x);
```

The routine contains the following parameter:

* *x*—The **valarray** object.

acos *(ANSI, Win 9x, Win NT)*
This routine calculates the arc cosine of each element of a **valarray** object and returns a **valarray** object containing the results.

```
template<class T>
    valarray<T> acos(const valarray<T>& x);
```

acos contains the following parameter:

* *x*—The **valarray** object.

asin *(ANSI, Win 9x, Win NT)*
The **asin** routine calculates the arc sine of each element of a **valarray** object and returns a **valarray** object containing the results.

```
template<class T>
    valarray<T> asin(const valarray<T>& x);
```

The routine contains the following parameter:

* *x*—The **valarray** object.

atan And atan2 *(ANSI, Win 9x, Win NT)*
These routines calculate the arc tangent of each element of a **valarray** object and return a **valarray** object containing the results.

```
template<class T>
    valarray<T> atan(const valarray<T>& x);
template<class T>
    valarray<T> atan2(const valarray<T>& x,
      const valarray<T>& y);
template<class T>
    valarray<T> atan2(const valarray<T> x, const T& y);
template<class T>
    valarray<T> atan2(const T& x, const valarray<T>& y);
```

atan and **atan2** contain the following parameters:

- *x*—The **valarray** object that gives the tangent, or the numerator of the tangent *x/y*.

- *y*—The **valarray** object that gives the denominator of the tangent *x/y*.

cos *(ANSI, Win 9x, Win NT)*
This routine calculates the cosine of each element of a **valarray** object and returns a **valarray** object containing the results.

```
template<class T>
    valarray<T> cos(const valarray<T>& x);
```

cos contains the following parameter:

- *x*—The **valarray** object.

cosh *(ANSI, Win 9x, Win NT)*
This routine calculates the hyperbolic cosine of each element of a **valarray** object and returns a **valarray** object containing the results.

```
template<class T>
    valarray<T> cosh(const valarray<T>& x);
```

cosh contains the following parameter:

- *x*—The **valarray** object.

exp *(ANSI, Win 9x, Win NT)*
This routine calculates the exponential of each element of a **valarray** object and returns a **valarray** object containing the results

```
template<class T>
    valarray<T> exp(const valarray<T>& x);
```

exp contains the following parameter:

- *x*—The **valarray** object.

log *(ANSI, Win 9x, Win NT)*
This routine calculates the natural logarithm of each element of a **valarray** object and returns a **valarray** object containing the results.

```
template<class T>
    valarray<T> log(const valarray<T>& x);
```

log contains the following parameter:

- *x*—The **valarray** object.

log10 (ANSI, Win 9x, Win NT)

This routine calculates the base-10 logarithm of each element of a **valarray** object and returns a **valarray** object containing the results.

```
template<class T>
    valarray&ttT> log10(const valarray<T>& x);
```

log10 contains the following parameter:

- *x*—The **valarray** object.

pow (ANSI, Win 9x, Win NT)

This routine calculates the power function x^y of each element of a **valarray** object and returns a **valarray** object containing the results.

```
template<class T>
    valarray<T> pow(const valarray<T>& x,
      const valarray<T>& y);
template<class T>
    valarray<T> pow(const valarray<T> x, const T& y);
template<class T>
    valarray<T> pow(const T& x, const valarray<T>& y);
```

pow contains the following parameters:

- *x*—The **valarray** object or constant that specifies the base.

- *y*—The **valarray** object or constant that specifies the power.

sin (ANSI, Win 9x, Win NT)

This routine calculates the sine of each element of a **valarray** object and returns a **valarray** object containing the results.

```
template<class T>
    valarray<T> sin(const valarray<T>& x);
```

sin contains the following parameter:

- *x*—The **valarray** object.

sinh (ANSI, Win 9x, Win NT)

This routine calculates the hyperbolic sine of each element of a **valarray** object and returns a **valarray** object containing the results.

```
template<class T>
    valarray<T> sinh(const valarray<T>& x);
```

sinh contains the following parameter:

* *x*—The **valarray** object.

sqrt (ANSI, Win 9x, Win NT)
This routine calculates the square root of each element of a **valarray** object and returns a **valarray** object containing the results.

```
template<class T>
    valarray<T> sqrt(const valarray<T>& x);
```

sqrt contains the following parameter:

* *x*—The **valarray** object.

tan (ANSI, Win 9x, Win NT)
This routine calculates the tangent of each element of a **valarray** object and returns a **valarray** object containing the results.

```
template<class T>
    valarray<T> tan(const valarray<T>& x);
```

tan contains the following parameter:

* *x*—The **valarray** object.

tanh (ANSI, Win 9x, Win NT)
This routine calculates the hyperbolic tangent of each element of a **valarray** object and returns a **valarray** object containing the results.

```
template<class T>
    valarray<T> tanh(const valarray<T>& x);
```

tanh contains the following parameter:

* *x*—The **valarray** object.

search.h
The **search.h** header file defines several routines that facilitate searching and sorting. The **stdlib.h** header file also defines these routines; programs that include **stdlib.h** do not need to also include **search.h**.

12. Collections

Routines

bsearch *(ANSI, Win 9x, Win NT)*
The **bsearch** routine performs a binary search of a sorted array.

```
void *bsearch(const void *key, const void *base, size_t num,
  size_t width,
  int (*compare) (const void *elem1, const void *elem2));
```

bsearch returns a pointer to the occurrence of *key* in the array. If no such occurrence exists or if the array is not properly ordered, the routine returns **NULL**.

It contains the following parameters:

- *key*—The object for which to search.

- *base*—A pointer to the base of the array to be searched.

- *num*—The number of elements in the array.

- *width*—The width of each element.

- *compare*—A pointer to a function that compares two elements of the array, *elem1* and *elem2*. The function must return the following values:

  - A negative value if *elem1* is less than *elem2*.

  - The value 0 if *elem1* is equal to *elem2*.

  - A positive value if *elem1* is greater than *elem2*.

- *elem1*—A pointer to the key for the search.

- *elem2*—A pointer to the array element to be compared with the key.

_lfind *(Win 9x, Win NT)*
This routine performs a linear search of a sorted or unsorted array.

```
void *_lfind(const void *key, const void *base,
  unsigned int *num, unsigned int width,
  int (cdecl *compare)
    (const void *elem1, const void *elem2));
```

_lfind returns a pointer to the occurrence of *key* in the array. If no such occurrence exists, the routine returns **NULL**.

It contains the following parameters:

- *key*—The object for which to search.
- *base*—A pointer to the base of the array to be searched.
- *num*—The number of elements in the array.
- *width*—The width of each element.
- *compare*—A pointer to a function that compares two elements of the array, *elem1* and *elem2*. The function must return the following values:
  - The value 0 if *elem1* is equal to *elem2*.
  - A non-zero if *elem1* is not equal to *elem2*.
- *elem1*—A pointer to the key for the search.
- *elem2*—A pointer to the array element to be compared with the key.

_lsearch *(Win 9x, Win NT)*

This routine performs a linear search of a sorted or unsorted array, adding the specified element to the array if the element is not already present.

```
void *_lsearch(const void *key, void *base,
  unsigned int *num, unsigned int width,
  int (*compare)(const void *elem1, const void *elem2));
```

_lsearch returns a pointer to the occurrence of *key* in the array. If no such occurrence exists, the routine adds the element at the end of the array and returns a pointer to the newly added element.

It contains the following parameters:

- *key*—The object for which to search.
- *base*—A pointer to the base of the array to be searched.
- *num*—The number of elements in the array.
- *width*—The width of each element.
- *compare*—A pointer to a function that compares two elements of the array, *elem1* and *elem2*. The function must return the following values:
  - The value 0 if *elem1* is equal to *elem2*.
  - A non-zero if *elem1* is not equal to *elem2*.

- **elem1**—A pointer to the key for the search.
- **elem2**—A pointer to the array element to be compared with the key.

qsort *(ANSI, Win 9x, Win NT)*
This routine sorts an array using the quicksort algorithm.

```
void qsort(void *base, size_t num, size_t width,
  int (*compare)(const void *elem1, const void *elem2 ));
```

It contains the following parameters:

- **key**—The object for which to search.
- **base**—A pointer to the base of the array to be searched.
- **num**—The number of elements in the array.
- **width**—The width of each element.
- **compare**—A pointer to a function that compares two elements of the array, **elem1** and **elem2**. The function must return the following values:
  - A negative value if **elem1** is less than **elem2**.
  - The value 0 if **elem1** is equal to **elem2**.
  - A positive value if **elem1** is greater than **elem2**.
- **elem1**—A pointer to the key for the search.
- **elem2**—A pointer to the array element to be compared with the key.

Internationalization

In Brief

Localizing Software

Because different cultures write monetary amounts and dates differently and use different character sets, it's difficult to write programs that can be easily adapted for use within a culture other than the one for which the program was originally written.

Immediate Solutions

clocale And locale.h

The **locale.h** header file defines constants, types, and routines that help you write programs that can be easily adapted to work with the character set and formatting conventions of a particular culture. The **clocale** header provides a convenient way to include the **locale.h** header file and define the contents of that file within the **std** namespace. You must reference the names introduced by **clocale** by qualifying them using the namespace (**std**) and the scope resolution operator. Alternatively, you can incorporate the members of the **std** namespace into the current namespace by including the following line after the **#include** directives:

```
using namespace std;
```

Variables And Constants

The constants defined in the **locale.h** header file are summarized in Table 13.1.

Types

The **locale.h** header file defines the structure type **lconv**, which contains the members described in Table 13.2. Tables 13.3 and 13.4 summarize the meanings of the values of the members that have coded values.

*Table 13.1   Constants defined in **locale.h**.*

Constant	Description
LC_ALL	Names the program's locale.
LC_COLLATE	Affects the behavior of **strcoll**, **_stricoll**, **wcscoll**, **_wcsicoll**, and **strxfrm**.
LC_CTYPE	Affects the behavior of the character-handling functions and multibyte functions, except **isdigit**, **isxdigit**, **mbstowcs**, and **mbtowc**.
LC_MONETARY	Affects the behavior of monetary formatting via **localeconv**.
LC_NUMERIC	Affects the behavior of numeric formatting via **localeconv**, including the behavior of formatted output routines such as **printf**.
LC_TIME	Affects the behavior of **strftime** and **wcsftime**.

Table 13.2 Members of the *lconv* structure.

Member	Value in "C" Locale	Description
char *decimal_point	"."	The decimal point character used for nonmonetary numbers.
char *thousands_sep	""	The character used to separate groups of digits to the left of the decimal of nonmonetary numbers.
char *grouping	""	The size of each group of digits in nonmonetary numbers. (See Table 13.3.)
char *int_curr_symbol	""	The international currency symbol; the first three characters specify the symbol and the fourth character specifies the character used to separate the currency symbol from the monetary number.
char *currency_symbol	""	The local currency symbol.
char *mon_decimal_ point	""	The decimal point character used for monetary numbers.
char *mon_ thousands_sep	""	The character used to separate groups of digits to the left of the decimal of monetary numbers.
char *mon_grouping	""	The size of each group of digits in monetary numbers. (See Table 13.3.)
char *positive_sign	""	The string used to indicate a nonnegative monetary number.
char *negative_sign	""	The string used to indicate a negative monetary number.
char int_frac_digits	CHAR_MAX	The number of fractional digits to be displayed in an international monetary number.
char frac_digits	CHAR_MAX	The number of fractional digits to be displayed in a noninternational monetary number.
char p_cs_precedes	CHAR_MAX	Set to 1 if **currency_symbol** precedes the value of a nonnegative monetary number; set to 0 if it follows such a number.
char p_sep_by_space	CHAR_MAX	Set to 1 if **currency_symbol** is separated by a space from the value of a nonnegative monetary number; set to 0 otherwise.

(continued)

Table 13.2   Members of the lconv structure (continued).

Member	Value in "C" Locale	Description
char n_cs_precedes	CHAR_MAX	Set to 1 if **currency_symbol** precedes the value of a negative monetary number; set to 0 if it follows such a number.
char n_sep_by_space	CHAR_MAX	Set to 1 if **currency_symbol** is separated by a space from the value of a negative monetary number; set to 0 otherwise.
char p_sign_posn	CHAR_MAX	Indicates the positioning of **positive_sign** for a nonnegative monetary number. (See Table 13.4.)
char n_sign_posn	CHAR_MAX	Indicates the positioning of **negative_sign** for a negative monetary number. (See Table 13.4.)

Table 13.3   Values for grouping and mon_grouping.

Value	Meaning
CHAR_MAX	No grouping is performed.
0	The previous element is used repeatedly for any remaining digits.
other	The integer value gives the number of digits that compose the group.

Table 13.4   Values for p_sign_posn and n_sign_posn.

Value	Meaning
0	Surround the number and currency symbol with parentheses.
1	Precede the number and currency symbol with the sign string.
2	Follow the number and currency symbol with the sign string.
3	Precede the currency symbol with the sign string.
4	Follow the currency symbol with the sign string.

Routines

***localeconv** (ANSI, Win 9x, Win NT)*
This routine retrieves detailed information on the current locale.

```
struct lconv *localeconv(void);
```

The routine returns a pointer to an **lconv** structure (see Table 13.2) that describes the current locale.

setlocale *(ANSI, Win 9x, Win NT)*
_wsetlocale *(Win 9x, Win NT)*
These routines define the current locale.

```
char *setlocale(int category, const char *locale);
wchar_t *_wsetlocale(int category, const wchar_t *locale);
```

They return a string associated with the specified locale and category, if the locale and category are valid; otherwise, they return **NULL**.

The **setlocale** and **_wsetlocale** routines contains the following parameters:

- *category*—The category affected by the locale (see Table 13.1).

- *locale*—The locale name. The special locale "" specifies the implementation-defined native environment.

Part III

The Visual C++ IDE

Visual C++ Basics

In Brief

The Visual C++ Toolkit

Visual C++ provides a rich assortment of tools, including:

- The ClassWizard, which acts as your assistant, automating routine programming tasks. (Chapters 17 and 18 describe the Visual C++ ClassWizard.)

- The Debugger, which lets you examine the state of your program as it executes. (Chapter 20 describes the Visual C++ Debugger.)

- Resource Editors, including:

NOTE: Chapter 20 describes the Visual C++ Resource Editors.

- The Accelerator Editor, which helps you work with accelerator key assignments.

- The Binary Editor, which lets you view and edit binary resources.

- The Dialog Editor, which lets you create and edit dialog boxes.

- The Graphics Editor, which lets you create and edit bitmaps, cursors, icons, and other images.

NOTE: The Graphics Editor is discussed in Chapter 22.

- The Menu Editor, which lets you create and edit menus.

- The String Editor, which lets you edit an application's string table.

- The Text Editor, which lets you create and edit source files.

NOTE: The Text Editor is the most important Visual C++ tool you'll work with, and is therefore covered in depth in this chapter. The section titled "The Text Editor" describes the commands supported by the Text Editor.

- The Toolbar Editor, which lets you create and edit toolbars.

- The Version Information Editor, which lets you create and maintain product identifiers, version numbers, and related information.

The Visual C++ environment lets you define *workspaces*, which contain the files that compose your application. More specifically, workspaces can contain:

- *Projects*—A project is a group of related files and typically includes all the files required to develop a single software component.

- *Configurations*—A configuration consists of settings, such as the identity of target platform, that determine the characteristics of the final output file for a project.

- *Subprojects*—A subproject is a dependent project. You can define a subproject in order to establish a dependency of one Visual C++ project on another project within the same workspace.

In addition to the tools mentioned earlier, Visual C++ includes an assortment of specialized tools. The section titled "Specialized Tools" briefly describes these tools.

14. Visual C++ Basics

Immediate Solutions

The Text Editor

The Visual C++ Text Editor helps you create and revise source files. Its operation is similar to that of other Windows-based programs, letting you select and edit text and search and navigate text files; it also includes a number of keystroke shortcuts that help you work efficiently. The text editor also lets you create bookmarks that mark your place in a file, making it quick and easy for you to return to commonly used locations within a text file.

Keystroke Shortcuts

The Visual C++ Text Editor includes keystroke shortcuts that help you:

- Create and manage bookmarks so that you can move between text in several source files.
- Select and edit text.
- Configure Text Editor options.
- Search for text.
- Navigate source files.

To view the available keystroke shortcuts from the Help menu, choose Keyboard Map. (Figure 14.1 shows the keyboard map.)

To view a sorted list, click on Category, Editor, Command, Keys, or Description to sort the keyboard shortcut list alphabetically by column.

To print the list, click on the Printer icon.

To copy the list to the Windows Clipboard, click on Copy to copy the list to the Clipboard so you can paste it into a word processor or other text editor.

To view only selected commands or all commands, click on the drop-down menu to filter the list to view either All Commands, Bound Commands, or commands sorted by menu.

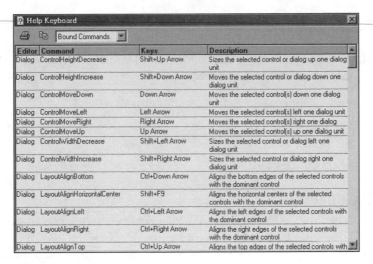

Figure 14.1 The keyboard map.

To assign a new keystroke shortcut:

1. On the Tools menu of the Visual C++ main window, click on Customize, and then click on the Keyboard tab of the Customize dialog box that appears.

2. In the Editor drop-down list, choose the editor to which you want to assign the shortcut key (for example, the Text Editor).

3. In the Categories list, choose the menu that contains the command to which you want to assign the shortcut key.

4. In the Commands list, choose the command to which you want to assign the shortcut key.

5. Click in the Press New Shortcut Key field, press on the keyboard the shortcut key or key combination that you want to assign to the command, and click on Assign.

   • If you press an invalid key or key combination, no key is displayed. You cannot assign key combinations with Esc, F1, or combinations that are already used by the operating system, such as Ctrl+Alt+Delete.

   • If you press a key or key combination that is currently assigned to another command, that command appears under Currently Assigned To.

To delete a keystroke shortcut:

1. On the Tools menu, click on Customize, and then click on the Keyboard tab.

2. On the Editor, Categories, and Commands lists, choose the location for the shortcut key you want to delete.

3. In the Current Keys list, choose the shortcut key you want to delete and click on Remove.

To reset all shortcut keys to their default values:

1. On the Tools menu, click on Customize, and then click on the Keyboard tab.

2. Click on Reset All.

Bookmarks

The Visual C++ Text Editor provides several commands that work with bookmarks. Bookmarks let you move between text in several source files. Table 14.1 summarizes the available bookmark commands. (Note that you can assign keystroke shortcuts to these commands for quick and easy access.)

Selection

The Visual C++ Text Editor provides an elaborate set of commands for selecting text. Table 14.2 summarizes the available selection commands. (Note that you can assign keystroke shortcuts to these commands.)

Table 14.1   Bookmark commands.

Command	Description
Bookmarks	Edits or navigates named bookmarks.
BookmarkClearAll	Clears all unnamed bookmarks.
BookmarkNext	Moves to the source line that contains the next named or unnamed bookmark.
BookmarkPrev	Moves to the source line that contains the previous named or unnamed bookmark.
BookmarkToggle	Toggles an unnamed bookmark for the current line.

Table 14.2   Selection commands.

Command	Description
CharLeftExtend	Extends the selection one character to the left.
CharRightExtend	Extends the selection one character to the right.
ConditionalDownExtend	Selects to the next matching preprocessor condition.

(continued)

Table 14.2   Selection commands (continued).

Command	Description
ConditionalUpExtend	Selects to the previous matching preprocessor condition.
DocumentEndExtend	Extends the selection to the end of the file.
DocumentStartExtend	Extends the selection to the beginning of the file.
HomeExtend	Extends the selection alternately between the start of the current line and the start of the text on that line.
LineDownExtend	Extends the selection one line down.
LineEndExtend	Extends the selection to the end of the text on the current line.
LineUpExtend	Extends the selection one line up.
PageDownExtend	Extends the selection one page down.
PageUpExtend	Extends the selection one page up.
SelectAll	Selects the entire document.
SelectChar	Starts the character-selection mode. When this mode is active, all other navigation commands select the characters from the position where the command was executed to the current cursor location.
SelectLine	Starts the line-selection mode. When this mode is active, all other navigation commands select lines from the position where the command was executed to the current cursor location.
SelectColumn	Starts the column-selection mode. In column-selection mode, the navigation keys act as if virtual space is enabled.
WordLeftExtend	Extends the selection backward one word.
WordRightExtend	Extends the selection forward one word.

14. Visual C++ Basics

Editing

The Visual C++ Text Editor provides an elaborate set of commands for editing text. Table 14.3 summarizes the available editing commands. (Note that you can assign keystroke shortcuts to these commands.)

Editor Configuration

The Visual C++ Text Editor provides several options that can be configured to suit your preferences. For example, searches can seek exact matches or matches that ignore capitalization. Table 14.4 summarizes the commands that set these options. If you like, you can

Table 14.3   Editing commands.

Command	Description
CharTranspose	Swaps characters adjacent to the cursor.
Copy	Copies the selection to the Clipboard.
Cut	Deletes the selection and copies it to the Clipboard.
Delete	Deletes the selection.
DeleteBack	Deletes the selection; or if there is no selection, deletes the character to the left of the cursor.
DeleteBlankLines	Deletes the blank lines adjacent to the cursor.
DeleteHorizontalSpace	Deletes spaces and tabs adjacent to the cursor.
SelectionFormat	Formats the selection using the smart indent settings.
IndentSelectionToPrev	Indents the selection to line up with the previous line's indentation.
LevelCutToEnd	Cuts the text between the cursor and the end of the next bracketed level.
LevelCutToStart	Cuts the text between the cursor and the beginning of the previous bracketed level.
LineCut	Deletes the selected lines and places them on the Clipboard.
LineDelete	Deletes the selected line.
LineDeleteToEnd	Deletes to the end of the current line.
LineDeleteToStart	Deletes to the beginning of the current line.
LineIndent	Indents the selected text one tab stop to the right.
LineOpenAbove	Opens a new line above the cursor.
LineOpenBelow	Opens a new line below the cursor.
LineTranspose	Swaps the current and previous lines.
LineUnindent	Indents the selected text one tab stop to the left.
SelectionLowercase	Changes the selection to all lowercase.
Paste	Inserts the Clipboard contents at the cursor.
SentenceCut	Deletes the remainder of the sentence.
SelectionTabify	Replaces spaces with tabs in the selection.
SelectionUntabify	Replaces tabs with spaces in the selection.
SelectionUppercase	Changes the selection to all uppercase.
WordCapitalize	Changes the first character to uppercase.
WordDeleteToEnd	Deletes the word to the right of the cursor.
WordDeleteToStart	Deletes the word to the left of the cursor.
WordLowerCase	Changes the current word to lowercase.
WordTranspose	Swaps the current and preceding words.
WordUpperCase	Changes the current word to uppercase.

Table 14.4   Editor configuration commands.

Command	Description
FindToggleCaseSensitivity	Toggles search case sensitivity.
FindToggleMatchWord	Toggles whole-word matching.
FindToggleOvertype	Toggles between insert and replace mode.
FindToggleRegExpr	Toggles the regular-expression search.
FindToggleAllDocs	Toggles searching across all open documents.
ToggleViewWhitespace	Toggles showing or hiding of tab characters.

assign a keystroke shortcut to any of these commands; however, most users configure the Text Editor only occasionally and prefer to reserve available keystroke shortcuts for other commands.

Go To

The Visual C++ Text Editor provides several commands that let you go to a specified location in a source file. In particular, several commands let you go directly to the line containing an error. The available Go To commands are summarized in Table 14.5. (Note that you can assign keystroke shortcuts to these commands.)

Searching

The Visual C++ Text Editor provides an elaborate set of commands, called *find commands*, that search for text. The available find commands are summarized in Table 14.6. Several of the find commands use regular expressions. Table 14.7 summarizes the regular-expression syntax. (Note that you can assign keystroke shortcuts to these commands.)

Navigation

The Visual C++ Text Editor provides a set of commands, called *navigation commands*, that move the cursor. These commands are frequently used, so programmers often associate them with keystroke shortcuts. The navigation commands are summarized in Table 14.8.

In addition, the Visual C++ Text Editor provides an additional set of navigation commands that require users to enter navigation criteria before the commands execute. These additional navigation commands are summarized in Table 14.9.

Table 14.5   Go To commands.

Command	Description
GoTo	Moves to a specified location.
GoToErrorTag	Moves to the line containing the current error or tag.
GoToNextErrorTag	Moves to the line containing the next error or tag.
GoToPrevErrorTag	Moves to the line containing the previous error or tag.
WindowList	Manages open windows.

Table 14.6   Find commands.

Command	Description
Find	Finds the specified text.
FindBackwardDlg	Opens the Find dialog box for searching backward.
FindForwardDlg	Opens the Find dialog box for searching forward.
FindNext	Continues searching forward, finding the next occurrence of the specified text.
FindNextWord	Finds the next whole-word occurrence of the selected text.
FindPrev	Finds the previous occurrence of the specified text.
FindPrevWord	Finds the previous whole-word occurrence of the selected text.
FindRegExpr	Finds the next string by using regular expressions.
FindRegExprPrev	Finds the previous string by using regular expressions.
FindRepeat	Continues the previous search.
FindReplace	Replaces specific text with different text.
FindReplaceRegExpr	Replaces specific text with different text, by using regular expressions.
SearchIncremental	Starts an incremental search forward.
SearchIncrementalBack	Starts an incremental search backward.

Table 14.7   Regular-expression syntax.

Regular Expression	Description
.	Any single character.
[ ]	Any one of the characters contained in the brackets, or any character in an ASCII range of characters separated by a hyphen (-). If the first character in the brackets is a caret (^), the regular expression matches any characters except those in the brackets.

(continued)

Table 14.7   Regular-expression syntax (continued).

Regular Expression	Description
^	The beginning of a line.
$	The end of a line.
\(\)	Indicates a tagged expression that is retained for replacement purposes. Each occurrence of a tagged expression is numbered according to its order in the Find What field; the corresponding replacement expression is \n, where 1 corresponds to the first tagged expression, 2 to the second, and so on. Up to nine tagged expressions are allowed.
\~	No match if the following character or characters occur.
\{c\!c\}	Any one of the characters separated by the alternation symbol (\!).
*	None or more of the preceding characters or expressions.
+	At least one or more of the preceding characters or expressions.
\{cc\}	Any sequence of characters between the escaped braces.
[^c]	Any character except those following the caret (^) character in the brackets, or any character in an ASCII range of characters separated by a hyphen (-).
\:a	Any single alphanumeric character [a–zA–Z0–9].
\:b	Any white space character.
\:c	Any single alphabetic character [a–zA–Z].
\:d	Any decimal digit [0–9].
\:n	Any unsigned number \{[0-9]+\.[0-9]*\![0-9]*\.[0-9]+\![0-9]+\}.
\:z	Any unsigned decimal integer [0–9]+.
\:h	Any hexadecimal number [0–9a–fA–F]+.
\:i	Any C/C++ identifier [a–zA–Z_$][a–zA–Z0–9_$]+.
\:w	Any alphabetic string [a–zA–Z]+.
\:q	Any quoted string \{"[^"]*"\!'[^']*'\}.
\	Removes the pattern match characteristic in the Find What field from the special characters listed previously, causing the special characters to be treated as ordinary.

14. Visual C++ Basics

Table 14.8   Navigation commands.

Command	Description
CharLeft	Moves the cursor one character to the left.
CharRight	Moves the cursor one character to the right.
ConditionalDown	Finds the next matching preprocessor condition.
ConditionalUp	Finds the previous matching preprocessor condition.
DocumentEnd	Moves the cursor to the end of the file.
DocumentStart	Moves the cursor to the beginning of the file.
GoToIndentation	Moves the cursor to the end of the indentation.
GoToMatchBrace	Finds the matching brace.
GoToMatchBraceExtend	Finds the matching brace and selects all text between the braces.
Home	Moves the cursor alternately between the beginning of the current line and the beginning of the text on that line.
IndentToPrev	Moves the cursor to the position of the next text that is on the previous line.
LevelDown	Searches forward to the end of the next bracketed level.
LevelUp	Searches backward to the beginning of the previous bracketed level.
LineDown	Moves the cursor one line downward.
LineEnd	Moves the cursor to the end of the text on the current line.
LineStart	Moves the cursor to the beginning of the current line.
LineUp	Moves the cursor one line upward.
PageDown	Moves the cursor one page downward.
PageUp	Moves the cursor one page upward.
ParaDown	Moves the cursor forward to the beginning of the next paragraph.
ParaUp	Moves the cursor backward to the beginning of the previous paragraph.
SentenceLeft	Moves the cursor backward to the beginning of the preceding sentence.
SentenceRight	Moves the cursor forward to the end of the next sentence.
WindowEnd	Moves the cursor to the bottom of the text window.
WindowStart	Moves the cursor to the top of the text window.
WordLeft	Moves the cursor backward one word.
WordRight	Moves the cursor forward one word.

Table 14.9   Additional navigation commands.

Command	Prompt	Response
Address	Enter address expression	Type a valid debugger expression.
Bookmark	Enter bookmark name	Type a bookmark name.
Definition	Enter identifier	Type an identifier. (Note: This requires browse information.)
Error/Tag	Enter error/tag	Select one of the listed error/tags.
Line	Enter line number	Type a line number.
Offset	Enter offset	Type a decimal or hexadecimal number.
Reference	Enter identifier	Type an identifier. (Note: This requires browse information.)

Workspaces

This section describes how to create, open, and close workspaces. (Chapter 15 describes how to work with projects, configurations, and subprojects.)

Creating A Workspace

Visual C++ lets you create a new project workspace in one of two ways:

- You can use the New Project Wizard to create the initial project. The wizard will automatically create a project workspace that includes the appropriate starter files.

- You can create a blank project workspace. In this case, you must create all the files, select the project(s) to be included in the project workspace, and add the appropriate files to the project. You must use this approach to create a workspace that has a name or location that is different from the name and location of every project it will contain. After you create the blank workspace, you can create a new project with any desired name and location and insert it into the workspace.

To use the New Project Wizard:

1. From the File menu, click on New.

2. In the New dialog box, click on the Projects tab and choose from the available project types to launch the wizard.

14. Visual C++ Basics

To create a blank project workspace:

1. On the File menu, click on New.

2. In the New dialog box, click on the Workspaces tab.

3. Choose Blank Workspace from the type list, and enter a name in the Workspace Name field (see Figure 14.2).

4. If necessary, use the Location field to specify the directory where the project workspace files are stored.

Opening An Existing Workspace

To open an existing project workspace:

1. On the File menu, click on Open Workspace.

2. In the Open dialog box, select the drive and directory containing the project workspace.

3. Select the DSW file for the project workspace from the File Name list and click on Open (see Figure 14.3).

Visual C++ maintains a list of the project workspaces that you've recently opened. This list makes opening one of these workspaces quicker and more convenient. You can reopen a recently used project workspace one of two ways:

- On the File menu, click on Recent Workspaces, and then click on the name of the recently used workspace.

- On the File menu, click on the name of the workspace.

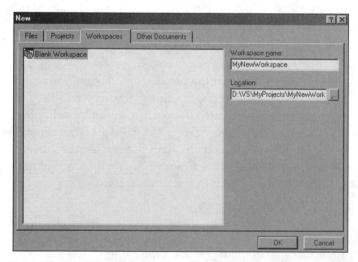

Figure 14.2   Using the Workspaces tab to create a blank project workspace.

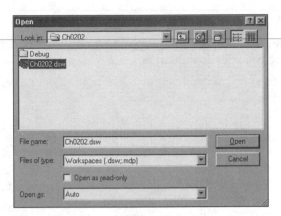

Figure 14.3   Opening an existing workspace.

Closing A Workspace

To close a project workspace, on the File menu, click on Close Workspace.

Displaying And Hiding The Workspace Window

Visual C++ lets you display or hide the workspace window. Of course, in order to view or hide the workspace window, you must have a workspace loaded.

To display the Workspace window, on the View menu, click on Workspace.

To hide the Project Workspace window:

1. Place the mouse cursor anywhere in the Project Workspace window and right-click to display the shortcut menu.

2. On the shortcut menu, click on Hide.

Unloading And Loading A Project From A Workspace

When Visual C++ builds your program, it builds every loaded project. You can unload a project from a workspace when the project is not immediately needed. Doing so can help you work more efficiently by reducing the time required to open and close or build the workspace. Unloading a project does not delete it from the workspace; you can easily reload a project so that builds will once again include the project's output files.

To unload or load a project:

1. On the FileView tab of the Project Workspace, right-click on the project you wish to unload or load.

2. From the pop-up menu, choose Unload Project or Load Project (see Figure 14.4).

NOTE: *Unload Project appears for loaded projects whereas Load Project appears for unloaded projects.*

When the project is unloaded, its icon changes to a folder and the words "not loaded" appear adjacent to it.

Figure 14.4   Unloading a project from a workspace.

Specialized Tools

In addition to its basic tools and wizards, Visual C++ includes several other useful tools. The following sections summarize the main features of the most commonly used tools. You start any of the tools in the same way:

1. Click on the Start button on the Windows Taskbar and choose Programs.

2. From the Programs submenu, choose Microsoft Visual C++ 6.0.

3. Choose Microsoft Visual C++ 6.0 Tools, then click on the tool you want to use.

DDESpy

The DDESpy tool, shown in Figure 14.5, monitors Dynamic Data Exchange (DDE) operations in the host operating system. DDE is a form of interprocess communication used by applications to exchange data.

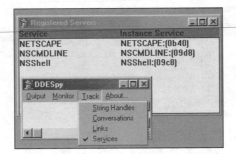

Figure 14.5   The DDESpy tool.

Because DDE employs shared memory (an efficient means of interprocess communication), applications can use DDE for one-time data transfers and for ongoing exchanges and updating of data.

After starting DDESpy, use its menus to specify the information you want to view. Use the Track menu to specify the activities you want to monitor. DDESpy displays a separate window for each activity. Supported activities are:

- String handles
- Conversations
- Links
- Services

DDESpy can also report the details of DDE activities as they occur. The Monitor menu lets you specify the types of information you're interested in, which can be any or all of the following:

- String handle data
- Sent DDE messages
- Posted DDE messages
- Callbacks
- Errors

To create a permanent record of monitored data and activity, you can use DDESpy's File menu to send DDESpy output to a file.

Process Viewer

The Process Viewer (PView) tool, shown in Figure 14.6, lets you examine and modify characteristics of processes and threads. The PView tool is particularly helpful in understanding how processes and threads are using memory. You can also use PView to kill processes and

14. Visual C++ Basics

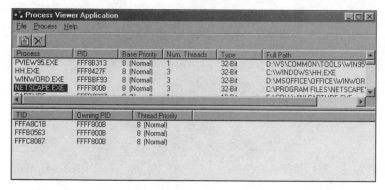

Figure 14.6   The Process Viewer tool.

threads; however, you should do so with caution, because killing processes or threads indiscriminately can crash your system.

The PView window has an upper pane and a lower pane. The upper pane displays a list of processes. If you click on a process, the lower pane of the PView window displays information about the threads owned by that process. Clicking on a column head in either part of the PView window causes PView to sort its output by the chosen column.

To kill a process:

1. Click on its row in the upper pane of the PView window.
2. Choose Kill from the Process menu.

You can kill a thread in a similar fashion, by first clicking on its row in the lower pane of the PView window.

Spy++

The Spy++ tool, shown in Figure 14.7, gives you a graphical view of processes, threads, windows, and window messages. Its functions are similar to those of DDESpy and PView; however, Spy++ cannot alter process or thread characteristics. Therefore, using Spy++ is somewhat safer than using PView.

Spy++ provides four distinct views:

- *Windows view*—Displays when Spy++ starts. It shows all windows in the system. The Windows view is organized as a tree in which each branch shows a child window and its children, if any. The current desktop window is at the top of the tree.

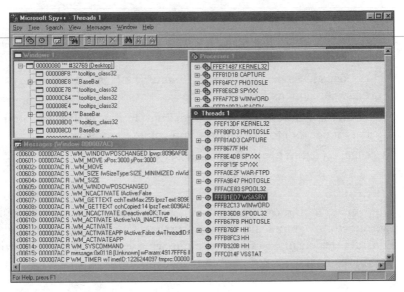

Figure 14.7   The Spy++ tool.

- *Processes view*—Shows processes and their threads. If a thread owns windows, the Processes view shows these as well. Like the Windows view, the Processes view is organized as a tree.

- *Threads view*—Shows threads and the windows they own. The Threads view does not show processes.

- *Messages view*—Shows messages associated with a window, thread, or process. You can designate which window, thread, or process a Messages view window monitors.

You can have multiple views open simultaneously. Use the Spy++ window to open any desired views. To open a Messages view for a particular window, thread, or process:

1. Move the focus to a Windows, Processes, or Threads view window.

2. Click on the window, process, or thread that you want to examine.

3. From the Spy menu, choose Messages.

4. Choose the message options you want.

5. Click OK to begin logging messages.

When you're done, choose Stop Logging from the Messages menu.

You can quickly associate a Messages view with any open window:

1. Arrange your windows so that both Spy++ and the window you want to monitor are visible.

2. Choose Messages from the Spy menu. The Message Options dialog box opens.

3. From the Windows tab of the Message Options dialog box, drag the Finder tool to the window you want to monitor.

4. Click on OK to begin logging messages.

WinDiff

The WinDiff tool, shown in Figure 14.8, compares two source files or two directories, graphically highlighting the differences between them. WinDiff is especially useful when comparing versions of a single program, making it easy to determine how they differ.

To use WinDiff:

1. Select Open from the File menu. A File Open dialog box appears.

2. Navigate to the first of the two files and click on Open. A new File Open dialog box appears.

3. Navigate to the second of the two files and click on Open. WinDiff displays a summary of the differences between the files.

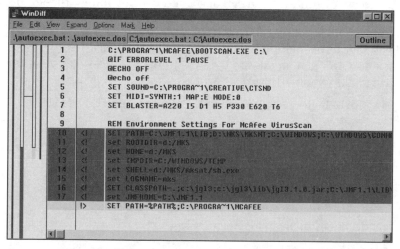

Figure 14.8   The WinDiff tool.

Table 14.10 summarizes the operations available by using WinDiff's menus.

Table 14.10   *WinDiff menus.*

Menu	Menu Item	Function
File	Compare Files	Displays the File Open dialog box, which lets you specify which files to compare.
	Compare Directories	Displays the Select Directories dialog box, which lets you specify which directories to compare.
	Abort	Terminates a file-scanning operation. This menu selection is available only during a scanning operation.
	Save File List	Displays the Save File List dialog box, which lets you specify the output file to which comparison results are written.
	Copy Files	Displays the Copy Files dialog box, which lets you specify the files to be copied from one directory to another.
	Print	Prints comparison results.
	Exit	Terminates WinDiff.
Edit	Edit Left File	Displays the contents of the first (left) file by using the currently specified editor.
	Edit Right File	Displays the contents of the second (right) file by using the currently specified editor.
	Edit Composite File	Displays both files by using the currently specified editor.
	Set Editor	Displays a WinDiff dialog box, which lets you specify the editor you want to use.
View	Outline	Displays only the list of file names.
	Expand	Displays comparison of the contents of selected files.
	Picture	Displays a graphical view of the contents of the two files.
	Previous Change	Finds the previous area of the file that was changed.
	Next Change	Finds the next area of the file that was changed.
	Rescan Selected File	Compares the selected file again.
Expand	Left File Only	Expands only the first (left) file.
	Right File Only	Expands only the second (right) file.
	Both Files	Expands both files.
	Left Line Numbers	Displays line numbers for the first (left) file.
	Right Line Numbers	Displays line numbers for the second (right) file.
	No Line Numbers	Turns off the line number display.

(continued)

Table 14.10   WinDiff menus (continued).

Menu	Menu Item	Function
Options	Ignore Blanks	Ignores white space in the expanded view, so that lines differing only in white space are treated as identical.
	Mono Colours	Displays differences in black and white only.
	Show Identical Files	In Outline view, displays files that are identical.
	Show Left-Only Files	In Outline view, displays files that appear only in the first (left) path.
	Show Right-Only Files	In Outline view, displays files that appear only in the second (right) path.
	Show Different Files	In Outline view, displays files that are in both paths, but are different.
Mark	Mark File	Marks selected comparison results.
	Mark Pattern	Displays the Mark Files dialog box, which lets you specify the file marking pattern.
	Hide Marked Files	Hides all marked files.
	Toggle Marked State	Reverses the marked status of marked and unmarked files.

ZoomIn

The ZoomIn tool, shown in Figure 14.9, lets you capture and enlarge an area of a window for better visibility.

To use ZoomIn:

1. Click within the ZoomIn window's client area and drag the zoom rectangle over the target area you want to view. The enlarged image appears in the ZoomIn window.

2. Use the ZoomIn window's scroll bar to adjust the magnification factor as desired.

Figure 14.9   The ZoomIn tool.

Other Tools

Visual C++ includes several other tools that you can launch from the Windows Taskbar. These tools are more specialized and less often used than the tools presented in the previous sections, so they're not presented here in detail. These tools include:

- *ActiveX Control Test Container*—This tool helps you test ActiveX controls.
- *AVI Editor*—This tool lets you edit Audio Video Interlaced (AVI) files.
- *DataObject Viewer*—This tool is used for viewing objects that support the **DataObject** interface.
- *Depends (Dependency Walker)*—This tool reports intermodular dependencies.
- *DocFile Viewer*—This tool displays the contents of an OLE2 DocFile.
- *Error Lookup*—This tool retrieves a system or module error message, based on an error code you enter.
- *Heap Walk Utility*—This tool reports the contents of the heap.
- *Help Workshop*—This tool is a graphical help authoring environment.
- *OLE Client Test*—This tool helps you test OLE clients.
- *OLE Server Test*—This tool helps you test OLE servers.
- *OLE View*—This tool views OLE and COM objects.
- *ROT Viewer*—This tool displays the contents of OLE's running-object table.
- *Stress Utility*—This tool acquires system resources so that you can test programs under low-resource conditions.
- *Tracer*—This tool works with the Debugger to provide trace information.

14. Visual C++ Basics

Projects

Working With Workspaces And Projects

Visual C++ workspaces can contain projects, configurations, and sub-projects. You can designate a project as the active project. When you use a Build command, Visual C++ builds the active project.

Visual C++ lets you add and remove projects from workspaces and add and remove files from projects. You can also move or copy files from one workspace to another. You can organize the contents of your workspaces by creating subprojects and folders within them.

Visual C++ provides a variety of options and configuration settings that control how it builds your projects. You can export these options and settings as makefiles.

Visual C++ lets you build all the projects in a workspace or build only selected projects. After all the projects of a workspace have been built, you can run the resulting program.

15. Projects

Immediate Solutions

Setting The Active Project

When you use the Build or Rebuild All commands, Visual C++ builds the active project. You can set the active project one of two ways:

- On the Project menu, click on Set Active Project and choose from the submenu of project names, as shown in Figure 15.1.

- On the Build toolbar, choose a project from the Select Active Project drop-down list. You can view the Build toolbar by right-clicking on an empty part of the menu bar and selecting Build.

Figure 15.1   Setting the active project.

Inserting Or Deleting Projects

You can insert a new or existing project into a project workspace and delete an existing project from the workspace.

Inserting A New Project Into An Existing Workspace

To insert a new project into an existing workspace:

1. Open the project workspace to which you want to add a new project.

2. On the File menu, click on New, and then click on the Projects tab (see Figure 15.2).

3. Select the project type.

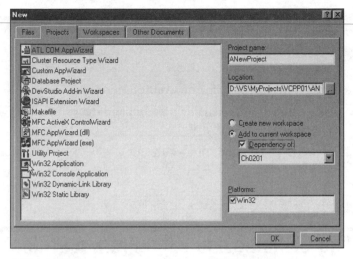

Figure 15.2   Inserting a new project into an existing workspace.

4. Enter the project name and location for the project.

5. Click on the Add To Current Workspace radio button.

6. Choose any of the available platforms for which you want to create initial Debug and Release configurations.

7. Click on OK.

The new project becomes the default project in the workspace.

Adding An Existing Project To An Existing Workspace

To add an existing project to an existing workspace:

1. Open the project workspace.

2. On the Project menu, click on Insert Project Into Workspace.

3. In the Insert Project Into Workspace dialog box, browse to the project you want to add.

4. If you want the project to be a subproject of another project, click on the Dependency Of checkbox and select the name of the other project from the list in the Dependency Of drop-down list (refer back to Figure 15.2).

Deleting A Project From A Workspace

To delete a project from a workspace, choose the project from the FileView pane of the Workspace window and press the Delete key.

15. Projects

WARNING!   *Deleting a project removes it as a subproject from any other project in the workspace.*

To delete a project configuration:

1. On the Build menu, click on Configurations.

2. In the Configurations dialog box, expand the project that you want to delete.

3. Choose each configuration you want to delete, and click on Remove.

Adding Or Removing Files From A Project

Projects are not static: You can add and remove files from projects. For example, you may want to add a source file prepared by another program. Or, you may combine the contents of two source files and remove one of them from the project.

Adding Files To A Project

To add a file to a project:

1. Open the project to which you want to add files.

2. On the Project menu, click on Add To Project, and then click on Files.

3. In the Files Of Type list, choose the type of files to add.

4. Choose one or more files you want to add.

5. Click on OK.

NOTE: *You can use the pop-up menu from FileView to add files quickly.*

When you add a file to a project, the file is added to all configurations for that project. If you add files from directories on a different drive than the project, Visual C++ places absolute paths for those files in the project's DSP file.

Such absolute paths may complicate sharing the project with other developers in your group, who may have other drive names. To support sharing files outside the project directory, you can use the Persist As field in the source file's property page. In the Persist As field, enter a replacement path for the shared file. You can include the value of an environment variable in the path by writing the name of the environment variable in uppercase letters, enclosing it within parentheses, and preceding the parentheses with a dollar sign (**$**). For example, to reference the environment variable **root**, you would write **$(ROOT)**.

Moving Or Copying Files From One Workspace To Another

To move or copy files from one workspace to another:

1. From the FileView pane, choose the files that you want to move or copy.

2. On the Edit menu, click on Cut if you want to move the files, or on Copy if you want to copy the files.

3. Close the current project workspace.

4. Open the destination project workspace.

5. Choose the project to receive the files.

6. On the Edit menu, click on Paste.

Removing Files From A Project

To remove files from a project:

1. From the FileView pane, choose the files that you want to remove.

2. On the Edit menu, click on Delete.

Working With Subprojects

A subproject is a project that has a dependency relationship with another project. This dependency may consist of shared files that need to be built in the subproject first; or it may include shared resources that need to be updated in the subproject first. The dependency relationship is established by configuration settings.

Creating A New Project As A Subproject

To create a new project as a subproject:

1. On the File menu, click on New, and then click on the Projects tab (refer back to Figure 15.2).

2. Choose the project name and location for the new project.

3. Click on Add To Current Workspace, click on the Dependency Of checkbox, and then choose from the drop-down list the name of the project you want the new project to be a sub-project of.

4. Double-click on the appropriate icon for your project type.

Including An Existing Project As A Subproject

To include an existing project as a subproject:

1. Open the workspace that contains the project to which you want to add an existing project as a subproject.

2. On the Project menu, click on Insert Project Into Workspace.

3. Choose the project (.dsp) file you want to insert as a sub-project.

4. Click on the Dependency Of checkbox, and then choose the parent project from the drop-down list.

5. Click on OK.

Removing A Subproject From A Project

To remove a subproject from a project, click on the project in the FileView pane and then choose Delete from the Edit menu.

Working With Folders

Subprojects help you organize your projects. A second way to organize your projects is by using folders.

Adding A Folder

Visual C++ organizes project files as folders in the FileView pane of the project workspace. Visual C++ creates folders for source files, header files, and resource files, but you can reorganize these folders and create new ones. For example, you can use folders to organize related sets of files within the hierarchy of a project.

When Visual C++ adds a new file to a project, it consults the File Extensions field of the folder's properties page. If the file extension of the added file is listed in the folder's File Extensions field, Visual C++ automatically adds the file to the folder that holds files of its type.

To add a folder to a project:

1. On the Project menu, click on Add To Project.

2. Click on New Folder.

3. Enter the name of the new folder.

4. Enter the file extensions for the folder.

Renaming A Folder

To rename a folder:

1. Right-click on the folder you want to rename.

2. Click on Properties.

3. On the General tab, type the new folder name.

Working With Makefiles

A makefile records information that describes how to build a project. You can load a makefile (conventionally named **MAKEFILE** or **filename.mak**) into the Visual C++ project system either as a separate workspace or as a project that is part of the current workspace. You can also add a makefile to a project.

Loading A Makefile As A Project

You can load a makefile as a project one of two ways:

• On the File menu, click on Open.

• On the File menu, click on Open Workspace.

To add a makefile as a project in the current workspace, click on Insert Project Into Workspace on the Project menu.

To add the makefile to an existing project, on the Project menu, click on Add To Project, then click on Files.

When you open a makefile as a project, Visual C++ does one of the following:

• For makefiles created in the current version of Visual C++, it opens the associated workspace.

• For makefiles that were created in an earlier version of Visual C++, it presents a message box that asks if you want to convert the project to the current format. If you click on No, Visual C++

does not open the file. If you click on Yes, Visual C++ upgrades the makefile project, adding it and any associated files to the workspace or creating a new workspace.

- For makefiles that were not created in the Visual C++ environment, presents a message box that asks if you want to create a project for the makefile. If you click on No, Visual C++ does not open the file. If you click on Yes, Visual C++ creates a project workspace file, with other associated project files for the external makefile, which becomes a part of the project workspace.

Exporting A Makefile

To export a makefile:

1. From the Project menu, choose Export Makefile.

2. In the Export Makefile(s) dialog box, choose the project(s) for which you want to create a makefile, as shown in Figure 15.3. A separate makefile is created for each project you select.

3. If you want Visual C++ to automatically update dependency information, check the Write Dependencies When Writing Makefiles checkbox.

When you direct Visual C++ to export a makefile, it performs two steps. First, it creates the MAK file, and then it creates or updates the corresponding DEP file. The first time you export a MAK file, Visual C++ creates an include file (*projectname*.dep) that contains information about any included files required to build the project. Within the MAK file, Visual C++ inserts an **!include** directive that references the *projectname*.dep file. Once the DEP file exists, you can specify whether you want Visual C++ to export the dependency information when it exports the MAK file.

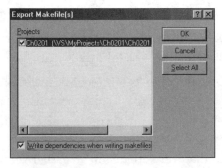

Figure 15.3   Exporting a makefile.

You can greatly increase the speed of exporting MAK files by exporting dependency information only when you want to update the DEP file. You may not need or wish to update dependency information when, for example, only compiler switches have changed.

By default, Visual C++ applies the information written to the DEP file to all build configurations. If you prefer, you can specify that the dependency information be written on a per-configuration basis.

Automatically Exporting A Makefile

If you want Visual C++ to automatically export the makefile each time you update the project, you can specify the export makefile option. To do this:

1. From the Tools menu, choose Options.
2. On the Build tab, check the Export Makefile When Saving Project File checkbox.

Selecting this option will increase the time required to save the project.

Automatically Writing Dependency Information

If you want Visual C++ to automatically write dependency information each time you update the project, you can specify the write dependencies option:

1. From the Tools menu, choose Options.
2. On the Build tab, check the Always Write Dependencies When Writing Makefiles checkbox.

Selecting this option will considerably increase the time required to write the MAK file.

Specifying Dependency Information

You can specify distinct dependency information for each configuration by using the All Per-Configuration configuration dependencies option in the Export Makefile dialog box. To set this option, on the General tab, check the Allow Per-Configuration Dependencies checkbox.

Selecting this option increases the time it takes to write the dependency information.

Adjusting The Build Settings

Visual C++ provides many configuration settings that you can apply to projects. You can also set configurations for specific files within a project.

Specifying Project Settings

To specify project configuration settings:

1. On the Project menu, click on Settings.

2. On the General tab, choose the project or projects you want to configure.

3. In the Settings For pane, choose the configuration, or choose All Configurations, as shown in Figure 15.4.

4. Click on OK to save the settings.

You can apply the options in the Project Settings dialog box to several projects, but the settings apply only to the selected project configuration, unless you select the All Configurations option.

Setting File Options

In general, the settings for a project configuration affect all files in that project. However, you can specify settings for a given file that are different from the project configuration's settings.

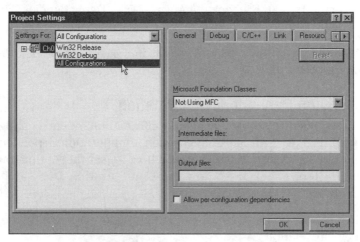

Figure 15.4   Specifying project settings.

To set file options:

1. On the Project menu, click on Settings, and then choose the General tab.

2. Under the Settings For drop-down control, expand the project or projects that contain the files for which you wish to specify settings.

3. Choose the files, and then, on any available tab, choose the options that you want to apply to the files.

   The available tabs depend on the files or configurations that you have selected. Only those tabs with settings common to the selections appear. Within each tab, only the settings common to all the files selected are available.

Setting The Active Project Configuration

You can build a project in several ways:

• You can build just the selected project.

• You can build all the projects.

• You can specific project configuration.

When you set the active project configuration, subsequent Build commands act on the active configuration and build its output.

You can set the active project one of two ways:

• On the Build menu, choose Set Active Configuration, and click on a project configuration in the Set Active Project Configuration dialog box, as shown in Figure 15.5.

• On the Build toolbar, choose a project configuration from the Select Active Configuration drop-down list.

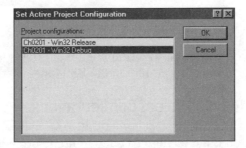

Figure 15.5   Setting the active configuration.

15. Projects

Building A Project

When you direct Visual C++ to build a project, Visual C++ compiles the source files to produce the result files.

Building The Active Project Configuration

To build the active project configuration, on the Build menu, click on Build *project*, where *project* is the program or library defined by the project configuration.

Rebuilding The Active Project Configuration

When you build a project, Visual C++ generates only files that it believes may be affected by changes to source files since the last time the project was built. Sometimes Visual C++ mistakenly fails to rebuild a file. You can cause Visual C++ to generate every file afresh by requesting that Visual C++ rebuild the project.

To rebuild a project, click on Rebuild All on the Build menu.

Visual C++ performs builds as a background task, so you can continue to use Visual C++ during a build. However, some menu commands and toolbar buttons may be disabled during a build. You can use the tabs at the bottom of the Output window to view the output from one phase of the build while another phase executes.

Visual C++ notifies you with a beep when the build is complete. If you have a sound card installed, you can use the Sound program in the Windows Control Panel to assign distinct sounds to the three standard system events listed below:

- *Asterisk (*)*—Indicates that the build completed without errors or warnings.
- *Question (?)*—Indicates that the build completed with warnings.
- *Exclamation (!)*—Indicates that errors occurred during the build.

Stopping A Build

Sometimes you may want to terminate a build that's in progress. To stop a build, click on Stop Build on the Build menu.

Building Multiple Project Configurations

You can build multiple project configurations as a single operation by using the Batch Build facility. To build multiple projects:

1. On the Build menu, click on Batch Build. The resulting dialog box is shown in Figure 15.6.

2. If you don't want to build certain project configurations, clear the associated checkboxes in the Project Configurations window.

3. Click on Build to build only those intermediate files of each project configuration that are out-of-date, or click on the Rebuild All button to build all intermediate files for each project configuration.

Building All The Projects In The Workspace

You can build all the projects in the workspace in a single operation. To do so, choose Build from the Build menu.

Building The Selected Project

If you like, you can build only a selected project:

1. From the FileView pane, highlight the project.

2. Right-click on the project, and choose Build (Selection Only) from the pop-up menu.

Cleaning The Active Project

Cleaning a project deletes intermediate and output files not needed to build the project. To clean the active project, choose Clean from the Build menu.

NOTE: *You can also clean a project by using the Clean button on the Batch Build dialog box.*

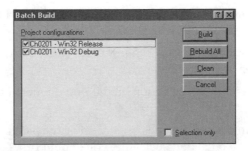

Figure 15.6   Building multiple project configurations.

15. Projects

Cleaning A Specific Project

To clean a specific project:

1. From the FileView pane, right-click on the project.

2. From the pop-up menu, choose Clean (Selection Only).

Building A Console Program From A Single Source File

You can create a single source file and then build a console program directly from it. This method is sometimes useful for relatively simple programs.

To build a console program from a single source file:

1. Close any open project workspace.

2. Create or open a source file in a text editor window.

3. On the Build menu, click on Build.

4. In the message box, click on Yes.

   If necessary, give the source file a new name, with an appropriate extension for a file type that Visual C++ can build, such as .CPP. If you don't provide a valid file extension, Visual C++ will not perform the build.

5. Click on OK.

Visual C++ creates a default project workspace using the base name of the source file as the base name for the project. It uses the default project configuration settings appropriate for a console program and builds the program.

Compiling Selected Files

You can select and compile desired files in any project in your project workspace. To compile selected files:

1. Choose the files in the FileView pane of the Project Workspace window.

2. Right-click on the selection on the pop-up menu, and click on Compile.

   If the project file depends on any other file, such as a precompiled header (.pch) file, you should first ensure that the dependent file is up to date.

Executing Programs

Visual C++ lets you run your program without exiting the Visual C++ environment. You can run the program normally or in debug mode.

Running A Program

To run a program, click on Execute on the Build menu.

Running A Program In The Debugger

To run a program in the Visual C++ Debugger:

1. Click on Start Debug on the Build menu

2. Click on Start Debug.

3. From the drop-down menu, click on Go|Step Into, or if you have an open source file open that has the focus, click on Run To Cursor.

Chapter 16

Working With ClassView

In Brief

ClassView And The ClassView Pane

When you open a project that contains a C++ class definition, the ClassView pane appears. ClassView graphically presents your classes, class members, globals, and COM interfaces. ClassView also lets you navigate source code: You can simply double-click on a ClassView icon to jump directly to the associated code.

ClassView also helps you:

- Create a new class or form.
- Create function or method declarations and implementations.
- Edit a dialog box by using the Dialog Editor.
- Edit COM interfaces.

ClassView works closely with the Text Editor. As you change code using the Text Editor, ClassView immediately updates its display.

Immediate Solutions

Working With The ClassView Pane

Figure 16.1 shows the ClassView pane, which shows all the C++ classes declared in a project header file for which definitions are available. The ClassView pane also shows the members of those classes. Figure 16.2 shows the icons that ClassView uses to depict classes and their members.

Sorting Class Members

By default, ClassView displays class members in alphabetical order. If you prefer, you can group class members by their access specifier—private, protected, or public.

To sort members in a class:

1. Choose a class icon.
2. Right-click to display the pop-up menu.

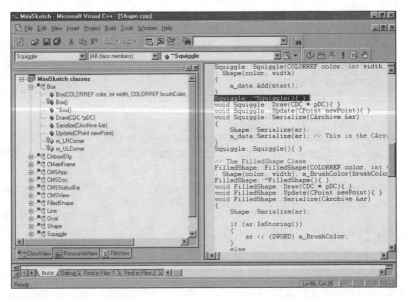

Figure 16.1   The ClassView pane.

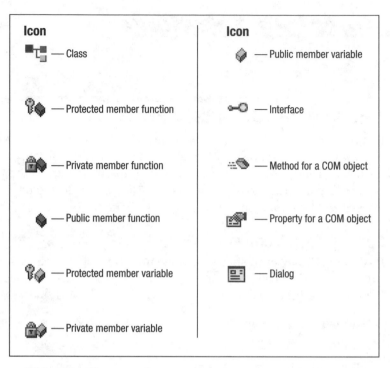

Figure 16.2 ClassView pane icons.

3. Choose Group By Access to toggle the grouping.

   If the Group By Access command is checked, the members are already grouped by access specifier; otherwise, they are grouped alphabetically.

Adding A Folder To ClassView

You can organize project classes simply by adding a new folder to ClassView. ClassView folders can contain any classes belonging to the project, but they cannot contain nonclass files such as text or resource files, which can be organized using FileView or ResourceView.

To add a folder to ClassView:

1. In ClassView, choose the project to which you want to add a folder.

2. Right-click and choose New Folder from the pop-up menu.

ClassView folders can contain other folders, but a class cannot contain a folder.

Once you create a new folder for a project, you can simply drag classes into the folder to organize your project classes. However, you cannot move classes from one project into a folder under a different project.

Adding A Class To A Project

ClassView makes it easy to open the New Class dialog box that assists you in adding a class to your project. To open the New Class dialog box:

1. Right-click on the project icon in ClassView.

2. Click on New Class on the pop-up menu.

The New Class dialog box has forms for four different classes:

- Generic classes
- MFC classes
- ATL classes
- Form-based classes

Visual C++ is aware of the type of the active project and presents an appropriate form of the New Class dialog box. Table 16.1 summarizes the class types available from the New Class dialog box for MFC and ATL projects.

Adding A Generic Class

A generic class is a class that you define or that is derived from a class that you define. To add a generic class to your project:

1. Open the New Class dialog box as described in the previous section.

Table 16.1   Class types supported by the New Class dialog box.

	MFC .exc Project	MFC .exe Project With ATL Support	ATL COM Project	ATL COM Project With MFC Support
New Generic Class	X	X	X	X
New MFC Class	X	X		X
New ATL Class		X	X	X
New Form Class	X	X		X

2. From the Class Type drop-down list, choose Generic Class (see Figure 16.3).

3. In the Name field, type the name of the new class.

   The name you specify is used to establish the file name, which is indicated in the read-only File Name field. By default, the header file and the implementation file share the same name as the class file; the header file has the extension .h, and the implementation file has the extension .cpp.

4. If you want to change the names of the header and implementation files for this class, click on the Change button and type the names into the Change Files dialog box.

5. If you want to add the new class to an existing file, click on Change, then click on the Browse button and locate the file you wish to add it to.

6. Type the name of the base class from which to derive the new class in the Derived From column under the heading Base Class(es). In the As column, click on the access you want the new generic class to have with regard to the base class: Public, Protected, or Private.

7. Click on OK to create the new class and add it to the project.

The new class immediately appears in ClassView, and you can view its header and implementation files in the FileView pane of the project workspace.

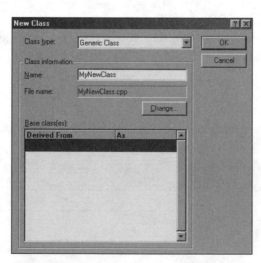

Figure 16.3   Adding a generic class.

Adding An MFC Class

An MFC class is a class derived from one or more MFC (Microsoft Foundation Classes) classes. To add an MFC class to your project:

1. Open the New Class dialog box as described in the section "Adding A Class To A Project" earlier in the chapter.

2. In the Class Type drop-down list, choose MFC Class (See Figure 16.4).

3. Type the name of the new class in the Name field.

   The name you specify is used to establish the file name, which is indicated in the read-only File Name field. By default, the header file and the implementation file share the same name as the class file; the header file has the extension .h, and the implementation file has the extension .cpp.

4. If you want to change the names of the header and implementation files for this class, click on the Change button and type the names into the Change Files dialog box.

5. If you want to add the new class to an existing file, click on Change, then click on the Browse button and locate the file you wish to add it to.

6. Choose a base class from which to derive the new class. There are two kinds of MFC classes:

   - Classes that do not require a resource ID

   - Classes that do require a resource ID

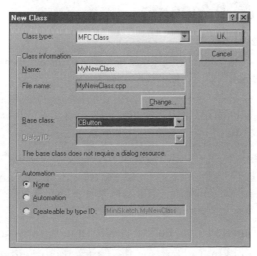

Figure 16.4   Adding an MFC class.

NOTE: *Classes, such as **CButton**, that are derived from base classes other than*
***CDaoRecordView**, **CDialog**, **CFormView**, **CPropertyPage**, or **CRecordView** do not require a*
resource ID. Because these classes do not require a resource ID, the Dialog ID drop-down list of
the New Class dialog box is not active. For classes that require a resource ID, you'll find it easier
to first use the Dialog Editor to create the resource and its ID. You can then use ClassWizard to
create a class associated with the resource ID.

---

7. For dialog-based classes, choose the resource with which the class is to be associated from the Dialog ID drop-down list.

8. Choose the desired type of Automation support—None, Automation, or Createable By Type ID:

    • Choose None if you want the new class to have no Automation capability.

    • Choose Automation if you want to expose the capabilities of the new class through Automation.

    • Choose Createable By Type ID if you want to allow other applications to create objects of this class using Automation.

9. Click on OK to create the new class and add it to the project.

The new class immediately appears in ClassView, and you can view its header and implementation files in the FileView pane of the project workspace.

Working With Member Functions And Variables

You can use ClassView to add or delete member functions and variables of a class.

Adding A Member Function

To add a member function using ClassView:

1. Choose the class to which you want to add a function.

2. Right-click on the class to display the pop-up menu, and choose Add Member Function. The Add Member Function dialog box appears (see Figure 16.5).

3. In the Function Type field, type the function's return type.

4. In the Function Declaration field, type the function declaration. Type only the function name, followed by a list of the names and types of formal parameters enclosed in parentheses.

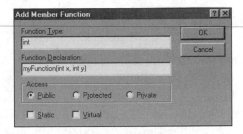

Figure 16.5   The Add Member Function dialog box.

5. Choose an access specifier for the function from the Access group of options.

6. If you want the function to be static, click on the Static checkbox. Or, if you want the function to be virtual, click on the Virtual checkbox.

7. Click on OK.

Adding A Member Variable

To add a member variable using ClassView:

1. In ClassView, choose the class to which you want to add a variable.

2. Right-click on the class to display the pop-up menu, and click on Add Member Variable. The Add Member Variable dialog box appears (see Figure 16.6).

3. In the Variable Type field, type the data type of the new member variable.

4. In the Variable Name field, type the name of the new member variable.

5. Choose an access specifier for the variable from the Access group of options.

6. Click on OK.

Figure 16.6   The Add Member Variable dialog box.

Overriding A Virtual Function

To override a virtual function by using ClassView:

1. From ClassView, right-click on a class and click Add Virtual Function on the pop-up menu.

2. The New Virtual Override dialog box appears (see Figure 16.7). Double-click on the virtual function you wish to add. If you click on Add Handler, the dialog adds a stub function—a syntactically valid but incomplete function to which you can add code as desired—to the class's implementation file.

3. If you want to edit the new virtual function, click on Add And Edit; Visual C++ will take you to the file in which the new virtual function is implemented.

4. If you want to edit an existing virtual function, choose a function from the Existing Virtual Function Overrides, and click on Edit Existing to navigate to the file that implements the virtual function.

Deleting A Member Function

To delete a member function by using ClassView:

1. Open the class that contains the function.

2. Right-click on the function you want to delete and choose Delete from the pop-up menu.

3. A dialog box will prompt you to confirm that you want to delete the function. Click on Yes to delete the specified function.

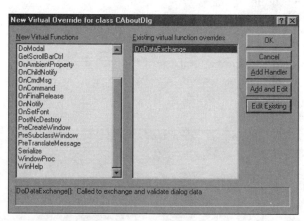

Figure 16.7 The New Virtual Override dialog box.

Deleting a function with ClassView:

- Removes the function declaration from the header (.h) file.
- Removes any associated map entry from the **MSG**, **MESSAGE**, or **DISPATCH** map.
- Comments out the function definition, if one exists.

Working With Code

Visual C++ lets you jump directly to code elements, such as definitions for classes, functions, and methods, by simply double-clicking on a ClassView icon or by choosing a command from the ClassView pop-up menu. You can also jump to declarations and references by using ClassView.

Jumping To A Definition

To jump to an object definition from ClassView:

1. In ClassView, right-click on the object whose definition you want to see.

2. From the ClassView pop-up menu, choose Go To Definition.

   For classes, Visual C++ takes you to the header (.h) file; for interfaces, it takes you to the IDL or ODL file.

NOTE: *Visual C++ updates the contents of ClassView as a background process. You may notice some delay from the time you open a project or save a revised file until the view is updated.*

Jumping To A Declaration

To jump to an object declaration from ClassView:

1. In ClassView, right-click on the object whose declaration you want to see.

2. From the ClassView pop-up menu, choose Go To Declaration.

   For classes, Visual C++ takes you to the declaration.

Jumping To A Reference

To jump to an object reference from ClassView:

1. In ClassView, right-click on the object whose references you want to see.

16. Working With ClassView

2. From the ClassView pop-up menu, choose References.

3. The Definitions And References browse information window box appears, as shown in Figure 16.8. You can double-click on a definition or reference to go to its code line.

NOTE: *If you did not specify that the application should build a browse information file, a message box appears, asking if you want to build one. If you click on Yes, Visual C++ builds the browse information file, and you can then find references. If you click on No, the references are not available.*

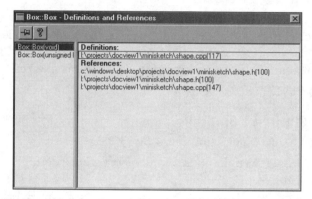

Figure 16.8   Jumping to a reference.

Working With Message Handlers

Message handlers are member functions that handle Windows messages. You can use ClassView to add a message handler to a class and map Windows messages to the message handler. You can also use ClassView to quickly add a message handler for any dialog box control.

Defining A Message Handler

To define a message handler:

1. From ClassView, right-click on a class and click on Add Windows Message Handler on the pop-up menu.

2. The New Windows Message And Event Handlers dialog box appears (see Figure 16.9).

3. From the Class Or Object To Handle list, choose an item.

4. The New Windows Messages/Events list lists messages that you can add to the chosen class or object. The Existing Message/

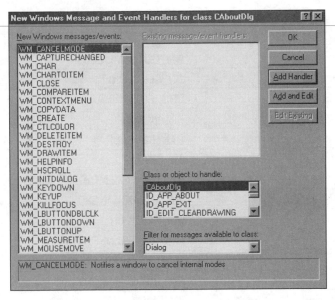

Figure 16.9   The New Windows Message And Event Handlers dialog box.

Event Handlers list lists the messages previously associated with the chosen class or object.

5. Choose an item from New Windows Messages/Events, and click on Add Handler to add the new handler function. Visual C++ automatically adds a stub function—a syntactically valid but incomplete function to which you can add code as desired—to the class's implementation file.

   Add And Edit performs the same function as Add Handler, except that it also navigates you to the file in which the message handler is implemented.

6. If you want to edit a message handler, choose an item from Existing Messages/Event Handlers, and click on Edit Existing to navigate to the file in which the message handler is implemented.

Adding The Default Message Handler For A Dialog Box Control

Each Windows control has an associated default event and corresponding message, as shown in Table 16.2.

To add a default message handler for a dialog box control:

1. Right-click on the dialog box in the ClassView pane, and choose Go To Dialog Editor from the pop-up menu.

2. Double-click on the control whose default message you want to handle.

Table 16.2 Default events.

Control Name	Default Event
Animate	**NM_OUTOFMEMORY**
CheckBox	**BN_CLICK ONED**
Combo Box	**CBN_EDITCHANGE**
Custom	(Not applicable)
Date Time Picker	**DTN_CLOSEUP**
Edit Box	**EN_CHANGE**
Hot Key	**NM_OUTOFMEMORY**
IP Address	**IPN_FIELDCHANGED**
List	**NM_CLICK ON**
List Box	**LBN_SELCHANGE**
Month Calendar	**MCN_GETDAYSTATE**
Progress	**NM_OUTOFMEMORY**
Push Button	**BN_CLICK ONED**
Radio Button	**BN_CLICK ONED**
Rich Edit	**NM_CLICK ON**
Scrollbar	(Not applicable)
Slider	**NM_OUTOFMEMORY**
Spin	**NM_OUTOFMEMORY**
Tab	**TCN_SELCHANGE**
Tree	**NM_CLICK ON**

3. The Add Member Function dialog box appears (see Figure 16.10), with the default handler already chosen.

   If the control has a handler defined for it already, double-clicking jumps you to the handler code in the Text Editor.

4. Click on OK to have Visual C++ generate the declaration and stub function—a syntactically valid but incomplete function to which you can add code as desired—for the new message handler function.

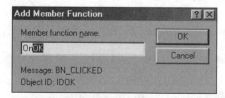

Figure 16.10 The Add Member Function dialog box.

Adding A Message Handler For A Control

To add a message handler (other than the default message handler) for a control:

1. Right-click on the icon for the dialog box in the ClassView pane, and choose Go To Dialog Editor from the pop-up menu.

2. Click on the control for which you want to add a message handler.

3. From the WizardBar Members drop-down list, choose an unimplemented (nonbold) message (see Figure 16.11).

4. The Add Member Function dialog box appears, with a proposed name for that message handler.

NOTE: *Choosing a bolded, or implemented, message from the Messages list jumps you to that handler function in the Text Editor.*

---

5. Click on OK to accept the default name for the handler, or type another name and click on OK. Visual C++ generates the function declaration and a stub function—a syntactically valid but incomplete function to which you can add code as desired—inside the dialog class.

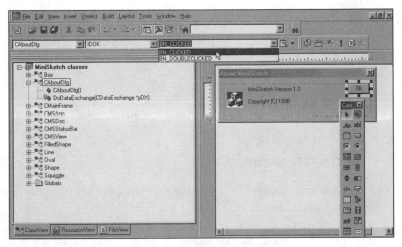

Figure 16.11   The WizardBar Members drop-down list.

16. Working With ClassView

Working With MFC Forms

A *form* is a dialog box with controls that let a user access or change data. You may want to develop an application in which the user chooses from a variety of forms. Commonly, a forms-based application lets the user access forms by choosing New from the File menu. However, a dialog-based application, which does not give the user access to a New option in the File menu, is also considered a forms-based application. Any application that supports the MFC libraries can include forms.

If the application does not support forms, Visual C++ will add this support when you insert a form. However, in the case of a dialog-based application, Visual C++ includes code that displays the initial form, but you must write code that provides the user with a way to view additional forms.

When you insert a new form into an application, Visual C++:

- Creates a class based on the form-style class that you choose (**CFormView**, **CRecordView**, **CDaoRecordView**, or **CDialog**). For dialog-based applications and other programs without a document/view architecture, the initial base class is always **CDialog**.

- Creates a dialog resource with appropriate styles. If you choose an existing dialog resource, you may need to set the styles by using the properties page for the dialog box. Styles for a dialog box must include:

  - **WS_CHILD=On**

  - **WS_BORDER=Off**

  - **WS_VISIBLE=Off**

  - **WS_CAPTION=Off**

For applications based on the document/view architecture, the New Form command also:

- Creates a **CDocument**-based class with a name based on the first three letters of the form class (skipping the leading "C"). However, if you prefer, you can use any existing **CDocument**-based class in your project.

- Generates a document template (derived from **CDocument**) with string, menu, and icon resources. If you prefer, you can create a new class on which to base the template.

- Adds a call to **AddDocumentTemplate** in the application's **InitInstance** member function. Visual C++ adds this call for each new form you create, so that your form is added to the list of available forms presented when the user chooses the New command. This code includes the form's associated resource ID, along with the names of the associated document, view, and frame classes that compose the new form object.

Inserting A Form Into A Project

To insert a form into your project:

1. From ClassView, right-click on the project to which you want to add the form.

2. From the pop-up menu, choose New Form.

NOTE: *If the New Form command is not available, your project may be based on the ActiveX Template Libraries (ATL). To add a form to an ATL project, you must specify MFC support when first creating the project.*

---

3. In the New Form dialog box, type a name for the form (see Figure 16.12). The remaining fields under Form Information are automatically generated from the form name.

4. Specify whether the form will support Automation by using the Automation area.

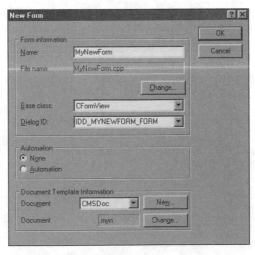

Figure 16.12   The New Form dialog box.

5. Use the Document Template Information fields to specify information about the document associated with the form. If you want to change the generated file extension or other information, click on Change.

6. Click on OK.

Visual C++ adds the form to your application and opens the Dialog Editor so that you can conveniently add controls or refine the design of the form.

Related solution:	Found on page:
Creating A Workspace	301

Working With ClassWizard

In Brief

Creating And Managing Classes With ClassWizard

The last chapter presented ClassView, which shows all defined C++ classes and the members of those classes, and helps you work with the classes and their members. This chapter presents ClassWizard, another Visual C++ tool that helps you create and manage classes. Like ClassView, ClassWizard lets you browse and edit the classes in your program. With ClassWizard, you can:

- Create new classes derived from MFC (Microsoft Foundation Classes) classes.

- Map messages associated with windows, dialog boxes, controls, menu items, and accelerators to functions.

- Create and delete message-handling member functions.

- See which messages have message handlers defined and jump to the handler program code.

- Define member variables that automatically initialize, acquire, and validate data entered into dialog boxes or form views.

- Add Automation methods and properties when creating a new class

- Work with existing classes and type libraries.

Immediate Solutions

Working With Classes

You launch ClassWizard by using the View menu. Once you've launched it, you can use it to create new classes. Unlike ClassView, ClassWizard does not immediately update its internal database when you make changes to your source code. Instead, you must use a special dialog to inform ClassWizard of such changes.

Launching ClassWizard

To launch ClassWizard, click on ClassWizard on the View menu.

The ClassWizard dialog box appears, as shown in Figure 17.1. You're then ready to use ClassWizard to create or modify classes.

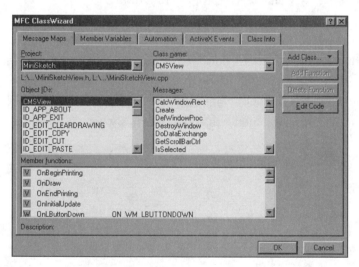

Figure 17.1   The ClassWizard dialog box.

Creating A New Class

The process of adding a new class by using ClassWizard is similar to adding a new class with ClassView. However, ClassWizard supports only MFC classes as base classes. Table 17.1 lists the classes available as base classes.

Table 17.1   Classes available to ClassWizard as base classes.

Class	Description
CAnimateCtrl	Encapsulates the Windows common animation control.
CasyncMonikerFile	Encapsulates access to asynchronous monikers in ActiveX controls (formerly OLE controls).
CAsyncSocket	Encapsulates a Windows socket.
CButton	Encapsulates a button control.
CcachedDataPathProperty	Encapsulates an ActiveX control property transferred asynchronously and cached in a memory file.
CCmdTarget	Encapsulates an object that can receive and respond to messages.
CColorDialog	Encapsulates a color selection dialog box.
CComboBox	Encapsulates a combination text box/list box with static or edit control.
CDaoRecordset	Encapsulates a set of records selected from a datasource. **CDaoRecordset** objects are available in three forms: table-type recordsets, dynaset-type recordsets, and snapshot-type recordsets.
CDaoRecordView	Encapsulates database records in controls. This form view is directly connected to a **CDaoRecordset** object.
CDataPathProperty	Encapsulates an ActiveX control property that can be loaded asynchronously.
CDialog	Encapsulates a dialog box.
CDocument	Encapsulates program data.
CEdit	Encapsulates a rectangular child window for text entry.
CEditView	Encapsulates a Windows edit control and can be used to implement simple text-editor functionality.
CFileDialog	Encapsulates a Windows common file dialog box that provides an easy way to implement File Open and File Save As dialog boxes.
CFontDialog	Encapsulates a font selection dialog box that displays a list of fonts that are currently installed in the system.
CFormView	Encapsulates a window that can contain dialog box controls.
CFrameWnd	Encapsulates a single document interface (SDI) frame window.
CHeaderCtrl	Encapsulates the Windows common header control.

(continued)

Table 17.1 Classes available to ClassWizard as base classes (continued).

Class	Description
CHotKeyCtrl	Encapsulates the Windows common hot key control.
CHttpFilter	Encapsulates a Hypertext Transfer Protocol (HTTP) filter object.
CHttpServer	Encapsulates an ISAPI-compliant HTTP server. Wraps ISAPI functionality and processes client requests, including extension DLLs but excluding CGI executables.
CListBox	Encapsulates a list box.
CListCtrl	Encapsulates the Windows common list view control.
CListView	Encapsulates a list control that simplifies use of **CListCtrl**, the class that encapsulates list-control functionality.
CMDIChildWnd	Encapsulates a multiple document interface (MDI) child frame window.
COleDocument	Encapsulates a document that consists of a collection of **CDocItem** objects that handle OLE items. Both container and server applications require this architecture because their documents must be able to contain OLE items.
COleLinkingDoc	Base class for OLE container documents that support linking to the embedded items they contain.
COleServerDoc	Encapsulates an OLE server document.
COleServerItem	Encapsulates a server interface to OLE items.
CPrintDialog	Encapsulates a Windows common dialog box for printing, which provides an easy way to implement Print and Print Setup dialog boxes.
CProgressCtrl	Encapsulates the Windows common progress bar control.
CPropertyPage	Encapsulates an individual page of a property sheet, otherwise known as a tab dialog box.
CPropertySheet	Encapsulates a property sheet (tab dialog box), which consists of a **CPropertySheet** object and one or more **CPropertyPage** objects.
CRecordset	Encapsulates access to a database table or query.
CRecordView	Encapsulates a window containing dialog box controls mapped to recordset fields.

(continued)

Table 17.1   Classes available to ClassWizard as base classes (continued).

Class	Description
CRichEditCtrl	Encapsulates a window in which the user can enter and edit text that can include character and paragraph formatting and embedded objects.
CRichEditView	Encapsulates the text and formatting characteristics of text.
CScrollBar	Encapsulates a scrollbar.
CScrollView	Encapsulates a scrolling window, derived from **CView**.
CSliderCtrl	Encapsulates a window containing a slider and optional tick marks.
CSocket	Encapsulates access to the **CSocketFile** and **CArchive** classes, which manage the sending and receiving of data.
CSpinButtonCtrl	Encapsulates a pair of arrow buttons that the user can click to increment or decrement a value.
CStatic	Encapsulates a simple text field, box, or rectangle used to label, box, or separate other controls.
CStatusBarCtrl	Encapsulates a horizontal window, usually displayed at the bottom of a parent window, in which an application can display status information.
CTabCtrl	Encapsulates functionality that lets an application display multiple pages in the same area of a window or dialog box.
CToolBarCtrl	Encapsulates the Windows toolbar common control.
CToolTipCtrl	Encapsulates a "tooltip control," a small pop-up window that displays a single line of text describing the purpose of a tool in an application.
CTreeCtrl	Encapsulates a hierarchical list of items.
CTreeView	Encapsulates a tree control that simplifies use of **CTreeCtrl**, the class that encapsulates tree control functionality.
CView	Encapsulates program data.
CWinThread	Encapsulates a thread of execution within an application.
generic	Encapsulates a **CWnd** custom window.
splitter	Encapsulates an MDI child window that contains a **CSplitterWnd** class, which lets the user split a window into multiple panes.

17. Working With ClassWizard

To create a new class by using ClassWizard:

1. Click on ClassWizard's Add Class button (see Figure 17.1).

2. On the drop-down menu, click on New. The New Class dialog box appears, as shown in Figure 17.2.

3. In the Name field, type the name of the new class.

4. Visual C++ uses the class name you specify to determine the file name, which it displays in the read-only File Name field. By default, the header file and the implementation file have the same name as the class file.

5. If you want to change the name of the header or implementation file for this class, click on Change, and type the revised name in the Change Files dialog box.

6. To add the new class to existing header and implementation files, click on Change, then click on the Browse button and locate the files to which you wish to add it.

7. Choose the base class from which to derive the new class. There are two kinds of MFC classes:

   • Classes that do not require a resource ID

NOTE: *Classes, such as **CButton**, that are derived from base classes other than **CDao-RecordView**, **CDialog**, **CFormView**, **CPropertyPage**, or **CRecordView**, do not require a resource ID. Because these classes do not require a resource ID, the Dialog ID drop-down list of the New Class dialog box is not active.*

   • Classes that do require a resource ID

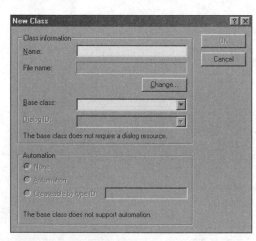

Figure 17.2   The New Class dialog box.

NOTE: For classes that require a resource ID, you'll find it easier to first use the Dialog Editor to create the resource and its ID, then use ClassWizard to create a class associated with the resource ID.

8. For dialog-based classes, select the resource with which the class is to be associated from the Dialog ID drop-down list.

9. Choose the desired type of Automation support: None, Automation, or Createable By Type ID:

   - Choose None if you want the new class to have no Automation capability.

   - Choose Automation if you want to expose the capabilities of the new class through Automation.

   - Choose Createable By Type ID if you want to allow other applications to create objects of this class using Automation.

10. Click on OK. Visual C++ creates the new class and adds it to the project.

When you exit the ClassWizard dialog box, the new class immediately appears in ClassView; you can view its header and implementation files in the FileView pane of the project workspace.

Keeping ClassWizard Information Current

ClassWizard stores information about your project's classes in a file with the file extension .clw. Unlike ClassView, ClassWizard does not immediately update this database when you modify source code. In stead, it tracks your code as you make changes and displays the Repair Class Information dialog box (shown in Figure 17.3) when you next edit the affected class. The dialog box asks you for updated information about classes and uses this information to:

- Delete obsolete classes from the ClassWizard file.

- Update the ClassWizard file with the name or location of classes that you have changed or moved.

Deleting A Class

Because of the help provided by the Repair Class Information dialog box, it's simple to delete a class created by ClassWizard. You can delete the class from the header (.h) and implementation (.cpp) files (if

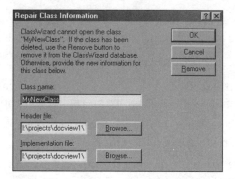

Figure 17.3   The Repair Class Information dialog box.

the class shares these files with other classes) or delete the H and CPP files altogether. In either case, you must update the information in the ClassWizard (.clw) file.

To delete a class:

1. Delete all references to the class from its H and CPP files, or delete the files themselves.

2. On the View menu, click on ClassWizard.

3. If ClassWizard appears, the active project does not contain the deleted class:

   • From ClassWizard's Project drop-down list, select the project that contains the deleted class.

   • If ClassWizard asks you to close any files, close ClassWizard, close the files, and then restart ClassWizard. A message box informs you that ClassWizard cannot find the deleted class.

   • Click on OK.

4. ClassWizard displays the Repair Class Information dialog box (refer to Figure 17.3).

5. Click on Remove. The class is deleted from the CLW file, and ClassWizard appears.

6. Click on OK.

Renaming Or Moving A Class

When you change the name of a class or move it from one implementation file to another, ClassWizard prompts you to update the information in the ClassWizard (.clw) file the next time you start ClassWizard.

To change the name of a class or move it from one file to another:

1. Make the desired changes to your source files.

NOTE: *When you change the name of a class, remember to change it everywhere, including in the special-format comments ClassWizard uses.*

---

2. On the View menu, click on ClassWizard.

3. If ClassWizard appears, the active project does not contain the renamed or moved class.

   - From ClassWizard's Project drop-down list, select the project that contains the renamed or moved class.

   - If ClassWizard asks you to close any files, close ClassWizard, close the files, and then restart ClassWizard. ClassWizard displays a message box warning you that the old class could not be found.

   - Click on OK.

4. The Repair Class Information dialog box appears (refer to Figure 17.3).

5. Type the new class information in the Class Name, Header File, and Implementation File fields. If necessary, use the Browse button to supply the correct name of the header file or the implementation file.

6. Click on OK to update the ClassWizard file.

Rebuilding The ClassWizard File

If you have made many changes to your code, you may find it simpler to rebuild the ClassWizard (.clw) file from scratch, rather than update it one class at a time.

To rebuild the ClassWizard file:

1. Delete your project's CLW file.

2. On the View menu, click on ClassWizard.

3. If ClassWizard appears, the project for which you deleted the CLW file is not the active project.

   - From ClassWizard's Project drop-down list, select the project that contains the renamed or moved class.

   - If ClassWizard asks you to close any files, close ClassWizard, close the files, and then restart ClassWizard.

   - Click on OK.

4. A message box asks if you want to rebuild the ClassWizard file from your source files. Click on Yes. The Select Source Files dialog box appears, as shown in Figure 17.4.

5. Use the Add and Add All buttons to transfer the project's H and CPP files and RC file from the File Name field to the Files In Project list. Click on Remove to remove any files other than H, CPP, or RC from the Files In Project list.

6. Click on OK. ClassWizard appears and builds a new CLW file.

7. Click on OK to close ClassWizard.

Associating A Resource With An Existing Class

When you associate a resource with an existing class, Visual C++ makes the resource command IDs available for mapping when the class is selected in the ClassWizard's Message Maps tab. You can use ClassWizard's Select Class dialog box to associate a new dialog box, menu, toolbar, or accelerator resource with an existing class.

To associate an existing class from the project with a resource:

1. Use the Dialog, Menu, Toolbar, or Accelerator Editor to create the new resource.

2. On the View menu, click on ClassWizard.

3. ClassWizard appears, along with the Adding A Class dialog box (shown in Figure 17.5), which prompts you to provide a class for the new resource. You can either create a new class or select an existing class.

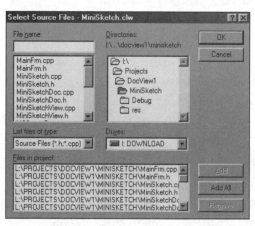

Figure 17.4   The Select Source Files dialog box.

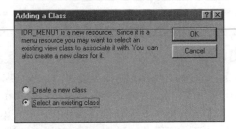

Figure 17.5   The Adding A Class dialog box.

4. Click on the Select An Existing Class radio button to select an existing class.

5. The Select Class dialog box appears, displaying a list of existing classes in the active project.

6. Select a class from the list, then click on the Select button. A message box asks if you want to substitute the resource ID for the class's current resource ID.

7. Click on OK. ClassWizard associates the resource with the specified class.

Importing The Elements Of A Type Library

A type library is a collection of controls. You can use ClassWizard to wrap the elements of a type library in an MFC class that you can conveniently add to a project.

To import the elements of a type library into the ClassWizard:

1. On the View menu, click on ClassWizard. ClassWizard appears.

2. On any of ClassWizard's tabs, click on Add Class, then click on From A Type Library on the drop-down menu that appears. The Import From Type Library dialog box appears.

3. Select a type library and click on Open. The Confirm Classes dialog box appears. ClassWizard generates a list of classes that it can create from information in the type library, and the dialog box displays this list.

4. If you want to rename a class, select it and use the Name field.

5. If you want to rename the H or CPP files that will hold the imported type library, use the Header File and Implementation File fields. You can use the Browse buttons to rename the files or cause the files to be generated in a different directory. All classes selected from the class list are added to these two files.

6. Click on OK. ClassWizard generates the specified class.

Working With Member Functions And Variables

You can use ClassWizard to add new member variables to a class, to override a virtual function, or to delete a member function. However, ClassWizard cannot add a member function or a generic member variable to a class; you must use ClassView for these operations. ClassWizard does let you add *control variables*, which are special member variables that shadow controls and facilitate data exchange and data validation; ClassView cannot add control variables to a class.

Adding A Control Variable

To add a control variable using ClassWizard:

1. On the View menu, click on ClassWizard. Click on the Member Variables tab. Select the class to which you want to add a variable.

2. Click on Add Variable.

3. The Add Member Variable dialog box appears, as shown in Figure 17.6.

4. In the Member Variable Name field, type the name of the variable. By convention, the names of member variables begin with the prefix **m_**.

5. In the Category drop-down list, select the appropriate type of variable.

6. In the Variable Type drop-down list, select the appropriate class that defines the variable's data type.

7. Click on OK.

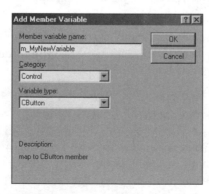

Figure 17.6   The Add Member Variable dialog box.

This procedure automatically adds an appropriate variable definition to the header file for the class.

Overriding A Virtual Function

You can use ClassWizard to override virtual functions defined in a base class. To override a virtual function with ClassWizard:

1. On the View menu, click on ClassWizard. ClassWizard appears.

2. On the Message Maps tab under Class Name, select the name of the class whose virtual function you want to override. (The Message Maps tab is shown in Figure 17.7.)

3. In the Object IDs list, select the class name. The Messages list displays a list of virtual functions you can override and a list of Windows messages. The virtual functions precede the messages and appear in mixed case.

4. In the Messages list, select the name of the virtual function you want to override.

5. Click on Add Function. The function is created and its name is displayed in the Member Functions list. The names of virtual overrides are preceded by a gray glyph containing the letter "V" (handlers have a "W").

6. Click on Edit Code to jump to the virtual function definition.

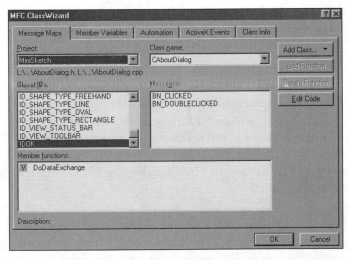

Figure 17.7   The ClassWizard dialog box with the Message Maps tab displayed.

Deleting A Member Function

When ClassWizard deletes a function, it deletes the function declaration from the class declaration in the header file, and deletes any message map entry from the class definition in the implementation file. However, you must manually remove the function definition, as well as any references to the function, from the implementation file. You can browse through the class structure with ClassWizard to locate these references.

To delete a member function with ClassWizard:

1. In the ClassWizard dialog box, click on the Message Maps tab.

2. In the Class Name list, select the class containing the member function you want to delete.

3. In the Member Functions list, select the name of the member function to delete.

4. Click on Delete Function. This deletes the function entries from the message map for the class from both the header and implementation files.

ClassWizard will remind you to edit the implementation file containing the member function. Use Text Editor to comment out or delete the function header and function body.

Working With Message Handlers

A message handler is a member function that handles Windows messages. You can use ClassWizard to add a message handler to a class and to map Windows messages to the message handler. You can also quickly add a message handler for any dialog box control. ClassWizard lets you browse the messages associated with user interface objects in your project. It automatically updates the message dispatch table, or message map, and your class header file when you define message-handling functions.

Defining A Default Message Handler

A default message handler provides default Windows handling for a Windows message. To define a default message handler with ClassWizard:

1. On the View menu, click on ClassWizard. ClassWizard appears and displays information about the currently selected class.

2. Click on the Message Maps tab.

3. From the Class Name drop-down list, select the class name of the control you want to work with. ClassWizard displays information about the currently selected control.

4. In the Object IDs list, select the name of the control for which you want to define a message handler.

5. In the Messages list, select the message for which you want to define a handler. Click on Add Function (or double-click on the message name). Messages with handlers already defined are displayed in bold. Selecting a message causes ClassWizard to display a brief description of the message at the bottom of the ClassWizard dialog box.

NOTE: *ClassWizard lists in the Messages list only those functions that are most appropriate to your class. If your class is not associated with the resource that contains the command you want to handle, set the focus on the resource, open ClassWizard, and then use the Class Name drop-down list to switch to the class from which you want the message handled.*

6. For messages that do not already have a predefined name for the handler function, the Add Member Function dialog box appears. If the Add Member Function dialog box appears, click on OK to accept the default name, or type a name for the member function and click on OK. Either action returns you to the ClassWizard's Message Maps tab.

The message name is now displayed in bold to show that a message handler has been defined. The name of the new message handler appears in the Member Functions list.

At this point, you do any of the following:

- Click on Cancel to avoid updating your source code with the selected member functions.

- Add more message handlers.

- Click on OK to close ClassWizard. Visual C++ updates your source code with the selected member functions .

- Click on Edit Code to jump to the definition of the function selected in the Member Functions list just created by ClassWizard.

17. Working With ClassWizard

When you choose OK or Edit Code, ClassWizard updates your source code by:

- Inserting a function declaration into the header file.
- Inserting a function definition with a skeletal implementation into the implementation file.
- Updating the class's message map to include the new message-handling function.

Adding A Handler Function

ClassWizard lets you create your own handler functions and connect them to the menu items, toolbar buttons, and accelerators whose commands they respond to. To connect a dialog box or other control to a menu command or toolbar button, you must first create the dialog box, menu entry, or toolbar button and its object ID using the appropriate resource editor.

It's often convenient to bind more than one control to a single function. For example, you can bind both a menu command and a toolbar button to a single function, provided that you want the same action to occur whenever either sends a message.

To add a function and edit its related code, you should make your selections in this order on the ClassWizard's Message Maps tab:

1. Select the project that contains the class you want to edit.
2. Select a class name.
3. Select an object ID.
4. Select a message.

You can then edit or delete the associated function, or click on the Add Function button to add a member function to the class. By convention, the names of all message-handling functions begin with the prefix **On**.

Overriding A Handler Function

You can override a virtual function in much the same way, also on the Message Maps tab:

1. Select a class name.
2. In the Object IDs list, select the class name again.
3. In the Messages list, select a virtual function to override.
4. Click on Add Function.

Adding Code From ClassWizard

After you've added a new member function in the ClassWizard dialog box, click on Edit Code to add the implementation code for your new function. The Text Editor opens with the file containing the class for the member function. A highlighted comment shows you where to add your code.

Defining A Message Handler For A Dialog Box Button

ClassWizard provides shortcuts that let you quickly define a message handler for a dialog box button or a member variable for a dialog control. To define a message handler for a dialog box button:

1. In the Dialog Editor, select the button with which you want to associate a message handler.

2. While holding down the Ctrl key, double-click on the button. ClassWizard automatically creates a message handler in the class associated with the dialog box. The message handler is named according to the control ID of the dialog box button. Finally, the insertion point moves to the newly created function in your source code.

Alternatively, you can follow this procedure:

1. In the Dialog Editor, double-click on the button with which you want to associate a message handler.

2. If a class is not already associated with the dialog box, ClassWizard appears, along with the Adding A Class dialog box, which prompts you to specify a class for the new resource. You can create a new class or select an existing class.

3. If a class is already associated with the dialog box, the Add Member Function dialog box opens if no message handler for the control has been implemented. If a message handler for the control has already been implemented, you navigate directly to that handler's definition.

Defining A Member Variable For A Dialog Box Control

To define a member variable for any dialog box control except a button, you can use the following shortcut. To define a member variable for a (nonbutton) dialog box control:

1. In the Dialog Editor, select a control.

2. While holding down the Ctrl key, double-click on the dialog box control. The Add Member Variable dialog box appears.

3. Type the appropriate information in the Add Member Variable dialog box (see "Adding A Control Variable" earlier in this chapter).

4. Click on OK. ClassWizard returns you to the Dialog Editor.

NOTE: *You can jump from any dialog box control to its existing handler by double-clicking on the control.*

Editing A Message Handler

To edit a message handler:

1. In the ClassWizard dialog box, select the Message Maps tab.

2. In the Class Name list, select the class containing the message-handling function you want to edit.

3. In the Member Functions list, select the function you want to edit.

4. Choose Edit Code, or double-click on the function name. The insertion point moves to the function.

Deleting A Message Handler

When ClassWizard deletes a message handler, it deletes the function declaration from the class declaration in the header file and deletes any message map entry from the class definition in the implementation file. However, you must manually remove the function definition, as well as any references to the function, from the implementation file. You can browse through the class structure with ClassWizard to locate these references.

To delete a message handler by using ClassWizard:

1. In the ClassWizard dialog box, click on the Message Maps tab.

2. In the Class Name list, select the class containing the message-handling function you want to delete.

3. In the Member Functions list, select the name of the member function to delete.

4. Click on Delete Function. This deletes the function entries from the message map for that class in both the header and implementation files.

ClassWizard will remind you to edit the implementation file containing the member function. Use a text editor to comment out or delete the function header and function body.

Working With Code

ClassWizard helps you work with code by taking you quickly to the definition of a class or member function.

Finding A Class

To go to a class definition:

1. In the ClassWizard dialog box, click on the Message Maps tab.
2. Select a class from the Class Name drop-down list.
3. Select the class name from the Object IDs list.
4. Click on the Edit Code button to jump to the class definition.

Finding A Function Definition

To go to a function definition:

1. In the ClassWizard dialog box, select the Message Maps tab.
2. Select a class from the Class Name drop-down list.
3. Select a function from the Member Functions list.
4. Click on the Edit Code button to jump to the function definition.

Understanding ClassWizard Comments

When ClassWizard creates a new class, it inserts specially formatted comments in the source code. These comments mark the sections of the header and implementation files that ClassWizard edits; Class-Wizard never modifies code that is outside these commented sections. ClassWizard creates the following types of comments:

- Message Map comments
- Virtual Function comments
- Data Map comments
- Field Map comments
- Active Dispatch Map comments

It's important that you do not disturb the code maintained by ClassWizard. The following sections will help you recognize the comments that ClassWizard places around the code it maintains. The common pattern is that all such comments begin with the sequence

*//{{***AFX_****XXX*** and end with the sequence *//}}***AFX_****XXX***, where ***XXX***
is a sequence of three or more characters that identify the type of
code block inserted by ClassWizard.

Message Map Comments

When ClassWizard creates member function definitions in the class
header file, it inserts comments that look like this:

```
//{{AFX_MSG(classname)
  afx_msg void OnAppAbout();
//}}AFX_MSG
```

ClassWizard inserts comments like the following around message map
entries in the class implementation file:

```
//{{AFX_MSG_MAP(classname)
  ON_COMMAND(ID_APP_ABOUT, OnAppAbout)
//}}AFX_MSG_MAP
```

Virtual Function Comments

ClassWizard inserts code into two files when you use it to override
a virtual function: the class header file and the class implementation file. The ClassWizard comments in the header file look like the
following:

```
//{{AFX_VIRTUAL(classname)
  virtual BOOL InitInstance();
//}}AFX_VIRTUAL
```

The ClassWizard section in the implementation file has no special
comments. Virtual function definitions in the CPP file look like other
function definitions, and you can freely edit them.

Data Map Comments

For dialog boxes, form views, and record views, ClassWizard creates
and edits three code sections that it marks with specially formatted
comments. Member variable declarations in the class header file look
like this:

```
//{{AFX_DATA
...
//}}AFX_DATA
```

Member variable initialization in the class implementation file looks like this:

```
//{{AFX_DATA_INIT
...
//}}AFX_DATA_INIT
```

Data exchange macros in the implementation file look like this:

```
//{{AFX_DATA_MAP
...
//}}AFX_DATA_MAP
```

Field Map Comments

For record field exchange, ClassWizard creates and edits three code sections that it marks with specially formatted comments. Member variable declarations in the class header file look like this:

```
//{{AFX_FIELD
...
//}}AFX_FIELD
```

Record exchange function calls in the implementation file look like this:

```
//{{AFX_FIELD_MAP
...
//}}AFX_FIELD_MAP
```

Member variable initializations in the class header file look like this:

```
//{{AFX_FIELD_INIT
...
//}}AFX_FIELD_INIT
```

Active Dispatch Map Comments

For active method dispatch, ClassWizard creates and edits four code sections it marks with specially formatted comments. Active events in the class header file look like this:

```
//{{AFX_EVENT
...
//}}AFX_EVENT
```

Active events in the class implementation file look like this:

```
//{{AFX_EVENT_MAP
...
//}}AFX_EVENT_MAP
```

Automation declarations in the class header file look like this:

```
//{{AFX_DISP
...
//}}AFX_DISP
```

Automation mapping in the class implementation file looks like this:

```
//{{AFX_DISP_MAP
...
//}}AFX_DISP_MAP
```

Working With Dialog Boxes

ClassWizard offers an easy way to take advantage of MFC's dialog data exchange (DDX) and dialog data validation (DDV) capabilities.

Dialog Data Exchange

Dialog data exchange (DDX) lets you define member variables in the dialog box, form view, or record view class and associate each of them with a dialog box control. The MFC framework transfers any initial values to the controls when the dialog box is displayed. When the user clicks on OK, MFC updates the variables with the data that the user entered. DDX validation is carried out after the user clicks on OK.

ClassWizard lets you create variables that use the framework's automatic DDX capabilities. When you want to set an initial value for, or gather data from, a dialog box control, use ClassWizard to define a data member in the dialog box class. The framework will transfer the initial value of the variable to the dialog box when it is created and update the associated member variable when the dialog box is dismissed.

NOTE: You can use **CWnd::UpdateData** to transfer data back and forth between controls and member variables while a dialog box is open.

Defining Data Members For Dialog Data Exchange

To define data members for dialog data exchange:

1. Create your dialog box, adding the controls you want and setting the appropriate control styles in the Properties window. Then, use ClassWizard to define a new dialog box class.

2. On the View menu, click on ClassWizard. In ClassWizard, click on the Member Variables tab.

3. In the Control IDs box, select the control for which you want to set up DDX, and click on Add Variable. The Add Member Variable dialog box appears (refer to Figure 17.6).

4. In the Member Variable Name list, type the name of the new variable. ClassWizard provides the conventional **m_** prefix that identifies the variable as a member variable.

5. In the Category drop-down list, select whether this variable is a control variable or a value variable. A *control variable* provides a handle to a dialog box control; a *value variable* provides access to the value of a control property.

6. For standard Windows controls, choose Value in the Category drop-down list to create a variable that contains the control's text or status as typed by the user. MFC automatically converts the data to the type selected in the Variable Type box.

7. If you want a control variable, choose Control in the Category drop-down list to create a control variable that gives you access to the control itself.

8. In the Variable Type drop-down list, choose from a list of variable types appropriate to the control. Table 17.2 shows the type of DDX value variables ClassWizard provides

9. Click on OK. The new member variable is added to the Control IDs list on the Member Variables tab.

After you've defined a DDX value variable for a standard Windows control, MFC automatically initializes and updates the variable for you.

You can use ClassWizard to bind a member variable to the value of a scrollbar control, using the Value property and the **int** data type, or to a **CScrollBar** object, using the Control property. The Value property binds the value of a scrollbar control (which indicates the position of the scrollbox, or "thumb"). ClassWizard enables DDX for a scrollbar by calling **DDX_Scroll** in your **DoDataExchange** override.

Table 17.2 Types of value properties provided by ClassWizard for DDX variables.

Control Variable	Type
Edit box	**BOOL**, **COleCurrency**, **COleDateTime**, **CString**, **double**, **DWORD**, **float**, **int**, **long**, **short**, **UINT**
Normal checkbox	**BOOL**
Three-state checkbox	**int** (possible values are 0 (off), 1 (on), and 2 (indeterminate))
Radio button (first in group)	**int** (values for a group of radio buttons range from 0 for the first button in the group to n–1 for a group with n buttons; a value of –1 indicates that no buttons are selected)
Nonsorted list box	**CString, int**
Drop-down list	**CString, int**
All other list box and drop-down list types	**CString**

If your **DoDataExchange** function calls **DDX_Scroll**, you must set the scrollbar range before that call, as shown in the following code:

```
void CMyDlg::DoDataExchange( CDataExchange* pDX )
{
    CScrollBar* pScrollBar = (CScrollBar*)GetDlgItem(
      IDC_SCROLLBAR1);
    pScrollBar->SetScrollRange( 0, 100 );
    CDialog::DoDataExchange( pDX );
    //{{AFX_DATA_MAP(CMyDlg)
    DDX_Scroll(pDX, IDC_SCROLLBAR1, m_nScroll );
    //}}AFX_DATA_MAP
}
```

Table 17.3 summarizes some special considerations in using DDX variables. Table 17.4 shows the types of DDX control variables you can define with ClassWizard.

Setting Values And Getting Values Of DDX Member Variables

You can set the initial value of DDX variables by editing the initialization code that ClassWizard places in the constructor for the dialog box class. You can also set initial values for DDX variables after your dialog class object has been constructed, but before **DoModal** or **CreateDialog** is called.

Table 17.3   Special considerations in using DDX variables.

Control Type	Considerations
Checkbox or radio button group	Set the Auto property from each control's property window.
Radio button group	Set the Group property for the first radio button in the group. Make sure all other radio buttons immediately follow it in the tab order.
Drop-down list or list box	To use an integer value, turn off the Sort property from each control's property window Styles tab.

Table 17.4   DDX control variables definable using ClassWizard.

Control	Variable Type
Edit box	**CEdit**
Checkbox	**CButton**
Radio button	**CButton**
Pushbutton	**CButton**
List box	**CListBox**
List or drop-down list	**CComboBox**
Static text	**CStatic**
Scrollbar	**CScrollBar**

After the dialog box is dismissed, you can access the values of the DDX variables just as you would any other C++ member variable.

Related solution:	Found on page:
Dialog Editor	438

Dialog Data Validation

With dialog data validation (DDV), dialog box information entered by the user is validated automatically. You can set the validation boundaries: the maximum length for string values in an edit box control or the minimum or maximum numeric values for a numeric input. DDV validation is performed as the user enters each input.

You can define the maximum length for a **CString** DDX variable or the minimum or maximum values for a numeric DDX variable at the time you create it. When you dismiss the Add Member Variable dialog box, ClassWizard provides an appropriate field (or fields) for entering such values, as shown in Figure 17.8. You simply enter the desired

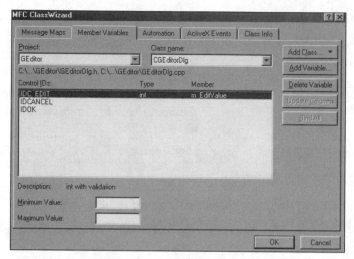

Figure 17.8   Validation fields in the ClassWizard dialog box.

value or values. At runtime, if the user enters a value that exceeds the range you specify, the framework immediately and automatically displays a message box asking the user to reenter the value. In contrast, the validation of DDX variables takes place only after the user dismisses the dialog box.

Advanced ClassWizard Functions

In Brief

ClassWizard provides some special functions in addition to those presented in Chapter 17. ClassWizard can help you write programs that:

- Access databases via Open Database Connectivity (ODBC) or Data Access Objects (DAO)
- Create ActiveX controls
- Work with Automation classes

Accessing Databases

To access a database via ODBC, you use two classes:

- **CRecordset**—Encapsulates a recordset, which is a set of records selected from a datasource.
- **CRecordView**—Supplies a record view, which is a database form (based on a dialog resource template) that contains controls that map to the field data members of a recordset object.

To access a database via DAO, you use two analogous classes:

- **CDaoRecordset**—Encapsulates a recordset.
- **CDaoRecordView**—Supplies a record view.

To access a database, you associate a record view class with a recordset and map the record view's controls to field data members of the recordset class. Dialog data exchange (DDX) provides a facility, known as a *foreign object*, that simplifies the transfer of data between the controls in a dialog box or record view and the corresponding data members of a recordset. When you associate a record view class with a recordset, you can name an existing recordset class or create a new one. ClassWizard adds a member variable of type **recordset** to the record view class. By default, it names the variable **m_pSet**. The recordset is the foreign object that facilitates data transfer between the record view and the recordset. Figure 18.1 illustrates the relationships between the record view, the record view object, and the recordset object.

When you use ClassWizard to create a recordset or record view class, ClassWizard creates the classes in the files you specify in the Add Class dialog box. The default file names are based on the class name

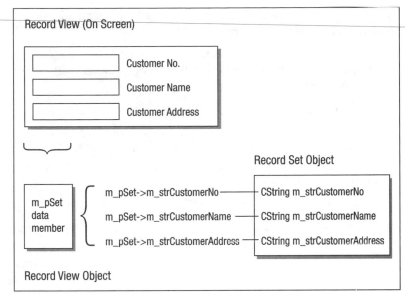

Figure 18.1   A foreign object links a record view to a recordset.

you enter. You can modify the default names, place the recordset and record view in the same files, or consolidate all recordsets in one set of files.

You can also browse and edit existing recordset and record view classes by using ClassWizard. When you edit a recordset class, ClassWizard provides a dialog box that lets you update the table columns bound to the recordset if the table's schema has changed since you created the class. You can also use this mechanism to specify the columns of additional tables for relational table joins.

Creating ActiveX Controls

If you've authored an ActiveX control, ClassWizard's ActiveX Events tab lets you specify actions that will cause your ActiveX control to fire events. If you're simply using an ActiveX control, rather than authoring one, you don't need to use the Events tab. You can simply use the Message Maps tab just as you would for handling messages.

Working With Automation Classes

An Automation class has a programming interface used by other applications (such as Microsoft Office or Microsoft Visual Basic, which are referred to in this context as *Automation clients*) to manipulate objects that your application implements. ClassWizard supports the following Automation features:

- Adding classes that support Automation. This makes your application an Automation server. The added classes will be available to Automation clients.

- Adding methods and properties to classes that support Automation.

- Creating a C++ class for another Automation object on your system, such as Microsoft Excel. This makes your application an Automation client.

Immediate Solutions

Working With Databases

Visual C++ facilitates working with databases by providing recordsets and record views. Recordsets encapsulate a database table (or the result of a query, such as a join). Record views provide a way to associate a user interface with a recordset.

Creating A Recordset Class

You must create a **CRecordset**-derived class (for ODBC) or **CDaoRecordset**-derived class (for DAO) for each table, join of tables, or predefined query you work with in your program. Each recordset class specifies a set of columns and may also specify parameters.

To create the recordset class:

1. On the View menu, click on ClassWizard.

2. Click on Add Class, and choose New from the drop-down list. The Add Class dialog box appears.

3. In the Name field, enter a name for the class; in the Filenames field, enter file names for its H and CPP files.

4. From the Base Class drop-down list, choose **CRecordset** (if you're using ODBC) or **CDaoRecordset** (if you're using DAO) as the base-class type of the new class.

5. Click on OK. The Database Options dialog box appears, as shown in Figure 18.2.

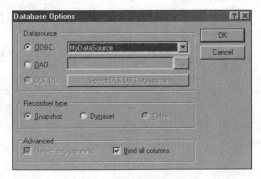

Figure 18.2   The Database Options dialog box.

6. Choose ODBC or DAO. Then, choose a datasource:

   • For ODBC, choose a datasource from the drop-down list.

   • For DAO, click on the Browse button beside the DAO edit control. Then, in the Open dialog box, navigate to the database file you want to use.

7. Under Recordset Type, choose Snapshot, Dynaset, or Table, and under Advanced, choose any additional features you want the class to have.

8. Click on OK.

9. The Select Database Tables dialog box appears, as shown in Figure 18.3. Choose the name(s) of the table(s) you want.

10. Click on OK. ClassWizard binds all of the table's columns to recordset field data members, as shown on its Member Variables tab, which appears as Figure 18.4.

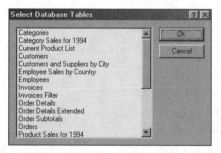

Figure 18.3   The Select Database Tables dialog box.

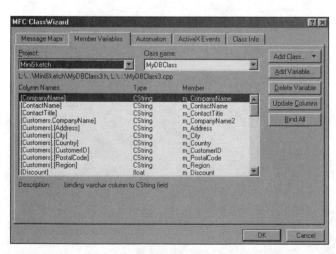

Figure 18.4   The ClassWizard's Member Variables tab.

11. When you finish, click on OK to close ClassWizard, which writes your class files in the specified directory and adds them to your project.

Binding Recordset Fields To Table Columns

ClassWizard binds all columns of your selected tables to the recordset. However, you can add and remove columns as you wish.

Removing Columns From Your Recordset

To remove a column from a recordset:

1. In ClassWizard, click on the Member Variables tab.

2. Click on a member variable name in the Members column of the Column Names list.

3. Click on Delete Variable.

The member variable is removed from your recordset class.

Adding Columns To Your Recordset

To add a column to the recordset:

1. In ClassWizard, on the Member Variables tab, choose the recordset class name in the Class Name drop-down list.

2. Choose a column in the Column Names list.

3. Click on Add Variable to open the Add Member Variable dialog box.

4. Type a name for the recordset data member that will represent the selected column. ClassWizard supplies a standard data member prefix, **m_**, for the name. You can complete the name as you desire or type over it. ClassWizard also supplies the variable's property and data type. The property for these variables is always "Value." The data type is based on the data type of the column.

5. Click on OK to close the Add Member Variable dialog box.

6. Click on OK to close ClassWizard.

ClassWizard writes the class files and adds them to your project.

Updating Your Recordset's Columns

When you make a number of changes to a table in a datasource, it may be cumbersome to add and delete the affected columns. In this case, you can use ClassWizard's Update Columns feature to rebuild the columns bound to the recordset.

18. Advanced ClassWizard Functions

To update the columns in your recordset:

1. On ClassWizard's Member Variables tab, click on your recordset class.

2. Click on Update Columns.

Any columns in the table that aren't bound to the recordset disappear from the refreshed recordset. ClassWizard doesn't disturb columns you've previously bound to recordset data members; to unbind a column, simply delete its data member. Any new columns are shown in the list but not yet bound to recordset field data members. To bind them, follow the procedure given in the section "Adding Columns To Your Recordset."

Creating A Database Form

A record view class provides a form view whose controls are mapped directly to the field data members of a recordset object, and thereby to the corresponding columns in a table on the datasource. Establishing this mapping enables dialog data exchanges (DDX) between the form's controls and the recordset's field data members.

To create a record view associated with a recordset:

1. Create the recordset class.

2. Create a dialog-template resource. In the Styles and More Styles property pages of the dialog template, set the following properties, as you would for a **CFormView** object:

   • In the Style field, specify Child (**WS_CHILD** on).

   • In the Border field, specify None (**WS_BORDER** off).

   • Clear the Visible checkbox (**WS_VISIBLE** off).

   • Clear the Titlebar checkbox (**WS_CAPTION** off).

3. Run ClassWizard with the Visual C++ Dialog Editor open to your dialog-template resource.

4. In the Adding A Class dialog box, click on Create A New Class (unless you are importing or using an existing class).

5. In the New Class dialog box (see Figure 18.5), specify the base class for the new class as **CRecordView** (for ODBC) or **CDaoRecordView** (for DAO).

6. Type a name for the class and file names for its H and CPP files. Choose any other options you need, such as Automation.

7. Click on Create.

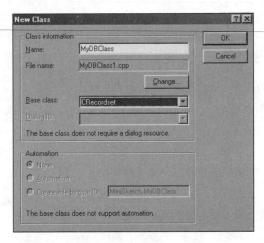

Figure 18.5   The New Class dialog box.

8. In the Choose A Recordset dialog box, choose the recordset class you created in Step 1, or click on New to create a new recordset class. If you choose to create a new recordset class, choose a datasource and table for the recordset; close the Choose A Recordset dialog box; and on returning to the Member Variables tab, choose your new recordset class.

9. Bind the desired columns to recordset field data members.

10. Click on Create to exit ClassWizard.

Mapping Form Controls To Recordset Fields

The DDX connection between a form view and a record view is different from the normal use of DDX, which connects the controls in a dialog box directly to the data members of the associated dialog class. As shown in Figure 18.1, DDX for a record view object is indirect: The connection goes from form controls (Customer No and so forth) through the record view object (**m_pSet**) to the field data members of the associated recordset object (**m_strCustomerNo**, and so forth).

To map form controls to recordset fields:

1. Click on ClassWizard's Member Variables tab.

2. In the Class Name drop-down list, choose the name of your record view class.

3. In the Control IDs list, choose a control ID.

4. Click on the Add Variable button to name the variable to be associated with the control.

5. In the Add Member Variable dialog box, choose a variable name by selecting a recordset data member in the Member Variable Name drop-down list. All variables of the recordset class appear in the list, not just variables of the currently selected data type. Be sure you choose the appropriate data member.

6. Click on OK to close the Add Member Variable dialog box.

7. Repeat Steps 3 through 6 for each control in the record view that you want to map to a recordset field data member.

8. Click on OK to close ClassWizard.

If you're running ClassWizard with the Visual C++ Dialog Editor open, you can use the following shortcut:

1. Choose a control on the form, then press Ctrl and double-click on the mouse. This opens ClassWizard's Add Member Variables dialog box.

2. Choose a recordset field data member to bind to the control.

3. Click on OK to close ClassWizard.

If you use this shortcut before you create a class for the dialog template, ClassWizard opens and displays the Add Class dialog box. If you follow this simple rule when placing controls on your record view form, ClassWizard is able to prechoose the most likely recordset member in the dialog box: Place the static text label for the control ahead of the corresponding control in the tab order.

You can also use the shortcut for push buttons. ClassWizard creates a message handler function in your record view class for the **BN_CLICKED** notification message. You can edit the code to specify the button's behavior.

Using Foreign Objects

The record view class shown in Figure 18.1 contains a member variable, which is a pointer whose type matches that of the foreign object. The DDX mapping is from three record view controls to corresponding members of the foreign object via the pointer, as illustrated by the following **DoDataExchange** function:

```
void CSectionForm::DoDataExchange(CDataExchange* pDX)
{
  CRecordView::DoDataExchange(pDX);
  //{{AFX_DATA_MAP(CSectionForm)
  DDX_FieldText(pDX, IDC_CUSTOMERNO,
    m_pSet->m_strCustomerNo, m_pSet);
```

```
    DDX_FieldText(pDX, IDC_ CUSTOMERNAME,
      m_pSet->m_strCustomerName, m_pSet);
    DDX_FieldText(pDX, IDC_ CUSTOMERADDRESS,
      m_pSet->m_strCustomerAddress, m_pSet);
    //}}AFX_DATA_MAP
}
```

Notice the indirect reference to recordset fields, via the **m_pSet** pointer, to a **CSections** recordset object:

```
m_pSet->m_strCourseID
```

You set the foreign class and object on ClassWizard's Class Info tab. You use the Foreign Class drop-down list to specify the class of the foreign object (**CRecordset** for ODBC or **CDaoRecordset** for DAO). You use the Foreign Variable field to specify the pointer variable that points to an object of that class. You can specify only one foreign object per class.

If you choose a class based on a dialog-template resource on ClassWizard's Member Variables tab, ClassWizard finds the appropriate pointer variable in the class and displays its type in the Foreign Class drop-down list and the variable name in the Foreign Variable field. You can change these values if you wish.

Creating ActiveX Controls

The **COleControl** class automatically fires stock events resulting from common actions, such as single and double clicks on the control, keyboard events, and changes to the state of the mouse buttons. Table 18.1 describes the stock events provided by **COleControl**.

Adding A Stock Event

To add a stock event using ClassWizard:

1. On the View menu, click on ClassWizard.
2. Click on the ActiveX Events tab.
3. Choose the name of your control class from the Class Name drop-down list.
4. Click on Add Event.
5. In the External Name list, click on the desired stock event.
6. Click on OK. Click on OK again to exit ClassWizard.

*Table 18.1   Stock events provided by **COleControl**.*

Event	Firing Function	Description/Event Map Entry
Click	**void FireClick( )**	Fired when the control captures the mouse, any **BUTTONUP** (left, middle, or right) message is received, and the button is released over the control. The stock **MouseDown** and **MouseUp** events occur before this event. Event map entry: **EVENT_STOCK_CLICK( )**
DblClick	**void FireDblClick( )**	Similar to **Click** but fired when a **BUTTONDBLCLK** message is received. Event map entry: **EVENT_STOCK_DBLCLICK( )**
Error	**void FireError()**	Fired when an error occurs within your ActiveX control outside of the scope of a method call or property access. Event map entry: **EVENT_STOCK_ERROREVENT( )**
KeyDown	**void FireKeyDown()**	Fired when a **WM_SYSKEYDOWN** or **WM_KEYDOWN** message is received. Event map entry: **EVENT_STOCK_KEYDOWN( )**
KeyPress	**void FireKeyPress()**	Fired when a **WM_CHAR** message is received. Event map entry: **EVENT_STOCK_KEYPRESS( )**
KeyUp	**void FireKeyUp()**	Fired when a **WM_SYSKEYUP** or **WM_KEYUP** message is received. Event map entry: **EVENT_STOCK_KEYUP( )**
MouseDown	**void FireMouseDown()**	Fired if any **BUTTONDOWN** (left, middle, or right) is received. The mouse is captured immediately before this event is fired. Event map entry: **EVENT_STOCK_MOUSEDOWN( )**
MouseMove	**void FireMouseMove()**	Fired when a **WM_MOUSEMOVE** message is received. Event map entry: **EVENT_STOCK_MOUSEMOVE( )**

(continued)

Table 18.1   Stock events provided by COleControl (continued).

Event	Firing Function	Description/Event Map Entry
MouseUp	**void FireMouseUp()**	Fired if any **BUTTONUP** (left, middle, or right) is received. The mouse capture is released before this event is fired.
		Event map entry: **EVENT_STOCK_MOUSEUP( )**
ReadyState-Change	**void FireReadyState-Change( )**	Fired when a control transitions to the next ready state due to the amount of data received.
		Event map entry: **EVENT_STOCK_READY-STATECHANGE( )**

Adding A Stock Property

To add a stock property using ClassWizard:

1. On the View menu, click on ClassWizard.

2. Click on the Automation tab.

3. Select the control's class from the Class Name drop-down.

4. Click on Add Property.

5. In the External Name list, click on the stock property you wish to add. Note that in the Implementation Group, Stock is automatically selected.

6. Click on OK to close the Add Property dialog box. Click on OK to exit ClassWizard.

Adding A Stock Method

To add a stock method using ClassWizard:

1. On the View menu, click on ClassWizard.

2. Choose the Automation tab.

3. Click on the control class in the Class Name drop-down list.

4. Click on Add Method.

5. In the External Name list, click on *XXX*, where *XXX* is the name of the stock method you wish to add.

6. Click on OK. Click on OK to exit ClassWizard.

Using Automation Support

Automation lets an application modify objects implemented in another application. An *Automation class* is a class that can be manipulated in that fashion. ClassWizard helps you create Automation classes and specify the properties and methods they expose to other applications.

Adding An Automation Class

To add an Automation class:

1. On the View menu, click on ClassWizard.

2. In ClassWizard, click on the Add Class drop-down list and click on New. The New Class dialog box appears.

3. Type a name for the class.

4. Choose a base class. Typically, new Automation classes are derived from **CCmdTarget**.

5. If you do not like the file names specified by ClassWizard, click on Change. The Change Files dialog box appears. Type new names for the H and CPP files. Click on OK to return to the New Class dialog box.

6. Click on the Automation option to expose this class to Automation clients. If you click on Createable By Type ID, you can specify a type ID for your Automation object. The Automation client will create an object of this class using the type ID.

7. When you have entered all the necessary information, click on OK. ClassWizard creates the necessary code and adds it to your project.

Adding A Property To An Automation Class

You can use member variable properties if you need to allocate storage for the values within an Automation class. The most common case for member variables is when there is no user interface that saves the revised state when changes occur.

To add a member variable property to your Automation class:

1. On the View menu, click on ClassWizard.

2. In ClassWizard, click on the Automation tab.

3. Choose the name of a class that supports Automation.

4. Click on Add Property, and type the following information:

   - External Name: Type the name that Automation clients will use to refer to this property.

   - Type: Choose any of the types found in the list.

   - Implementation: Click on Member Variable.

   - Variable Name: Type the name of the C++ class data member.

5. Click on OK to close ClassWizard.

Adding A **Get/Set** Method Property To An Automation Class

You can use **Get/Set** method properties if your Automation class deals with calculated properties. The most common use of **Get/Set** properties is cause in the user interface to reflect updates of calculated properties.

To add a **Get/Set** method property:

1. On the View menu, click on ClassWizard.

2. In ClassWizard, click on the Automation tab.

3. Choose the name of a class that supports Automation.

4. Click on Add Property, and supply the following information:

   - External Name: Type the name that Automation clients will use to refer to this property.

   - Type: Choose the appropriate type from among those found in the list.

   - Implementation: Click on Member Variable.

   - Get Function: Type the name of the member function used to get the property value.

   - Set Function: Type the name of the member function used to set the property value. This function can include special processing for when the property value is changed. If you want to create a read-only property, delete the name of the set function.

5. Add any method parameters you need, using the grid control:

   - Double-click in the first empty row under the Name label to activate an edit control, then type the parameter name.

   - Double-click in the row under the Type label to activate a drop-down list, then choose the parameter's type.

6. Continue this procedure until you have entered all the parameters you need. To delete a parameter, delete its row by clicking in the row and pressing the Delete or Back Space key.

7. Click on OK to create the necessary code.

Adding A Method To An Automation Class

To add a method to an Automation class:

1. On the View menu, click on ClassWizard.

2. In ClassWizard, click on the Automation tab.

3. Choose the name of a class that supports Automation.

4. Click on Add Method to open the Add Method dialog box, and then supply the following information:

   • External Name: Type the name that Automation clients will use to refer to this property.

   • Internal Name: Type the name of the C++ member function you want to add to the class.

   • Return Type: Choose the appropriate type from among those found in the list.

5. Double-click in the first empty row under the Name label to activate an edit control, then type the parameter name.

6. Double-click in the row under the Type label to activate a dropdown list, then choose the parameter's type.

7. Continue this procedure until you have entered all the parameters you need. To delete a parameter, delete its row by clicking in the row and pressing the Delete or Back Space key.

8. Click on OK to create the member function.

Accessing Automation Servers

Automation clients must have information about server objects' properties and methods in order to let clients manipulate the server's objects. Clients must know the data types of properties, method parameters, and method return values. Type libraries store this information in a form readable by ClassWizard. ClassWizard uses the information to create a dispatch class derived from **COleDispatchDriver**. An object of that class has shadow properties and operations that replicate those of the server object. Your application calls this object's properties and operations, and methods inherited from **COleDispatchDriver** route these calls to the OLE system, which in turn routes them to the server object.

ClassWizard automatically maintains the type library file for you if you specify support for Automation when you create your project. As part of each build, Visual C++ builds the TLB file with MkTypLib.

To create a dispatch class from a type library (.tlb) file:

1. On the View menu, click on ClassWizard.

2. In ClassWizard, click on the Add Class button and select From A Type Library from the drop-down list. The Import From Type Library dialog box appears.

3. In the Import From Type Library dialog box, choose the TLB file.

4. Click on OK. The Confirm Classes dialog box appears. The list contains the external names of the classes contained in the type library file. The Confirm Classes dialog box also shows the proposed names for the dispatch classes and for the header and implementation files for those classes. When you choose a class in the list, the Class Name list displays the name of the corresponding class.

   You can use the Browse buttons to choose other files, if you prefer to have the header and implementation information written in files or a directory other than those proposed by ClassWizard.

5. In the Confirm Classes dialog box, edit the names of the new dispatch classes and their files.

6. Click on OK to exit the Confirm Classes dialog box.

The Type Library tool writes header and implementation files for your dispatch class, using the class names and file names you have supplied, and adds the CPP file to your project.

WizardBar

In Brief

Using WizardBar To Access ClassView And ClassWizard Functions

WizardBar is a dockable toolbar that provides ready access to ClassView and ClassWizard functions. WizardBar also extends ClassView functionality by "tracking" your context, updating what's displayed in the WizardBar toolbar when your focus shifts. For example, WizardBar changes its display when you move the cursor from one function to another in the Text Editor.

To view WizardBar, right-click in an unused portion of the toolbar area, and choose WizardBar in the shortcut menu that appears. Figure 19.1 shows WizardBar.

The WizardBar interface includes three combo boxes and a combination of a button and drop-down menu that are referred to as the Action control. Clicking on the Action control prompts WizardBar to take an action, known as the default action, that varies from context to context.

Tooltips for the combo boxes are labeled:

- *Class*—The Class combo box displays the classes in the active project. If your workspace contains multiple projects, or a subproject, you can change the active project by choosing a new project from the Class combo box.

  When the Class control has focus, choosing the default action jumps you to the alphabetically first member of the selected class. If the selected class implements no functions or methods,

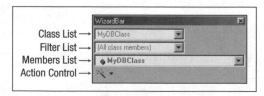

Figure 19.1   The Visual C++ WizardBar.

WizardBar displays a dialog box that lets you create a new function or method. For C++ global classes, the dialog box prompts you to create a new class.

- *Filter*—The Filter combo box provides useful filters related to the current class. You can choose from the All Class Members filter or specific resource IDs.

  When the focus is on a resource ID, WizardBar updates the Members combo box to reflect all valid Windows messages for the selected resource ID. Choosing the default action jumps you to the first implemented message handler in alphabetical order. If the class includes no message handlers, WizardBar opens a dialog box that lets you create one.

- *Members*—The Members combo box displays the result of the filter selected—for example, the specified class members or the Windows message handlers defined for the selected resource ID.

  When the Members control has focus, choosing the default action jumps you to the definition of the selected member.

The Action control provides a direct way to perform common tasks, such as navigating code. The task performed when you choose the Action button (the default action) is displayed in the tooltip for the button. The Action button has one of three possible states:

- *Tracking*—The Tracking state indicates that WizardBar is currently tracking your context.

- *Active*—The Active state indicates the WizardBar itself is active, but is not currently tracking your context. When the ClassView focus is on a project rather than a class, the Action control will be in the Active state, rather than the Tracking state.

- *Disabled*—The Disabled state indicates there is no open project.

The WizardBar Action menu appears when you click on the arrow next to the Action button, or when you click the right mouse button when the focus is on one of the WizardBar combo boxes. The Action menu shows the default action (which WizardBar performs when you click on the Action button) in bold. For controls, WizardBar also performs the default action when you double-click on the control in the Dialog Editor.

During a development session, you may switch focus from the Text Editor to the C++ Dialog Editor, to ClassView, and back to the Text Editor. Because WizardBar cannot track your context from every possible location in the Visual C++ IDE, WizardBar provides visual cues that indicate whether or not it is currently in Tracking mode. For example, the Action button changes color to indicate the current state of the WizardBar. Similarly, when your cursor is in a Text Editor window, WizardBar tracks and displays the current class or C++ member function. But, if you move the cursor to a section that contains code comments or C++ **include** statements, the display of the WizardBar Members combo box dims.

Immediate Solutions

Adding A Class To A Project

Like ClassView and ClassWizard, WizardBar uses the New Class dialog box to assist you in adding classes to your projects. To open the New Class dialog box, click on New Class on the WizardBar Action menu.

Working With Code

You can use WizardBar to quickly navigate your source code. Several navigational commands are available from the WizardBar Action menu. By choosing commands from this menu, you can:

- Jump to C++ class or function definitions or declarations.
- Jump to the next or previous function or method.
- Open a C++ include file from the current project.
- Jump to the Dialog Editor (only from a class that implements a dialog box).

You can also jump directly to the definition of a class member by choosing the member from WizardBar's Members combo box and pressing Enter, or by typing the name of the member into a WizardBar control.

Jumping To The Dialog Editor

To jump from a class that implements a dialog box to the Dialog Editor, do any of the following:

- Choose the class that implements the dialog box in WizardBar's Classes combo box.
- Choose the dialog ID from WizardBar's Members combo box.
- Choose Go To Dialog Editor from WizardBar's Action menu.

The Debugger

In Brief

Overview Of The Visual C++ Debugger

Visual C++ includes a debugger that can help you identify the source of problems and errors in your programs. To make effective use of the Visual C++ Debugger, you should build a Debug version of your program. By default, Visual C++ builds both a Debug and Release version of programs. The main differences between the Debug and Release versions are:

- The Debug version object files include full symbolic debugging information in Microsoft format. However, the compiler does not optimize code included in a Debug version, because optimization generally makes debugging more difficult.

- The Release version object files lack symbolic debugging information. However, the compiler optimizes the code for maximum execution speed.

You control the Debugger by means of commands found on the Visual C++ Build, Debug, View, and Edit menus:

- *Build menu*—Includes the Start Debug command, which offers a subset of the commands on the full Debug menu. These four commands (Go, Step Into, Run To Cursor, and Attach To Process) start the debugging process.

- *Debug menu*—Appears in the menu bar only while the Debugger is running or stopped at a breakpoint, taking the place of the Build menu that otherwise appears. The Debug menu lets you control program execution and access the QuickWatch window.

- *View menu*—Includes commands that display various Debugger windows, such as the Variables window and the Call Stack window.

- *Edit menu*—Provides access to the Breakpoints dialog box, with which you can insert, remove, enable, or disable breakpoints.

Several special Debugger windows display debugging information. When debugging, you can access these windows using the View menu. These information windows are:

- *Output window*—Displays information about the build process, such as errors or output from the **OutputDebugString** function, and thread termination codes.

- *Watch window*—Displays names and values of variables and expressions.

- *Variables window*—Displays the values of nearby variables and function returns.

- *Registers window*—Displays the contents of the general-purpose and CPU status registers.

- *Memory window*—Displays current memory contents.

- *Call Stack window*—Displays the stacks of all function calls that have not returned

- *Disassembly window*—Displays assembly language code equivalent to that of compiled program statements.

The Debugger also provides several dialog boxes that let you manipulate breakpoints, variables, threads, and exceptions:

- *Breakpoints dialog box*—Displays a list of all breakpoints assigned to your project. You can use the tabs in the Breakpoints dialog box to create new breakpoints.

- *Exceptions dialog box*—Displays system and user-defined exceptions. You can use the Exceptions dialog box to control the way the Debugger handles exceptions.

- *QuickWatch dialog box*—Displays a variable or expression. You can use the QuickWatch dialog box to view or modify a variable or expression or to add it to the Watch window.

- *Threads dialog box*—Displays application threads. You can use the Threads dialog box to suspend and resume threads and to set focus.

You access the Breakpoints dialog box using the Breakpoints command on the Edit menu. You access other Debugger dialog boxes by using the commands on the Debug menu. The Debugger interface also supports intelligent drag-and-drop operations. For example, you can drag variables from the Variables window to the Watch window, where the variable information will be updated each time the Watch window is updated. If you drag a variable to a text window, the variable information is converted into text. If you drag a variable to the Memory window or the Disassembly window, the variable is used as a pointer, and the window scrolls to display the memory contents or instructions at the indicated address.

The Watch window, Variables window, and QuickWatch dialog box use *spreadsheet fields,* which are special fields that resemble the cells of a spreadsheet program such as Microsoft Excel. The Variables window lets you edit cells in its Value column. The Watch window lets you edit cells in its Name and Value columns.

Spreadsheet fields contain special controls that simplify viewing of arrays, objects, structures, and pointer variables. Figure 20.4 (shown later in this chapter) shows the spreadsheet fields of the Variables window, which work somewhat like directory icons in the Windows Explorer. Some variables (arrays, objects, and structures) are marked with a box containing a plus sign (+) in the Name column. You can expand the variable by clicking on the plus sign, which opens a tree that shows the elements or members of the variable. These too may contain additional boxes. When a variable is expanded, the box in the Name column contains a minus sign (–). You can collapse an expanded variable by clicking on the minus sign. Alternatively, you can expand a variable by selecting it and pressing the Shift and + keys or the right arrow key. You can collapse a variable by selecting it and pressing the - key or left arrow key.

For pointer variables, the branch immediately below the variable contains the value pointed to. Scalar variables, which have no components to expand, do not have boxes in the Name column.

Just as in the Windows Explorer, if you want to make a column wider or narrower, you can size it by dragging the divider at the right edge of the column.

20. The Debugger

Immediate Solutions

Starting The Debugger And Running The Program

In order to activate the Debugger, you must start your program in a special way. Once the Debugger is active, you can use it to control the way your program runs. You can also halt your program or hide the debugging toolbar.

Starting Debugging

To start debugging:

1. Click on Start Debug on the Build menu.

2. Click on Go, Step Into, or Run To Cursor.

Running To A Location

To run to the cursor (while the Debugger is not running):

1. Move the insertion point in the Text Editor window to the location in the source code where you want the Debugger to break.

2. From the Build menu, choose Start Debug, then choose Run To Cursor.

To run to the cursor (while the Debugger is running but halted):

1. Move the insertion point in the Text Editor window to the location in the source code where you want the Debugger to break.

2. From the Debug menu, choose Run To Cursor.

To run to the cursor location in disassembly code (while the Debugger is running but halted):

1. In the Disassembly window (see Figure 20.1), move the insertion point to the line where you want the Debugger to break.

2. On the Debug menu, click on Run To Cursor.

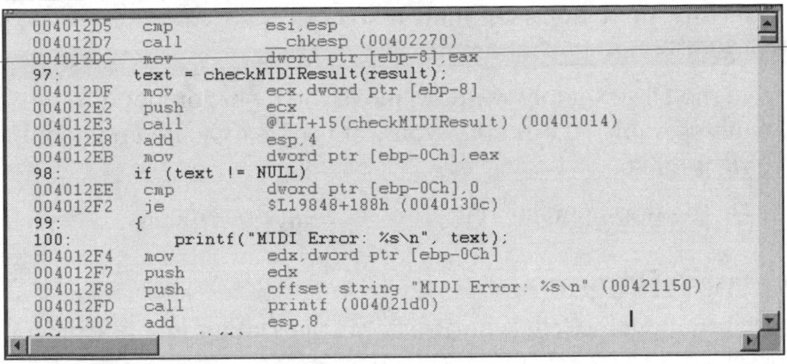

```
004012D5   cmp          esi,esp
004012D7   call         __chkesp (00402270)
004012DC   mov          dword ptr [ebp-8],eax
97:     text = checkMIDIResult(result);
004012DF   mov          ecx,dword ptr [ebp-8]
004012E2   push         ecx
004012E3   call         @ILT+15(checkMIDIResult) (00401014)
004012E8   add          esp,4
004012EB   mov          dword ptr [ebp-0Ch],eax
98:     if (text != NULL)
004012EE   cmp          dword ptr [ebp-0Ch],0
004012F2   je           $L19848+188h (0040130c)
99:     {
100:        printf("MIDI Error: %s\n", text);
004012F4   mov          edx,dword ptr [ebp-0Ch]
004012F7   push         edx
004012F8   push         offset string "MIDI Error: %s\n" (00421150)
004012FD   call         printf (004021d0)
00401302   add          esp,8
```

Figure 20.1   The Disassembly window.

To run to the cursor location in the call stack code (while the Debugger is running but halted):

1. In the Call Stack window (see Figure 20.2), choose the function name.

2. From the Debug menu, choose Run To Cursor.

To run to a specified function:

1. In the Find field on the standard toolbar, type the function name.

2. On the Build menu, click on Start Debug.

3. On the Start Debug menu, click on Run To Cursor.

To set the next statement to execute (while the Debugger is running but halted):

1. In a source window, move the insertion point to the statement or instruction that you want to be executed next and right-click.

2. On the pop-up menu, click on Set Next Statement.

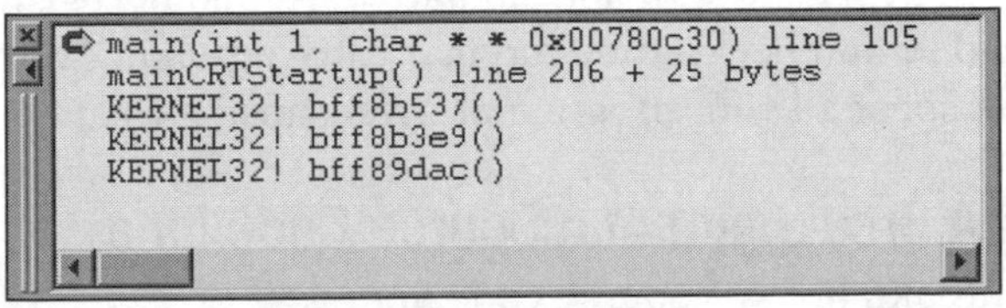

```
main(int 1, char * * 0x00780c30) line 105
mainCRTStartup() line 206 + 25 bytes
KERNEL32! bff8b537()
KERNEL32! bff8b3e9()
KERNEL32! bff89dac()
```

Figure 20.2   The Call Stack window.

To set the next disassembled instruction to execute (while the Debugger is running but halted):

1. In the Disassembly window, move the insertion point to the disassembled instruction you want to be executed next and right-click.

2. On the pop-up menu, click on Set Next Statement.

Halting A Program

To halt debugging, click on Break on the Debug menu. Control returns to the Microsoft Visual C++ IDE.

Displaying And Hiding The Debug Toolbar

The Debug toolbar provides quick access to several of the same functions provided by menus. To display or hide the Debug toolbar:

1. Click on Customize on the Tools menu.

2. Choose the Toolbars tab.

3. Select the box marked Toolbar to display the Debug toolbar; clear the box to hide the Debug toolbar.

4. Click on Close.

Some Debugger functions are found on the Build toolbar, which you can display or hide in a similar fashion.

Setting Breakpoints

You can use the Breakpoints dialog box to set, remove, disable, enable, or view breakpoints. The breakpoints you set will be saved as a part of your project.

Debugging involves use of special hardware debug registers, which are limited in number. Setting too many breakpoints can reduce the execution speed of your program or even cause it to appear to hang.

Setting A Breakpoint At A Source Code Line

To set a breakpoint at a source code line:

1. In a source window, move the insertion point to the line where you want the program to break. If you want to set a breakpoint

on a source statement extending across two or more lines, you must set the breakpoint on the last line of the statement.

2. Click on the Insert/Remove Breakpoint button on the Build toolbar.

A red dot appears in the left margin, indicating that the breakpoint is set.

Running Until A Breakpoint Is Reached

To run until a breakpoint is reached:

1. Set the breakpoint.

2. On the Build menu, click on Start Debug.

3. From the Start Debug menu, choose Go.

Setting A Breakpoint At The Beginning Of A Function

To set a breakpoint at the beginning of a function:

1. In the Find field on the Standard toolbar, type the function name.

2. Click on the Insert/Remove Breakpoint button on the Build toolbar.

A red dot appears in the left margin of your source code, at the beginning of the function, indicating that the breakpoint is set.

Setting A Breakpoint At The Return Point Of A Function

To set a breakpoint at the return point of a function:

1. Start the Debugger and pause it in break mode.

2. On the View menu, click on Debug Windows, then click on Call Stack.

3. In the Call Stack window, move the insertion point to the function where you want the program to break.

4. Click on the Insert/Remove Breakpoint button on the Build toolbar .

A red dot appears in the left margin of your source code, indicating that the breakpoint is set.

Setting A Breakpoint At A Label

To set a breakpoint at a label:

1. In the Find field on the Standard toolbar, type the name of the label.

2. Click on the Insert/Remove Breakpoint button on the Build toolbar.

A red dot appears in the left margin of your source code, at the line containing the label, indicating that the breakpoint is set.

TIP: *If you set multiple location breakpoints on a line, enabling some and disabling others, a gray dot appears in the left margin in the Source window, Disassembly window, and Call Stack window. When you click on the Enable/Disable Breakpoint button on the Build toolbar, all breakpoints on the line become disabled, and the gray dot changes to a hollow circle. If you click again on the Enable/Disable Breakpoint button on the Build toolbar, all breakpoints on the line become enabled and the hollow circle changes to a red dot.*

Viewing The Current Breakpoints

To view the list of current breakpoints:

1. On the Edit menu, click on Breakpoints.

2. Use the scrollbar to move up or down the Breakpoints list.

Disabling A Breakpoint

To disable a breakpoint:

1. For a location breakpoint in a source code window or in the Call Stack or Disassembly window, move the insertion point to the line containing the breakpoint you want to disable.

2. Click on the Enable/Disable Breakpoint button on the Build toolbar button, or click the right mouse button and choose Disable Breakpoint from the pop-up menu.

Alternatively, you can follow this procedure:

1. For any breakpoint in the Breakpoints dialog box, find the breakpoint in the Breakpoints list.

2. Clear the checkbox corresponding to the breakpoint that you want to disable.

3. Click on OK.

For a location breakpoint, the red dot in the left margin changes to a hollow circle.

Disabling All Location Breakpoints

To disable all location breakpoints, click on the Disable All Breakpoints button on the Build toolbar. The red dots in the left margin change to hollow circles.

NOTE: *You can also use the spacebar to toggle the state of one or more breakpoints in the Breakpoints list.*

Enabling A Breakpoint

To enable a breakpoint:

1. For a location breakpoint in a source code window or in the Call Stack or Disassembly window, move the insertion point to the line containing the breakpoint you want to enable.

2. Click on the Enable/Disable Breakpoint button on the Build toolbar, or click the right mouse button and choose Enable Breakpoint from the shortcut menu.

Alternatively, you can follow this procedure:

1. In the Breakpoints dialog box, find the breakpoint in the Breakpoints list.

2. Choose the empty checkbox corresponding to the breakpoint that you want to enable.

3. Click on OK.

For a location breakpoint, the hollow circle in the left margin changes to a red dot.

NOTE: *You can also use the spacebar to toggle the state of one or more breakpoints in the Breakpoints list.*

Removing A Breakpoint

To remove a breakpoint:

1. For a location breakpoint in a source window or in the Call Stack or Disassembly window, move the insertion point to the line containing the breakpoint you want to remove.

2. Click on the Insert/Remove Breakpoint button on the Build toolbar, or click the right mouse button and choose Remove Breakpoint from the shortcut menu.

Alternatively, you can follow this procedure:

1. In the Breakpoints dialog box, choose one or more breakpoints in the Breakpoints list.

2. Click on the Remove button, or press the Delete key.

3. Click on OK.

For a location breakpoint, the red dot in the left margin disappears.

Viewing The Source Code Where A Breakpoint Is Set

To view the source code where a breakpoint is set:

1. In the Breakpoints dialog box, choose a location breakpoint in the Breakpoints list.

2. Click on the Edit Code button.

The Debugger takes you to the source code for a breakpoint set at a line number or function name. In the case of function names, the Debugger must be running for this to work.

Setting A Breakpoint At A Memory Address

To set a breakpoint at a memory address:

1. From the View menu, click on Debug Windows and then click on Disassembly. The Disassembly window opens.

2. In the Disassembly window, move the insertion point to the line where you want the program to break.

3. Click on the Insert/Remove Breakpoint button on the Build toolbar .

A red dot appears in the left margin, indicating that the breakpoint is set.

Setting A Conditional Breakpoint

To set a conditional breakpoint:

1. From the Edit menu, click on Breakpoints. The Breakpoints dialog box appears.

2. Choose the Location tab.

3. In the Break At field, type the location (source line number, memory address, or function name) at which you want to set the breakpoint.

4. Click on Condition. The Breakpoint Condition dialog box appears.

5. Type the appropriate text in the Expression and Number Of Elements fields.

6. In the Breakpoint Condition dialog box, click on OK to set the condition.

7. In the Breakpoints dialog box, click on OK to set the breakpoint.

Setting A Conditional Breakpoint With A Skip Count

To set a conditional breakpoint with a skip count:

1. From the Edit menu, click on Breakpoints. The Breakpoints dialog box appears.

2. Choose the Location tab.

3. In the Break At field, type the location (source line number, memory address, or function name) at which you want to set the breakpoint.

4. Click on Condition. The Breakpoint Condition dialog box appears.

5. Type the appropriate text in the Expression and Number Of Elements fields.

6. Complete the Enter The Numbers Of Times To Skip Before Stopping field. If you want your program to break every nth time the condition is met at the specified location, set the number of times to $n - 1$.

7. In the Breakpoint Condition dialog box, click on OK to set the condition.

8. In the Breakpoints dialog box, click on OK to set the breakpoint.

Setting Breakpoints Outside The Current Scope

You can set a breakpoint on a location or variable that is not within the current scope in either of two ways:

• By using the Advanced Breakpoint dialog box.

• By using Advanced Breakpoint Syntax.

Using the Advanced Breakpoint dialog box is usually the better approach, because the dialog box handles many details for you and does not require you to learn any special syntax. To break on a location outside the current scope by using the Advanced Breakpoint dialog box:

1. From the Edit menu, click on Breakpoints.

2. Click on the Location tab on the Breakpoints dialog box.

3. Choose the drop-down menu next to the Break At field and click on Advanced. The Advanced Breakpoint dialog box appears.

4. In the Location field, type the location (source line number, memory address, or function name) at which you want to set the breakpoint.

5. Under Context, type any necessary information in the Function, Source File, and Executable File fields.

6. Click on OK to close the Advanced Breakpoint dialog box. The information that you specified appears in the Break At field of the Breakpoints dialog box.

7. In the Breakpoints dialog box, click on OK to set the breakpoint.

To use advanced breakpoints syntax, you must qualify a breakpoint location or variable with a special context operator, using this syntax:

```
{[function],[source],[exe] } location
{[function],[source],[exe] } variable_name
{[function],[source],[exe] } expression
```

The context operator is a pair of braces ({}) that encloses two commas and some combination of function name, source file name, and executable file name. Even if you omit either *function* or *exe*, you must nevertheless include both commas. However, if you omit both *source* and *exe*, you can omit the commas. The *location* can be any line number, function, or memory address at which you can set a breakpoint.

If the *source* or *exe* file name includes a comma, an embedded space, or a brace, you must use double quotation marks around the file name.

An alternative syntax for advanced breakpoints uses the exclamation point instead of the context operator:

```
source!.location
```

This form of advanced breakpoint syntax lacks the function name and *.exe* specifiers. If you use this syntax to specify a file name that contains an exclamation point, you must surround the file name with double quotes.

Setting Breakpoints When Values Change Or Become True

You can set breakpoints that halt program execution when an expression changes value or evaluates to true. These types of breakpoints are referred to as *data breakpoints*. You can set a data breakpoint on any valid C or C++ expression. Breakpoint expressions can include memory addresses and register mnemonics. The Debugger interprets all constants as decimal numbers unless they begin with 0 (octal) or 0x (hexadecimal).

Setting A Breakpoint When A Variable Changes Value
To set a breakpoint when a variable changes value:

1. From the Edit menu, click on Breakpoints.

2. Click on the Data tab of the Breakpoints dialog box.

3. In the Expression field, type the name of the variable.

4. Click on OK to set the breakpoint.

Setting A Breakpoint When An Expression Changes Value
To set a breakpoint when an expression changes value:

1. From the Edit menu, click on Breakpoints.

2. Click on the Data tab of the Breakpoints dialog box.

3. In the Expression field, type an expression, such as $x*y$.

4. Click on OK to set the breakpoint.

Setting A Breakpoint When An Expression Is True
To set a breakpoint when an expression is true:

1. From the Edit menu, click on Breakpoints.

2. Click on the Data tab of the Breakpoints dialog box.

3. In the Expression field, type an expression, such as **x==1**, that evaluates to true or false.

4. Click on OK to set the breakpoint.

Breaking On A Variable Outside The Current Scope

To break on a variable outside the current scope:

1. From the Edit menu, click on Breakpoints.

2. Click on the Data tab of the Breakpoints dialog box.

3. In the Expression field, type the variable name.

4. Choose the drop-down menu to the right of the field and click on Advanced. The Advanced Breakpoint dialog box appears.

5. In the Expression field, type the function name and (if necessary) the file name of the variable.

6. Click on OK to close the Advanced Breakpoint dialog box. The information that you specified appears in the Expression field in the Breakpoints dialog box.

7. In the Breakpoints dialog box, click on OK to set the breakpoint.

Breaking When Initial Element Of Array Changes Value

To break when the initial element of an array changes value:

1. From the Edit menu, click on Breakpoints.

2. Click on the Data tab of the Breakpoints dialog box.

3. In the Expression field, type the first element of the array (for example, **theArray[0]**).

4. In the Number Of Elements field on the Data tab, type "1".

5. Click on OK to set the breakpoint.

Breaking When Initial Element Of Array Has Specific Value

To break when the initial element of an array has a specific value:

1. From the Edit menu, click on Breakpoints.

2. Click on the Data tab of the Breakpoints dialog box.

3. In the Expression field, type an expression containing the initial element of the array (for example, **theArray[0]==1**).

4. In the Number Of Elements field, type "1".

5. Click on OK to set the breakpoint.

Breaking When A Particular Element Of An Array Changes Value

To break when a particular element of an array changes value:

1. From the Edit menu, click on Breakpoints.

2. Click on the Data tab of the Breakpoints dialog box.

3. In the Expression field, type the element of the array (for example, **theArray[10]**).

4. In the Number Of Elements field, type "1".

5. Click on OK to set the breakpoint.

Breaking When Any Element Of An Array Changes Value

To break when any element of an array changes value:

1. From the Edit menu, click on Breakpoints.

2. Click on the Data tab of the Breakpoints dialog box.

3. In the Expression field, type the first element of the array (for example, **theArray[0]**).

4. In the Number Of Elements field, enter the number of elements in the array.

5. Click on OK to set the breakpoint.

Breaking When First Elements Of An Array Change Value

To break when any of the first n elements of an array change value:

1. From the Edit menu, click on Breakpoints.

2. Click on the Data tab of the Breakpoints dialog box.

3. In the Expression field, type the first element of the array (for example, **theArray[0]**).

4. In the Number Of Elements text box, type the number n.

5. Click on OK to set the breakpoint on **theArray[0]** through **theArray[4]**.

Breaking When Location Value Of Pointer Changes

To break when the location value of a pointer changes:

1. From the Edit menu, click on Breakpoints.

2. Click on the Data tab of the Breakpoints dialog box.

3. In the Expression field, type the pointer variable name (for example, **p**).

4. Click on OK to set the breakpoint.

Breaking When Value At The Location Pointed To Changes

To break when the value at a location pointed to changes:

1. From the Edit menu, click on Breakpoints.

2. Click on the Data tab of the Breakpoints dialog box.

20. The Debugger

3. In the Expression field, type the dereferenced pointer variable expression (for example, ***p** or **p->data**).

4. Click on OK to set the breakpoint.

Breaking When An Array Pointed To By A Pointer Changes

To break when an array pointed to by a pointer changes:

1. From the Edit menu, click on Breakpoints.

2. Click on the Data tab of the Breakpoints dialog box.

3. In the Expression field, type the dereferenced pointer variable name (for example, ***p**).

4. In the Number Of Elements field, enter the length of the array in elements. For example, if the pointer is a pointer to **int**, and the array pointed to contains 10 values of type **int**, type "10".

5. Click on OK to set the breakpoint.

Breaking When Value At Specified Memory Address Changes

To break when the value at a specified memory address changes:

1. From the Edit menu, click on Breakpoints.

2. Click on the Data tab of the Breakpoints dialog box.

3. In the Expression field, type the memory address for the byte. For a word or doubleword memory address, enclose the address in parentheses, and precede it with a cast operator, using **WO** for a word, or **DW** for a doubleword. For example, use **WO(120456)** for a word address.

4. In the Number Of Elements field, type the number of bytes, words, or doublewords you want to monitor. Specify the number of bytes, words, or doublewords, using the unit of measure appropriate to the type you specified in Step 3.

5. Click on OK to set the breakpoint.

Breaking When A Register Changes

To break when a register changes:

1. From the Edit menu, click on Breakpoints.

2. Click on the Data tab of the Breakpoints dialog box.

3. In the Expression field, type a register mnemonic, such as **DS**.

4. In the Number Of Elements field, type the number of bytes you want to monitor.

5. Click on OK to set the breakpoint.

Breaking When A Register Expression Is True

To break when a register expression is true:

1. From the Edit menu, click on Breakpoints.

2. Click on the Data tab of the Breakpoints dialog box.

3. In the Expression field, type an expression that contains a Boolean comparison operator, such as **DS==0**.

4. In the Number Of Elements field, type the number of bytes you want to monitor.

5. Click on OK to set the breakpoint.

Setting A Breakpoint On A Specified **WndProc** Message

To set a breakpoint on a specified **WndProc** message:

1. From the Edit menu, click on Breakpoints. The Breakpoints dialog box appears.

2. Click on the Messages tab.

3. In the Break At WndProc field, type the name of the Windows function that handles the **WndProc** message. If you are setting a breakpoint during a debug session, the list contains the exported functions in your project.

4. In the Set One Breakpoint For Each Message To Watch list, choose the message.

5. To set another breakpoint, press Enter, and then repeat Steps 3 and 4. The Breakpoints list displays the currently active breakpoints.

6. Click on OK to set the breakpoints.

WARNING! *If you interrupt execution while Windows or other system code is running, the results can be unpredictable.*

Stepping Into Functions

To run the program and execute the next statement, referred to as "stepping into":

1. While the program is paused in break mode (that is, waiting for user input after completing a debugging command), click on Step Into from the Debug menu.

2. The Debugger executes the next statement, then pauses execution in break mode. If the next statement is a function

call, the Debugger steps into that function, then pauses execution at the beginning of the function.

3. Repeat Step 1 to continue executing the program one statement at a time.

Stepping Over Or Out Of Functions

To step over a function:

1. Open a source file, and start debugging.

2. Execute the program to a function call.

3. On the Debug menu, click on Step Over.

The Debugger executes the next function, but pauses after the function returns. You can repeat Step 3 to continue executing the program one statement at a time.

To step out of a function:

1. Start debugging, and execute the program to some point inside the function.

2. On the Debug menu, click on Step Out.

The Debugger continues until the function returns, then the Debugger pauses.

Using Edit And Continue

Edit And Continue lets you make changes to your source code while your program is being debugged. You can make code changes while the program is running or halted under the Debugger. Edit And Continue is subject to a few limitations. For example, you can add new variables totaling no more than 64 bytes to an active function. Moreover, Edit And Continue cannot handle some types of code changes, for example:

- Changes to resource files

- Changes to code in read-only files

- Changes to optimized code

WARNING!   You should not use Edit And Continue on optimized code, because results are unpredictable.

- Changes to exception-handling blocks
- Changes to data types, including class, structure, union, or enumeration definitions
- Additions of new data types
- Removal of functions or changes to function prototypes
- Most changes to global or static code
- Changes to executables that are copied from another machine rather than built locally

In some cases, Edit And Continue may be able to apply the code changes later if you continue debugging. In such instances, Edit And Continue gives you two options:

- Cancel the Go or Step command. You may then reverse the change or stop the debugging session and recompile the program for a clean start.
- Finish executing the current call using the original code. Edit And Continue can apply the code changes to the modified function when the current call completes.

Applying Code Changes

To apply code changes to a program you are debugging, click on Apply Code Changes from the Debug menu.

When your code change affects a control statement, the program's point of execution may move to a new location when Edit And Continue applies the changes. Edit And Continue places the point of execution as accurately as possible, but the results may be approximate rather than precise. A dialog box warns you of this possibility; you should verify that the new location is correct before you continue debugging, using Set Next Statement to correct the location, if necessary.

Enabling/Disabling Automatic Edit And Continue

To enable/disable Automatic Edit And Continue:

1. From the Tools Menu, click on Options.
2. In the Options dialog box, choose the Debug tab.
3. On the Debug tab, choose or clear the Debug Commands Invoke Edit And Continue checkbox, as appropriate.

You do not need to rebuild your application after changing this setting. You can change the setting even while debugging. However, altering this setting affects all projects you work on.

To enable/disable Edit And Continue for the current project:

1. From the Project menu, click on Settings.

2. In the Project Settings dialog box, choose the C/C++ tab and the General category.

3. On the C/C++ tab, choose the Debug Info list box. Choose Program Database For Edit And Continue to enable Edit And Continue, or choose another option to disable it.

4. Click on OK to close the dialog box.

5. Rebuild your application.

Related solutions:	Found on page:
Building A Project	326

Viewing Program State Information

The Debugger lets you view or modify the value of program variables and registers. You can also view type information and disassembly code.

Viewing A Value

To view the value of a variable or expression or contents of a register:

1. Wait for the Debugger to stop at a breakpoint. Or click on Break on the Debug menu to halt the Debugger.

2. On the Debug menu, click on QuickWatch.

3. Type or paste the variable or register name or an expression into the Expression field, and click on Recalculate.

4. Click on Close.

As a convenience, the Expression drop-down list contains the most recently used QuickWatch expressions.

To view the value of a variable using QuickWatch:

1. When the Debugger is stopped at a breakpoint, switch to a source window, and right-click on a variable.

2. On the pop-up menu, click on QuickWatch *XXX*, where *XXX* is the name of the variable you selected in Step 1.

3. Click on Close.

To view the value of a variable or expression or the contents of a register in the Watch window (which is shown in Figure 20.3):

1. Start debugging and pause the Debugger in break mode.

2. On the View menu, click on Debug Windows, then click on Watch.

3. Choose a tab for the variable or expression.

4. Type, paste, or drag the variable or register name, or an expression into the Name column on the tab. If you typed the entry, press Enter.

The Watch window immediately evaluates the variable or expression and displays the value or an error message.

To view a variable in the Variables window (which is shown in Figure 20.4):

1. Start debugging, and pause the Debugger in break mode.

2. On the View menu, click on Debug Windows, then click on Variables.

3. Click on the Auto tab, Locals tab, or This tab, according to the type of variables you want to see.

The Registers window lets you view the contents of CPU registers, as shown in Figure 20.5. To view the registers by using the Registers

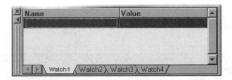

Figure 20.3   The Watch window.

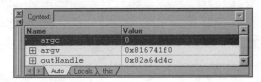

Figure 20.4   The Variables window.

20. The Debugger

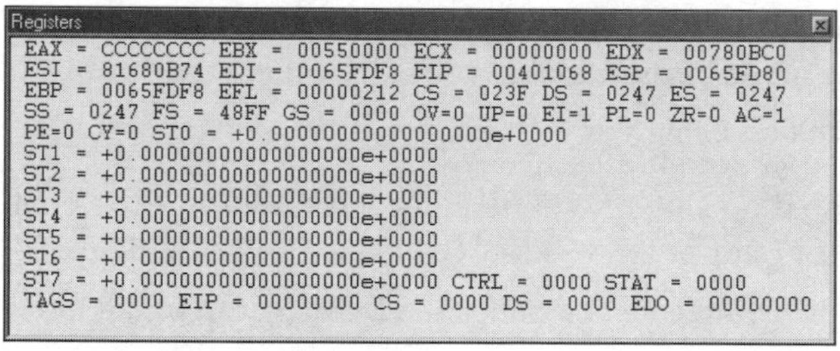

```
Registers                                                                    ⊠
EAX = CCCCCCCC EBX = 00550000 ECX = 00000000 EDX = 00780BC0
ESI = 81680B74 EDI = 0065FDF8 EIP = 00401068 ESP = 0065FD80
EBP = 0065FDF8 EFL = 00000212 CS = 023F DS = 0247 ES = 0247
SS = 0247 FS = 48FF GS = 0000 OV=0 UP=0 EI=1 PL=0 ZR=0 AC=1
PE=0 CY=0 ST0 = +0.00000000000000000e+0000
ST1 = +0.00000000000000000e+0000
ST2 = +0.00000000000000000e+0000
ST3 = +0.00000000000000000e+0000
ST4 = +0.00000000000000000e+0000
ST5 = +0.00000000000000000e+0000
ST6 = +0.00000000000000000e+0000
ST7 = +0.00000000000000000e+0000 CTRL = 0000 STAT = 0000
TAGS = 0000 EIP = 00000000 CS = 0000 DS = 0000 EDO = 00000000
```

Figure 20.5   The Registers window.

window, choose Debug Windows And Registers from the View menu, then click on Debug Windows and Registers.

The Debugger's Memory window lets you view program memory, as shown in Figure 20.6.

To view memory by using the Memory window:

1. Click on the View menu, then click on Debug Windows and Memory. The Memory window appears.

2. Click on the Memory window to select it.

3. Type a memory address into the Address field and press Enter.

The Memory window displays the contents of the specified memory location.

Viewing Type Information

To view type information for a variable in the Watch window:

1. In the Watch window, choose the line that contains the variable whose type you want to see.

2. On the View menu, click on Properties.

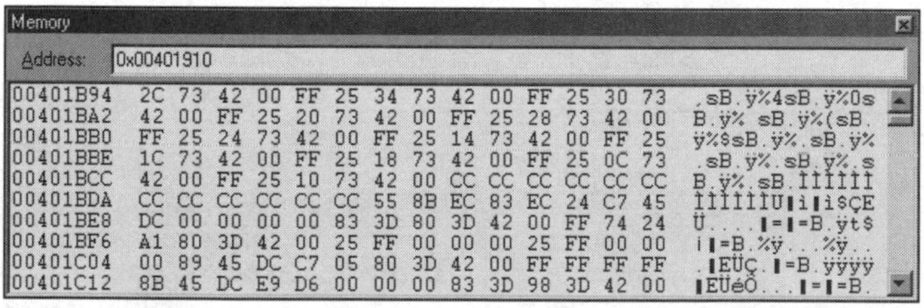

```
Memory                                                                       ⊠
Address:  0x00401910
00401B94   2C 73 42 00 FF 25 34 73 42 00 FF 25 30 73   ,sB.ÿ%4sB.ÿ%0s  ▲
00401BA2   42 00 FF 25 20 73 42 00 FF 25 28 73 42 00   B.ÿ% sB.ÿ%(sB.  ▬
00401BB0   FF 25 24 73 42 00 FF 25 14 73 42 00 FF 25   ÿ%$sB.ÿ%.sB.ÿ%
00401BBE   1C 73 42 00 FF 25 18 73 42 00 FF 25 0C 73   .sB.ÿ%.sB.ÿ%.s
00401BCC   42 00 FF 25 10 73 42 00 CC CC CC CC CC CC   B.ÿ%.sB.ÌÌÌÌÌÌ
00401BDA   CC CC CC CC CC CC 55 8B EC 83 EC 24 C7 45   ÌÌÌÌÌÌU¦¦¦¦¦$ÇE
00401BE8   DC 00 00 00 00 83 3D 80 3D 42 00 FF 74 24   Ü....¦=¦=B.ÿt$
00401BF6   A1 80 3D 42 00 25 FF 00 00 00 25 FF 00 00   ¦¦=B.%ÿ...%ÿ..
00401C04   00 89 45 DC C7 05 80 3D 42 00 FF FF FF FF   .¦EÜÇ.¦=B.ÿÿÿÿ
00401C12   8B 45 DC E9 D6 00 00 00 83 3D 98 3D 42 00   ¦EÜéÖ...¦=¦=B.   ▼
```

Figure 20.6   The Memory window.

To view type information for a variable in the Variables window:

1. In the Variables window, click on the Auto tab, Locals tab, or This tab.

2. Choose the line that contains the variable whose type you want to see.

3. On the View menu, click on Properties.

Modifying Values

When you pause the program at a breakpoint or between steps, you can change the value of any non-**const** variable or the contents of any register. To modify the value of a variable or contents of a register using QuickWatch:

1. On the Debug menu, click on QuickWatch.

2. In the Expression field, type the variable or register name.

3. Click on the Recalculate button.

4. If the variable is an array or object, use the + box to expand the view until you see the value you want to modify.

5. Use the Tab key to move to the value you want to modify.

6. Type the new value and press Enter.

7. Click on Close.

You cannot edit an entire array at once. To change the value of an array, modify the individual fields or elements.

To modify the value of a variable or contents of a register using the Watch window:

1. In the Watch window, double-click on the value. Or use the Tab key to move the insertion point to the value you want to modify.

2. If the variable is an array or object, use the + box to expand the view until you see the value you want to modify.

3. Type the new value, and press Enter.

To modify the value of a variable in the Variables window:

1. In the Variables window, click on the Auto tab, Locals tab, or This tab.

2. Choose the line that contains the variable whose type you want to modify.

3. If the variable is an array or object, use the + box to expand the view until you see the value you want to modify.

4. Double-click on the value, or use the Tab key to move the insertion point to the value you want to modify.

5. Type the new value and press Enter. The new value appears in red.

Viewing Thread Information

You can view the Thread Information Block for the current thread. The Debugger uses a pseudoregister called **TIB** to refer to the Thread Information Block. You can view the contents of the **TIB** pseudo-register in the Watch window or QuickWatch dialog box by using the standard procedures for displaying registers.

You can also view the last error code for the current thread. The Debugger uses a pseudoregister called **ERR** to refer to the last error code for the current thread. You can view the contents of the **ERR** pseudoregister in the Watch window or QuickWatch dialog box using the standard procedures for displaying registers. To display the error code in meaningful form, use the **hr** format specifier with **ERR**:

```
ERR, hr
```

Displaying Meaningful Values For A Custom Data Type

The contents of the file autoexp.dat specify how the Debugger displays data types in windows, QuickWatch, and DataTips. You can modify this file to add meaningful displays for your own data types. For details, see the autoexp.dat file itself, which is located in the /bin subdirectory beneath the directory in which you installed Visual C++.

Viewing Disassembly Code

The Debugger lets you view the assembly code that corresponds to specified source code. It also lets you view the call stack for a function.

Viewing Specific Source Code

To view specific source code in the Disassembly window:

1. Start debugging, and pause the Debugger in break mode.

2. On the View menu, click on Debug Windows, then click on Disassembly.

Viewing The Call Stack For A Function
To view the call stack for a function:

1. Place the Text Editor window insertion point in the function.

2. On the Debug menu, click on Run To Cursor to execute your program up to the location of the insertion point.

3. The Debugger automatically updates the Locals tab of the Variables window to display the local variables for the function or procedure.

4. On the View menu, click on Debug Windows, then click on Call Stack.

The Debugger lists the calls in the calling order, with the current function at the top.

Changing The Call Stack Display
To change the call stack display:

1. On the Tools menu, click on Options.

2. Click on the Debug tab.

3. Under Call Stack Window, choose either or both of the checkboxes labeled Parameter Values and Parameter Types.

20. The Debugger

Chapter 21

The Resource Editors

In Brief

Visual C++ Resource Editors

Visual C++ includes nine Resource Editors:

- Accelerator Editor, which lets you create and maintain accelerator key assignments.
- Binary Editor, which lets you edit resources as binary data.
- Dialog Editor, which lets you create and edit dialog boxes.
- Graphics Editor, which lets you create and edit graphics objects, such as icons, bitmaps, and cursors.

NOTE: *Because the Graphics Editor is so sophisticated and powerful, it is not discussed in this chapter. Instead, Chapter 22 focuses on the Graphics Editor alone, describing its capabilities and presenting instructions for its use.*

- Menu Editor, which lets you create and edit menus.
- String Editor, which lets you edit your application's string table.
- Text Editor, which—in addition to helping you create and edit source files—lets you create and edit HTML pages that are contained as resources within your project.
- Toolbar Editor, which lets you create and edit toolbars.
- Version Information Editor, which lets you create and maintain such program information as the company identification, product identification, product release number, and copyright and trademark information.

21. The Resource Editors

Immediate Solutions

Common Techniques

For ease of use, the various Resource Editors share common functions and facilities, letting you apply common techniques to edit the range of resources that the Editors address. Each Resource Editor lets you:

- View resources
- Create new resources
- Use resource templates
- Copy resources
- Edit resources
- Open a resource file as text

Viewing Resources

To view a resource:

1. From the ResourceView pane, expand the folder for the project.
2. Expand the folder that contains the resource you want to view.
3. Double-click on the resource. The appropriate Resource Editor opens and displays the resource, ready for editing.

Creating A New Resource

To create a new resource:

1. From the Insert menu, choose Resource.
2. Choose a resource from the Resource Type list, and click on New.

Visual C++ creates the new resource and assigns it a unique ID, which you can change if you like.

Working With Resource Templates

A *template file* is a copy of a resource that you can use to create additional resources. You can save time by creating resource templates that share useful characteristics.

Creating A Resource Template

To create a resource template:

1. From the Insert menu, choose Resource.

2. Choose a resource from the Resource Type list, and click on New. Or copy a resource from another resource file.

3. Modify the resource as desired.

4. From the File menu, choose Save As.

5. In the Save File As Type drop-down list, choose Resource Template (*.rct).

6. Choose the Template subdirectory under the SharedIDE subdirectory of your Visual C++ installation.

7. Click on Save to save the template.

Creating A Resource From A Template

To create a new resource from a template:

1. From the Insert menu, choose Resource.

2. Choose a resource type. Double-click on the resource icon to create a default resource template object.

Alternatively, you can click on the plus sign (+) next to a resource. Visual C++ moves down the hierarchy to the template files grouped under that resource. Then, double-click on a specific template file under that resource to create a resource.

Copying An Existing Resource

To copy an existing resource:

1. Choose the resource you want to copy.

2. From the Edit menu, choose Copy, and then choose Paste.

Copying A Resource From One File To Another

To copy resources from one file to another:

1. Open both files.

2. If necessary, adjust the workspace so that both resource files are visible at the same time.

3. In the source file, choose the resource you want to copy.

4. Hold down the Ctrl key and drag the resource to the target file.

NOTE: *Dragging the resource without holding down the Ctrl key moves the resource.*

Opening A Resource For Editing

To open an existing resource for editing, choose the resource you want to edit from the Resource View tab, and press Enter.

Saving An Edited Resource

To save an edited resource file, choose Save from the File menu. Visual C++ saves the resource using its current name.

Alternatively, you can:

1. Choose Save As from the File menu.
2. Choose the target drive in the Drives list.
3. Choose the directory path in the Directories list.
4. Type the desired file name in the File Name field.
5. Click on OK. Visual C++ saves the resource.

Deleting A Resource

To delete an existing resource:

1. Choose the resource you want to delete.
2. From the Edit menu, choose Delete.

Opening A Resource File As Text

To open a resource file as text:

1. From the File menu, choose Open and locate the resource file you want to view.
2. From the Open As drop-down list, choose Text.

Opening a resource as text lets you, for example, use Text Editor functions to search for and modify information. Because a resource file contains many resources, you avoid having to open and separately work with each resource.

Accelerator Editor

The Accelerator Editor lets you add, delete, change, and browse your project's accelerator-key assignments. Figure 21.1 shows the Accelerator Editor and the Accel Properties page.

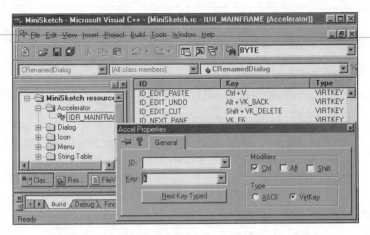

Figure 21.1   The Accelerator Editor and the Accel Properties page.

Adding An Accelerator Table Entry

To add an accelerator table entry:

1. Choose the new-item entry (the blank line at the end of the list).

2. Type the key you want to use as an accelerator, without any accompanying shift keys. The Accel Properties page appears.

3. Choose an ID from the ID drop-down list.

4. Change the modifier and type, if necessary. The modifier specifies whether the key you chose is a combination formed with Ctrl, Alt, or Shift. The type indicates whether the key is an ASCII or a virtual key value.

5. Press Enter.

Deleting An Accelerator Table Entry

To delete an entry from an accelerator table:

1. Choose the entry you want to delete.

2. From the Edit menu, choose Delete.

Moving Or Copying An Accelerator Table Entry

To move or copy an accelerator table entry to another resource file:

1. Open the Accelerator Editor windows in both resource files.

2. Choose the entry you want to move.

3. From the Edit menu, choose Copy (to copy the entry) or Cut (to cut the entry).

4. Choose an entry in the target resource file.

5. From the Edit menu, choose Paste.

Finding An Accelerator Table Entry

To find an entry in an accelerator table:

1. From the Edit menu, choose Find.

2. In the Find What field, type the accelerator key you want to find, or type a regular expression to match a pattern. For convenience, the Accelerator Editor presents your most recent search strings in a drop-down list.

3. Choose any of the Find options.

4. Click on Find Next.

Changing Properties Of Multiple Accelerator Keys

To change the properties of multiple accelerator keys:

1. Choose the accelerator keys you want to change by holding down the Ctrl key and clicking on each of them.

2. From the View menu, choose Properties. The Multiple Selection Accel Properties page appears.

3. Make the desired property changes, which are automatically reflected on each item selected. If you want to undo a change, choose Undo from the Edit menu.

Binary Editor

The Binary Editor lets you edit resources at the binary level, using either hexadecimal or ASCII format. Figure 21.2 shows the Binary Editor.

Creating A New Custom Or Data Resource

You're not limited to the resource types for which Visual C++ provides built-in support. You can create a new custom or data resource by placing the resource in a separate file using normal resource (.rc) file syntax, and then including the file in your project by using the Resource Includes command on the View menu.

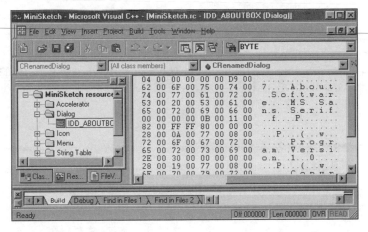

Figure 21.2   The Binary Editor.

To create a new custom or data resource:

1. Create an RC file that contains the custom or data resource. You can type custom data in an RC file as null-terminated quoted strings, or as integers in decimal, hexadecimal, or octal format.

2. From the View menu, choose Resource Includes. The Resource Includes dialog box appears.

3. In the Compile-Time Directives list, type a **#include** statement that specifies the name of the file that contains your custom resource.

4. Click on OK to record your changes.

Opening A Resource For Binary Editing

To open a resource for binary editing:

1. If you want to use the Binary Editor on a resource being edited in another Editor window, close the other Editor window first.

2. Open the project that contains the resource to be edited.

3. Choose the specific resource file you want to edit, and right-click on it.

4. Choose Open Binary Data.

Editing Binary Data

To edit a resource in the Binary Editor:

1. Choose the byte (hexadecimal) or character (ASCII) you want to edit. The Tab key moves the focus between the hexadecimal

and ASCII sections of the Binary Editor. You can use the Page Up and Page Down keys to move through the resource one screen at a time.

2. Type the new value. The value changes immediately in both the hexadecimal and ASCII sections of the Binary Editor window.

Dialog Editor

The Dialog Editor lets you create and maintain dialog boxes in which you can place controls. Figure 21.3 shows the Dialog Editor.

Adding, Editing, And Deleting Controls

Using the Dialog Editor, you can add, edit, and delete dialog box controls. The following sections show you how to perform these operations.

Adding A Control To A Dialog Box

To add a control to a dialog box, follow these steps:

1. From the Controls toolbar, choose the control you want.

2. Either click on the dialog box at the location where you want to place the control or drag the control to that location.

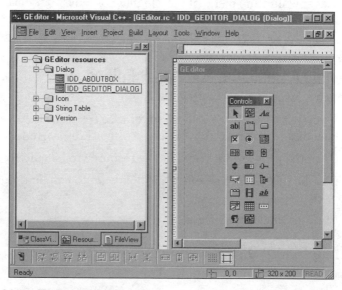

Figure 21.3   The Dialog Editor.

Sizing A Control

To size a control while you add it:

1. Choose the control from the Controls toolbar, and place the pointer where you want the control's upper-left corner to be.

2. Drag to the right and down until the control is the size you want.

Adding Multiple Controls

To add multiple controls:

1. Hold down Ctrl and choose a control from the Controls toolbar.

2. Click on the dialog box as many times as you want to add an instance of the control.

3. Press Esc to stop placing controls.

Adding An ActiveX Control To A Dialog Box

To add an ActiveX control to a dialog box:

1. Position the cursor over the dialog box, and click the right mouse button.

2. From the pop-up menu, choose Insert ActiveX Control.

3. Choose a control to insert, and click on OK. The Dialog Editor adds the control to the dialog box.

Adding An ActiveX Control To The Controls Toolbar

To add an ActiveX control to the Controls toolbar of an MFC project:

1. From the Project menu, choose Add To Project, then Components And Controls.

2. In the Components And Controls Gallery dialog box, open the Registered ActiveX Controls folder and choose a control.

3. To add the selected control to the Controls toolbar, click on Insert, and then click on Yes in the confirmation dialog box. The Confirm Classes dialog box appears.

4. Click on OK to accept the default names for the control classes, or type new names and click on OK.

5. When you are finished adding ActiveX controls, click on Close. The controls you have inserted now appear on the Controls toolbar.

Editing A Control's Properties

To edit the properties of a control or controls:

1. Select one or more controls in the dialog box.

2. Choose Properties from the View menu, and make the desired changes. If you have multiple controls selected, only the properties common to all the controls can be edited. To undo a change, choose Undo from the Edit menu.

Deleting A Control

To delete a control, choose the control from the dialog box and press the Delete key.

Formatting A Dialog Box

To align controls:

1. Choose the controls you want to align by holding down the Ctrl key and clicking on them.

2. Make sure the correct dominant control is selected. The final position of the group of controls depends on the position of the dominant control. The dominant control is the last control selected. The Dialog Editor indicates the dominant control by displaying it with solid, rather than hollow, sizing handles. You can select a new dominant control by holding down the Ctrl key and clicking on the control you want to become the dominant control.

3. From the Layout menu, choose Align, and then choose one of the following alignment options:

   - *Left*—Aligns the selected controls along their left side
   - *Right*—Aligns the selected controls along their right side
   - *Top*—Aligns the selected controls along their top edges
   - *Bottom*—Aligns the selected controls along their bottom edges

To align controls on their center, vertically or horizontally:

1. Choose the controls you want to center.

2. Make sure the correct dominant control is selected.

3. From the Layout menu, choose Align, and then choose Horiz. Center or Vert. Center.

To make the spacing between controls equal:

1 Choose the controls you want to rearrange.

2. From the Layout menu, choose Space Evenly, and then choose one of the following spacing alignments:

- *Across*—Spaces controls evenly between the leftmost and the rightmost control selected

- *Down*—Spaces controls evenly between the topmost and the bottommost control selected

To center controls in the dialog box:

1. Choose the control or controls you want to rearrange.

2. From the Layout menu, choose Center In Dialog, and then choose one of the following arrangements:

- *Vertical*—Centers controls vertically in the dialog box

- *Horizontal*—Centers controls horizontally in the dialog box

To arrange push buttons along the right or bottom of the dialog box:

1. Choose one or more push buttons by holding down the Ctrl key and clicking on them.

2. From the Layout menu, choose Arrange Buttons, and then choose one of the following arrangements:

- *Right*—Aligns push buttons along the right edge of the dialog box

- *Bottom*—Aligns push buttons along the bottom edge of the dialog box

Using Guides And Margins To Format A Dialog Box

Guides help you align controls accurately within a dialog box. They appear as blue dotted lines across the dialog box displayed in the Dialog Editor and corresponding arrows in the rulers. When you create a dialog box, Visual C++ provides four margins. Margins are modified guides, also appearing as blue dotted lines.

The sizing handles of controls snap to guides when you move the controls, and guides likewise snap to controls. When you move a guide, any controls that are snapped to it move as well. Controls snapped to multiple guides are resized when one of the guides is moved.

The tick marks in the rulers that indicate the position and spacing of guides and controls are defined by dialog units (DLUs). A DLU is based on the size of the dialog box font, which is normally 8-point MS Sans Serif. A horizontal DLU is the average width of the dialog box font divided by four. A vertical DLU is the average height of the font divided by eight.

When arranging controls in a dialog box, you can use the layout grid for more precise positioning. When the grid is turned on, controls snap to the dotted lines of the grid. You can turn this snap-to-grid feature on and off and change the size of the layout grid cells.

Creating And Setting A Guide

To create and set a guide:

1. Click anywhere within the rulers to create a guide.

2. Drag the new guide into position. The Dialog Editor displays the number of DLUs in the ruler and on the status bar below. Hold the cursor over the guide's arrow in the ruler to see the exact position of the guide.

Deleting A Guide

To delete a guide, drag the guide out of the dialog box.

Moving A Guide

To move a guide:

1. Drag the guide to the new position.

2. The Dialog Editor displays the coordinates of the guide in the status bar at the bottom of the window and in the ruler. You can move the pointer over the arrow in the ruler to display the exact position of the guide.

Moving Margins

To move margins:

1. Drag the margin to the new position.

2. To make a margin disappear, move the margin to the zero position. To restore the margin, place the cursor over the margin's zero position and move the margin into position.

Sizing A Group Of Controls

To size a group of controls with guides:

1. Snap one side of the controls to a guide.

2. Drag a guide to the other side of the controls.

3. If necessary, size each control to snap to the second guide.

4. Move either guide to size the controls on that side.

Changing The Tick Mark Intervals
To change the intervals of the tick marks:

1. From the Layout menu, choose Guide Settings.

2. In the Grid Spacing field, specify the new width and height in DLUs.

3. Click on OK.

Disabling The Snapping Effect
To disable the snapping effect of the guides, drag the control while holding down the Alt key.

Moving Guides Without Moving The Snapped Controls
To move guides without moving the snapped controls, drag the guide while holding down the Shift key.

Clearing All Guides
To clear all the guides:

1. Right-click in the ruler bar.

2. From the shortcut menu, choose Clear All.

Turing Off Guides
To turn off the guides:

1. From the Layout menu, choose Guide Settings.

2. Under Layout Guides, choose None.

3. Click on OK.

Turning The Layout Grid On Or Off
To turn the layout grid on or off:

1. From the Layout menu, choose Guide Settings.

2. Set or clear the Grid radio button. You can control the grid in individual Dialog Editor windows by using the Toggle Grid button on the Dialog toolbar.

Changing The Size Of The Layout Grid
To change the size of the layout grid:

1. From the Layout menu, choose Guide Settings.

2. Type the height and width in DLUs for the cells in the grid.

Editing A Dialog Box

A dialog box has a property page, a tab order, and mnemonic keys. The tab order is the order in which focus moves from control to control when the user presses the Tab key. Usually, the tab order proceeds from left to right in a dialog box, and from top to bottom. A keyboard user can press a mnemonic key to move the input focus to a particular control.

Each control has a Tabstop checkbox on its property page. The checkbox determines whether the control actually receives input focus. Even controls that do not have the Tabstop property set must be part of the tab order.

Changing The Tab Order
To change the tab order for all controls in a dialog box:

1. From the Layout menu, choose Tab Order. A number in the upper-left corner of each control shows the control's place in the current tab order.

2. Set the tab order by clicking each control in the order you want the Tab key to follow.

3. Press Enter to exit Tab Order mode.

Changing The Tab Order For Two Or More Controls
To change the tab order for two or more controls:

1. From the Layout menu, choose Tab Order.

2. Specify where the change in order will begin. To do so, press and hold the Ctrl key, and click on the control prior to the one where you want the changed order to begin. To set a specific control as the first in tab order (number 1), double-click on the control.

3. Reset the tab order by clicking the controls in the order you want the Tab key to follow.

4. Press Enter to exit Tab Order mode.

Defining A Mnemonic Key For A Control
To define a mnemonic key for a control with a visible caption:

1. Choose the control.

2. From the View menu, choose Properties. The control's property page opens.

3. In the Caption field, type an ampersand (&) in front of the letter you want as the mnemonic for that control.

An underline appears in the displayed caption to indicate the mnemonic key.

To define a mnemonic for a control without a visible caption:

1. Create a caption for the control by using a static text control. In the static text caption, type an ampersand (&) in front of the letter you want as the mnemonic.

2. Make the static text control immediately precede the control it labels in the tab order.

Jumping To Code

To jump to code from the Dialog Editor:

- Double-click on the dialog box to jump to its class definition.

- Double-click on a control within the dialog box to jump to the declaration for its most-recently implemented message-handling function.

Adding A Message Handler For A Control

To add a message handler for a control:

1. With a dialog box or control selected, click the right mouse button, and then click on Events in the pop-up menu that appears. The New Windows Message And Events Handlers dialog box appears.

2. Use the Class Or Object To Handle list to choose the control for which you want to create a handler. You can also choose the dialog box.

3. The New Windows Messages/Events list displays all possible Windows messages for which you can create handlers. The Existing Message/Event Handlers list shows the Windows messages and events for which handlers have already been created. You can either:

   - Choose a new message or event. Then, choose Add Handler to create a new stub handler function; or, choose Add And Edit to create the stub function, then exit, jumping directly to the handler code in the Text Editor.

   - Choose an existing message or event. Then, choose Edit Existing to jump to the existing handler code in the Text Editor.

Testing A Dialog Box

To test a dialog box:

1. From the Layout menu, choose Test.

2. To end the test session:

   - Press Esc.

   - Close the dialog box by clicking on its Close button.

   - Choose a push button with a symbol name of **IDOK** or **IDCANCEL**.

Editing HTML Resources

An HTML resource is an HTML page that is stored as part of a project's resource (.rc) file and as part of a compiled application's EXE or DLL file. HTML resources are a convenient way of storing hypertext information. Visual C++ does not provide a special editor for working with HTML resources; you can create and edit them using the Text Editor.

You can also include in the resource file the images needed by an HTML page. To refer to such images, you can use the special HTML protocol **res**, rather than the more typical **http** or **file** protocol. The handler for the **res** protocol can access images stored in either DLL or EXE files.

Creating A New HTML Resource

To create an HTML resource:

1. From the Insert menu, choose Resource.

2. In the Resource Type list, choose HTML, then click on New. Visual C++ creates the new HTML resource, giving it a unique resource ID.

Importing An Existing HTML File As A Resource

To import an existing HTML file as a resource

1. From the Insert menu, choose Resource.

2. In the Resource Type list, choose HTML, then click on Import.

3. In the Import Resource dialog box, locate the HTML file and click on Import. Visual C++ creates the new HTML resource, giving it a unique resource ID.

Menu Editor

The Menu Editor lets you create and modify menus and menu items. Figure 21.4 shows the Menu Editor. As you can see in the figure, the Menu Editor lets you work with menus in a way that closely resembles their appearance in an application.

Creating Menus And Menu Items

To create a menu on the menu bar:

1. Choose the new-item box (the empty rectangular outline) on the menu bar. Or, move the new-item box to a blank spot by using the right arrow and left arrow keys.

2. Type the name of the menu. When you start typing, focus automatically shifts to the Menu Item property page, where the text you type appears in the Caption field and in the Menu Editor window.

   You can define a mnemonic key that lets the user choose the menu with the keyboard. To do so, type an ampersand (&) in front of a letter to specify it as the mnemonic. Make sure all the mnemonics on a menu bar are unique.

   Once you have given the menu a name, the new-item box automatically shifts to the right and another new-item box opens for adding menu items.

NOTE: To create a single-item menu on the menu bar, clear the Pop-up checkbox on the Menu Item property page.

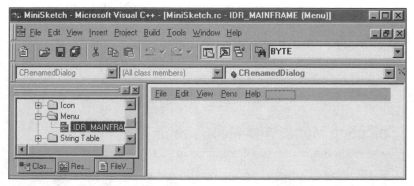

Figure 21.4   The Menu Editor.

To create a menu item:

1. Create a menu or open an existing menu.

2. Choose the menu's new-item box, or choose an existing menu item and press the Insert key. The new-item box is inserted before the selected item.

3. Type the name of the menu item. When you start typing, focus automatically shifts to the Menu Item property page, where the text you type appears in the Caption field.

    You can define a mnemonic key that lets the user choose the menu command. Type an ampersand (&) in front of a letter to specify it as the mnemonic.

4. On the property page, choose the menu item styles that apply.

5. In the Prompt field on the property page, type the prompt string you want to appear in your application's status bar. The Menu Editor creates an entry in the string table with the same resource identifier as the menu item you created.

6. Press Enter. The new-item box is selected so you can create additional menu items.

To create a cascading (hierarchical) menu:

1. Choose the new-item box on the menu where you want the cascading menu to appear.

2. Type the name of the menu item that, when selected, will cause the cascading menu to appear. When you start typing, focus automatically shifts to the Menu Item property page, where the text you type appears in the Caption field.

    Or, choose an existing menu item as the parent item of the cascading menu, and double-click.

3. On the property page, choose the Pop-up checkbox. This marks the menu item with the cascading menu symbol. A new-item box appears to the right.

4. Add any additional needed menu items to the cascading menu.

Selecting Menus And Menu Items

To select a menu and display its menu items:

1. Click on the menu caption on the menu bar, or click on the parent item of the cascading menu.

2. Click on the menu item you want.

To choose one or more menu items:

1. Click on the menu or cascading menu you want.

2. Click to choose a menu item, or hold down the Shift key while clicking to choose multiple menu items. Hold down the Shift key and click on a selected menu item to deselect it.

   Or, with the cursor outside the menu, drag to draw a selection box around the menu items you want to select.

Moving And Copying Menus And Menu Items

To move or copy menus or menu items using drag-and-drop:

1. Drag or copy the item you want to move to either a new location on the current menu or a different menu.

2. Drop the menu item when the insertion guide shows the item to be in the position you want.

To move or copy menus or menu items using the menu commands:

1. Choose one or more menus or menu items.

2. From the Edit menu, choose Cut (to move) or Copy (to copy).

3. If you want to move the items to another menu resource or resource file, make that Menu Editor window active.

4. Choose the position of the menu or menu item you want to move or copy to.

5. From the Edit menu, choose Paste. The moved or copied item is placed before the item you selected.

String Editor

An application's string table stores a list of strings as resources, which can be loaded and used by a program. Using a string table rather than hard coding string literals in your program makes it easier to change the values of the strings, because changing the value of a string resource does not require recompilation of the application. Moreover, it's much simpler to localize an application for a new language when all its string data resides in the application's resource file. The String Editor lets you edit an application's string table. Figure 21.5 shows the String Editor.

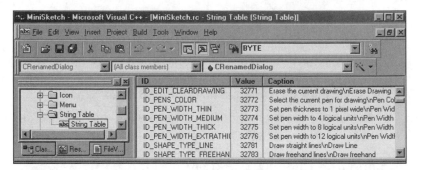

Figure 21.5   The String Editor.

WARNING!   Null strings are forbidden in Windows string tables. If you create an entry in the string table that contains a null string as its value, the String Editor deletes the entry when you close the String Editor.

Finding A String

To find a string in the string table:

1. In ResourceView, open the string table by double-clicking its icon.

2. From the Edit menu, choose Find.

3. In the Find What field, either:

   - Choose a previous search string from the drop-down list.

   - Type the caption text or resource identifier of the string you want to find.

   - Type a regular expression to match a pattern.

4. Choose a Find option.

5. Click on Find Next.

Adding Or Deleting A String

To add a string table entry:

1. Choose the new-item box (an empty line) at the end of a string segment.

2. Type the new string. As you type, the focus shifts to the String Properties page. The text appears entered in the Caption field, and the string is given the next identifier in sequence.

3. Press Enter to place the new string in the string table.

To delete a string table entry:

1. Choose the string you want to delete.

2. From the Edit menu, choose Delete.

Changing A String Or Its Identifier

To change a string or its identifier:

1. Choose the string you want to edit.

2. From the View menu, choose Properties, and modify the string in the Caption field.

3. In the ID field, modify the string's identifier:

   • Type a new ID, or choose one from the list.

   • To change a string's value, type the ID followed by an equal sign and the new value; for example:

   ```
   ID_PENS_COLOR=32671
   ```

NOTE: *The String Editor cannot change the value of a string that is used more than once. To change the value of such a string, you must edit the resource header file manually.*

4. Press Enter.

Toolbar Editor

The Toolbar Editor is a graphic tool that lets you create toolbar resources and convert bitmaps into toolbar resources. Figure 21.6 shows the Toolbar Editor.

As you can see, the Toolbar Editor has a window separated into two panes by a split bar. The Toolbar Editor also displays an image of the subject toolbar.

Creating A New Toolbar

To create a new toolbar resource:

1. From the Insert menu, choose Resource.

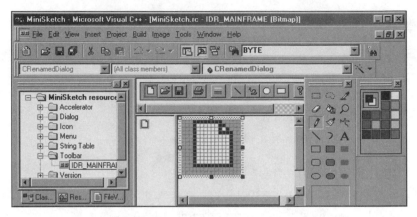

Figure 21.6   The Toolbar Editor.

2. In the Resource Type list, choose Toolbar, and click on OK. If a plus sign (+) appears next to the Toolbar resource type, toolbar templates are available. Click on the plus sign to expand the list of templates, choose a template, and click on OK.

Converting A Bitmap To A Toolbar

To convert a bitmap to a toolbar:

1. Open an existing bitmap resource in the Graphics Editor by right-clicking on the resource in the Visual C++ ResourceView tab and then choosing Open from the pop-up menu.

2. From the Image menu, choose Toolbar Editor. The New Toolbar Resource dialog box appears. Change the width and height of the icon images to match the bitmap. The toolbar image is then displayed in the Toolbar Editor.

3. Change the command IDs of the buttons on the toolbar:

   • From the View menu, choose Properties to open the property page for the toolbar button.

   • Type in the new ID, or choose an ID from the drop-down list.

Creating A Toolbar Button

To create a new toolbar button, assign an ID to the empty button at the right of the toolbar; then, open the property page on the toolbar button to edit the button ID. Or, choose the empty button at the right end of the toolbar, and begin drawing; the Toolbar Editor assigns a default button ID.

By default, the Toolbar Editor displays a new or blank button at the right of the toolbar. You can move this button before editing it. When you create a new button, a new empty button appears to the right of the edited button. When you save a toolbar, the empty button is not saved.

Moving A Toolbar Button

To move a toolbar button, drag the button to the desired new location on the toolbar.

Copying A Toolbar Button

To copy a button from a toolbar:

1. Hold down the CTRL key.

2. Drag the button to the desired new location on the toolbar or to a location on another toolbar.

Deleting A Toolbar Button

To delete a toolbar button, choose the toolbar button and drag it off the toolbar.

Inserting And Closing Up Space Between Buttons

To insert a space between buttons on a toolbar:

- If the button is not followed by a space, drag the button to the right (or down) until it overlaps the next button about halfway.

- If the button is followed by a space and you want to retain the space following the button, drag the button until the right (or bottom) edge just touches the next button or just overlaps it.

- If you want to insert a space before a button that is followed by a space and you want to close up the following space, drag the button to the right (or down) until it overlaps the next button about halfway.

To close up a space between buttons on a toolbar:

- Drag the button on one side of the space toward the button on the other side of the space until one button overlaps the other button about halfway.

    If there is no space on the side of the button that you are dragging away from and you drag the button more than halfway past the adjacent button, the Toolbar Editor inserts a space on the opposite side of the button that you are dragging.

21. The Resource Editors

Version Information Editor

Version information consists of company and product identification, a product release number, and copyright and trademark notification. The Version Information Editor is a simple tool for creating and maintaining this data. You can use its Find command to search for version information that you want to change. The Version Information Editor lets you add or delete string blocks, search for values, and modify individual string values within the version information.

NOTE: *The Windows standard is that a program should have only one version resource, named VS_VERSION_INFO.*

Figure 21.7 shows the Version Editor, which you can access by double-clicking the version resource in the ClassView window.

If you want to access the version information from within your program, your application can make use of the **GetFileVersionInfo** function or the **VerQueryValue** function.

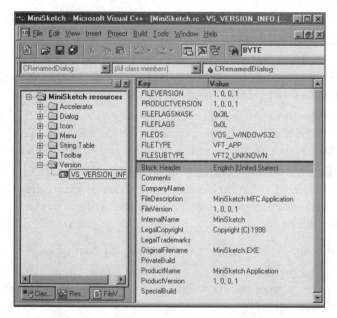

Figure 21.7 The Version Editor.

The Graphics Editor

In Brief

Graphical Resources And The Graphics Editor

Visual C++ refers to the images you create for your application as *graphical resources* and provides the Graphics Editor for creating and editing them. Using the Graphics Editor, you can create bitmaps and toolbars, and edit GIF and JPEG images. Figure 22.1 shows the major components of the Graphics Editor, which include:

- *Image Editor window*—This window has two panes: One shows an actual size view of the image, and the other shows an enlarged view. You can drag the split bar to adjust the relative sizes of the panes.

- *Graphics toolbar*—This component is located in the Image Editor window. Its tools lets you edit images. The Graphics toolbar has two parts:

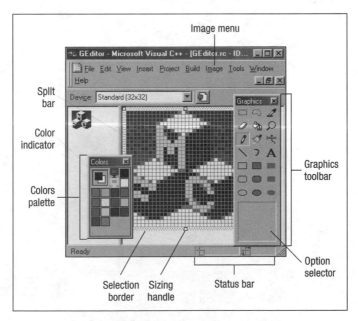

Figure 22.1   The Graphics Editor components.

- The toolbar, which contains tools for working with images.
- The option selector, which lets you choose brush widths and drawing options.

- *Colors palette*—This component lets you set the color in which you draw or paint. The Colors palette also has two parts:

  - The color indicator, which indicates the current foreground and background colors and provides selectors for the screen color and the inverse color.

  - The color palette, which lets you choose the foreground and background colors.

- *Status bar*—This component's two panes display useful information during editing. For example, when the mouse pointer is over an image, the left pane shows the cursor's current position (in pixels) relative to the upper-left corner of the image. During a drag operation, the status bar's right pane shows the size (in pixels) of the selected area.

- *Image menu*—This component includes commands for editing images, managing color palettes (sets of colors), and setting image editor window options. The Image menu is visible only when the Graphics Editor is active.

Immediate Solutions

Drawing And Erasing Images

The Graphics Editor provides several freehand drawing and erasing tools, but all the tools work in the same way. First, you choose a tool. Then, if necessary, you choose foreground and background colors and size and shape options. Finally, you move the mouse pointer to the image and click or drag to draw and erase.

Using A Drawing Tool

To choose and use a drawing tool:

1. Click on a tool button on the Graphics toolbar. You can choose:

    • The pencil tool, which draws freehand lines with a width of 1 pixel.

    • The brush tool, which draws freehand lines whose shape and size you determine by using the option selector.

    • The airbrush tool, which randomly distributes color pixels in the vicinity of the brush.

    • The eraser tool, which paints over the image in the current background color.

NOTE: *To use the eraser tool, press the left mouse button. If you press the right mouse button, the eraser tool replaces the current foreground color of a pixel with the current background color.*

---

2. If necessary, choose foreground and background colors and a brush:

    • Click the left mouse button on a swatch in the Colors palette to choose its color as the foreground color; click the right mouse button to choose a background color.

    • On the options selector, click on a shape representing the brush you want to use.

3. Move the mouse pointer to the place on the image where you want to start drawing or painting. The pointer changes shape to indicate the tool you selected.

4. Press the left mouse button (for the foreground color) or the right mouse button (for the background color), and hold it down as you drag to draw or paint.

Changing The Size Of A Tool

To change the size of a brush, airbrush, or the eraser, choose a shape in the option selector, which presents an assortment of sizes.

Drawing Lines And Figures

Drawing lines and figures is almost as easy as freehand drawing. You simply place the insertion point at one location and drag to another. For lines, these points are the endpoints. The current brush selection determines the width of a drawn line; the current width selection determines the width of a frame figure. To draw with the foreground color, drag using the left mouse button; to draw with the background color, drag using the right mouse button.

Drawing A Line

To draw a line:

1. Choose the line tool from the Graphics toolbar.

2. If necessary, choose colors and a brush:

   • Click the left mouse button on a swatch in the Colors palette to choose its color as the foreground color; click the right mouse button to choose a background color.

   • On the options selector, click on a shape representing the brush you want to use.

3. Place the mouse pointer where you want the line to begin.

4. Click and drag to the line's endpoint.

Drawing A Figure

To draw a closed figure:

1. Choose a closed-figure drawing tool from the Graphics toolbar. The closed-figure drawing tools have icons that resemble the figure each creates. You can draw a rectangle, a rounded

rectangle, or an ellipse. Your figure can be outlined, filled, or outlined and filled.

2. If necessary, choose colors and a brush:

   - Click the left mouse button on a swatch in the Colors palette to choose its color as the foreground color; click the right mouse button to choose a background color.

   - On the options selector, click on a shape representing the brush you want to use.

3. Move the mouse pointer to where you want to place a corner of the rectangular area in which you want to draw the figure.

4. Click and drag the pointer to the diagonally opposite corner.

Selecting An Image Or Part Of An Image

The selection tools let you cut, copy, clear, resize, invert, or move a portion of an image or an entire image.

Selecting An Image

To select an entire image, click on the image outside the current selection.

Selecting Part Of An Image

To select a part of an image:

1. In the Graphics toolbar, click on the selection tool you want: the rectangular selection tool or the irregular area selection tool.

2. Move the insertion point to one corner of the image area that you want to select. Crosshairs appear when the insertion point is over the image.

3. Click and drag the insertion point to the opposite corner of the area you want to select. A marquee rectangle shows which pixels will be selected. All pixels within the marquee, including those under the rectangle, are included in the selection.

4. Release the mouse button. The selection border encloses the selected area. Any subsequent operation you perform will affect only the pixels within the rectangle.

Editing An Image

The Graphics Editor works with the Windows Clipboard to let you cut, copy, clear, and move a selection, which can be part of an image or an entire image. You can also use the Windows Clipboard to transfer an image to another application.

Cutting The Selection To The Clipboard

To cut the current selection and move it to the Clipboard, choose Cut from the Edit menu.

Pasting An Image From The Clipboard

To paste the Clipboard contents into an image:

1. Choose Paste from the Edit menu. The Clipboard contents appear in the upper-left corner of the pane, surrounded by a selection border.

2. Position the mouse pointer inside the selection border; click and drag the image to the desired location.

3. To fix the image at its new location, click outside the selection border.

Clearing The Selection

To clear the current selection without moving it to the Clipboard, choose Clear from the Edit menu. The Graphics Editor fills the original area of the selection with the current background color.

Moving The Selection

To move the selection:

1. Position the mouse pointer inside the selection border (or anywhere on it except the sizing handles).

2. Click and drag the selection to its new location.

3. To fix the selection at its new location, click outside the selection border.

Copying The Selection

To copy the selection:

1. Position the mouse pointer inside the selection border (or anywhere on it except the sizing handles).

2. Press and hold the Ctrl key as you click and then drag the selection to a new location.

3. To fix the selection at its current location, click outside the selection cursor.

Drawing With The Selection

To draw with the selection:

1. Position the mouse pointer inside the selection border (or anywhere on it except the sizing handles).

2. Press and hold the Shift key as you click and then drag the selection.

3. Copies of the selection appear along the dragging path. The more slowly you drag, the more copies appear.

Flipping An Image

The Graphics Editor lets you flip an image horizontally or vertically. It also lets you rotate an image.

Flipping An Image Horizontally

To flip the selection horizontally, choose Flip Horizontal from the Image menu.

Flipping An Image Vertically

To flip the selection vertically, choose Flip Vertical from the Image menu.

Rotating An Image

To rotate the selection 90 degrees, choose Rotate 90 from the Image menu.

Resizing An Image

The Graphics Editor lets you resize an image in either of two ways: You can shrink the image to reduce its size, or you can stretch the image to increase its size. The effect of resizing an image depends on whether the selection includes the entire image or only a part of an image. If the selection includes only part of an image, the Graphics Editor shrinks the selection by deleting pixels and filling the vacated regions with the current background color; it stretches the selection by duplicating rows or columns of pixels.

You can resize an image either by using the resizing handles or the property page. You can simply drag the solid resizing handles of an image to resize the image or a part of the image. You can use the property page to resize only the entire image, not a part of it.

Resizing An Entire Image

To resize an entire image using the property page:

1. Open the image whose properties you want to change.

2. Choose Properties from the View menu.

3. Type the new dimensions in the Width and Height fields.

   If you increase the size of the image, the Graphics Editor will extend the image to the right, downward, or both. It will also fill the new region with the current background color.

   If you decrease the size of the image, the Graphics Editor will crop the image on the right or bottom edge, or on both edges.

NOTE: *You can use the property page to resize only the entire image, not a part of it.*

Cropping Or Extending An Image

To crop or extend an image:

1. Choose the entire image. If part of the image is currently selected, you can select the entire image by clicking anywhere on the image outside the current selection border.

2. Drag a sizing handle until the image reaches the desired size. The Graphics Editor crops or enlarges an image when you resize the image by moving a sizing handle.

NOTE: *If you press and hold the Shift key as you move a sizing handle, the Graphics Editor will shrink or stretch the image. See the next section to see how to shrink or stretch an image.*

Shrinking Or Stretching An Image

To shrink or stretch an entire image:

1. Choose the entire image. If part of the image is currently selected, you can select the entire image by clicking anywhere on the image outside the current selection border.

2. Press and hold the Shift key as you drag a sizing handle until the image is the desired size.

Shrinking Or Stretching Part Of An Image

To shrink or stretch part of an image:

1. Choose the part of the image you want to resize.

2. Drag a sizing handle until the selection reaches the desired size.

Working With A Custom Brush

A custom brush is a rectangular part of an image that you use to paint, in the same way you use one of the Graphics Editor's ready-made brushes. You can use a custom brush like a stamp or a stencil, creating a variety of special effects.

Creating A Custom Brush

To create a custom brush:

1. Choose the part of the image that you want to use for a brush.

2. Press Ctrl+B.

Drawing In The Background Color With A Custom Brush

To draw custom brush shapes in the background color:

1. Choose an opaque or transparent background.

2. Choose the background color in which you want to draw.

3. Place the custom brush at the point where you want to start drawing.

4. Right-click to fill opaque regions of the custom brush with the background color.

Changing The Size Of A Custom Brush

To increase or decrease the custom brush size, on the keyboard's number pad press the plus (+) key to double the brush size or the minus (–) key to halve it.

Canceling A Custom Brush

To cancel the custom brush, press Esc or simply choose another drawing tool.

Changing Image Properties And Format

The Graphics Editor lets you change image properties, such as width, height, and color model. It also lets you change the format in which the image is stored.

Changing Image Properties

To change an image's properties:

1. Open the image whose properties you want to change.

2. Choose Properties from the View menu.

3. Change any or all of the properties on the General tab:

   - You can modify the resource's identifier in the ID field.

   - You can modify the image's width and height (in pixels) in the Width and Height fields.

   - You can choose the image's color model in the Colors list. Possible values are Monochrome, 16, or 256.

   - You can modify the name of the file in which the image is stored, by using the File Name field.

   - You can use the Save Compressed checkbox to specify that the image should be saved in a compressed format.

4. Change any or all of the color properties on the Palette tab:

   - You can double-click to choose a color from the Custom Color Selector dialog box.

   - You can type an RGB or HSL value in the appropriate field.

Saving An Image In A Different Format

By default, Visual C++ creates a new image in the bitmap format. However, you can save your image as a GIF or JPEG.

To save an image in a different file format:

1. Choose Save As from the File menu.

2. In the File Name field, type the name of the file in which you want to store the image. The file extension you specify

determines the file format (.gif for a GIF file or .jpg for a JPEG file).

3. Click on Save.

Converting An Image To A Different Format

To convert an image from one format to another:

1. Open the image in the Graphics Editor.

2. Choose Save As from the File menu.

3. In the File Name field, type the name of the file in which you want to store the image. The file extension you specify determines the file format (.bmp for a bitmap file, .gif for a GIF file, or .jpg for a JPEG file).

4. Click on Save.

Working With Color

By default, the Graphic Editor's Colors palette displays 24 colors: 16 standard colors and 8 dithered colors. However, you can also create your own custom colors. You can save your customized color palettes on disk and reload them.

The Graphics Editor's Palette tab—which you can view by choosing Adjust Colors from the Image menu—displays up to 256 colors. Changing a color on the Palette tab will immediately change the corresponding color in the image.

Selecting Colors

To choose a foreground color, on the Colors palette, click the left mouse button on the color you want.

To choose a background color, on the Colors palette, click the right mouse button on the color you want.

Filling An Area

To fill an area:

1. Choose the fill tool from the Graphics toolbar.

2. Choose drawing colors from the Colors palette by clicking the left mouse button to choose a foreground color or the right mouse button to choose a background color.

3. Move the fill tool to the area you want to fill.

4. Click the left or right mouse button to fill with the foreground color or the background color, respectively.

Picking Up A Color

The color-pickup tool lets you choose a color from an image as the current foreground or background color.

To pick up a color:

1. Choose the color-pickup tool, which resembles an eyedropper, from the Graphics toolbar.

2. Choose the color you want to pick up from the image by moving the mouse pointer over a pixel having that color.

3. Click the left mouse button to make the chosen color the foreground color, or click on the right mouse button to make it the background color.

Choosing The Background Type

In a custom brush, pixels that match the current background color do not paint over an existing image. Likewise, when you move or copy a selection from a cursor or icon, pixels in the selection that match the background color are transparent. Therefore, they do not obscure underlying pixels in the image. However, you can change this behavior so that such pixels paint over the existing image.

To toggle the background-color transparency, click on the appropriate button in the Graphics toolbar option selector:

• *Opaque background*—Causes the existing image to be obscured by all parts of the selection, regardless of color.

• *Transparent background*—Causes the existing image pixels to show through parts of the selection that match the current background color.

NOTE: *You can change the background color while a selection is in effect.*

Inverting Colors

The Graphics Editor provides a convenient way to invert colors in the selected part of the image, so that you can see the effect that color inversion produces. To invert colors in the current selection, choose Invert Colors from the Image menu.

Customizing Colors

To change colors on the Colors palette or Palette tab:

1. Choose Adjust Colors from the Image menu.

2. Specify the desired color by typing RGB or HSL values in the appropriate fields.

3. Specify the luminosity by moving the slider on the luminosity bar.

4. A custom color may be dithered. If you want to avoid this by choosing the solid color closest to the dithered color, double-click the Color preview window.

5. Click on OK to add the new color.

Working With Color Palettes

The Graphics Editor lets you save a customized Color palette as a file. It also lets you load a customized Color palette from a file.

Saving A Color Palette

To save a custom Colors palette:

1. Choose Save Palette from the Image menu.

2. Use the dialog box controls to navigate to the directory where you want to save the palette, and type a name for the file in which to store the palette.

3. Click on Save.

TIP: *The Graphics Editor has no facility for restoring the default Colors palette. You should save the default Colors palette in a file name such as Standard.pal or Default.pal so that you can easily restore the default settings.*

Loading A Color Palette

To load a custom Colors palette:

1. Choose Load Palette from the Image menu.

2. Use the dialog box controls to navigate to the correct directory, and choose the palette you want to load.

3. Click on OK.

22. The Graphics Editor

The Graphics Editor Workspace

When working with a large image or an image that contains small details, you may need to customize the Graphics Editor. You can change the Graphics Editor's magnification factor, display and hide the pixel grid, and display and hide the Graphics toolbar.

Changing The Magnification Factor

By default, the Graphics Editor displays in its left pane a view of the image at actual size and in its right pane a view of the image at six times actual size. However, you can select different magnification factors.

To change the magnification factor:

1. Choose the image editor pane whose magnification factor you want to change.

2. Click the magnify tool on the Graphics toolbar. The pointer changes to the magnify tool and magnification-factor options appear in the option selector of the Graphics toolbar.

3. Click on the desired magnification factor.

Displaying And Hiding The Pixel Grid

When the image editor panes have a magnification factor of 4 or greater, you can display a grid that delimits the individual pixels in the image. To display or hide the pixel grid:

1. Choose Grid Settings from the Image menu.

2. Use the Pixel Grid checkbox to display or hide the grid.

Displaying And Hiding The Graphics Toolbar

To show or hide the Graphics toolbar:

1. Place the mouse pointer over the toolbar, and click the right mouse button.

2. Choose Graphics from the pop-up menu.

Index

A

I

P

U

V